AF595864
ANZ·979
TG977
ARB
4X4 ACCESSORIES

MAKE TRAX 4WD VICTORIA ATLAS

First Published 2020

Published and distributed by
Australian Fishing Network
PO Box 544 Croydon, Victoria 3136
Telephone: (03) 9729 8788 Facsimile: (03) 9729 7833
Email: sales@afn.com.au Website: www.afn.com.au

ISBN: 9781 8651 3339 3

CONTENTS

VICTORIA

HOW TO USE THIS BOOK

Our TRACK SNAPSHOT identifies the vital requirements for each trek, listing them in a boxed format.

The detailed maps are all orientated with north to the page top, and an integral distance bar to give a sense of scale. Towns, together with the road and track network linking them are clearly displayed, with broken lines indicating unsealed surfaces. For the sake of clarity we have omitted contour lines, but have included waterways and State / National Park boundaries. Camping areas, lookouts and other points of interest are indicated by boxed captions and the tour route and direction have been highlighted in yellow with orange arrows.

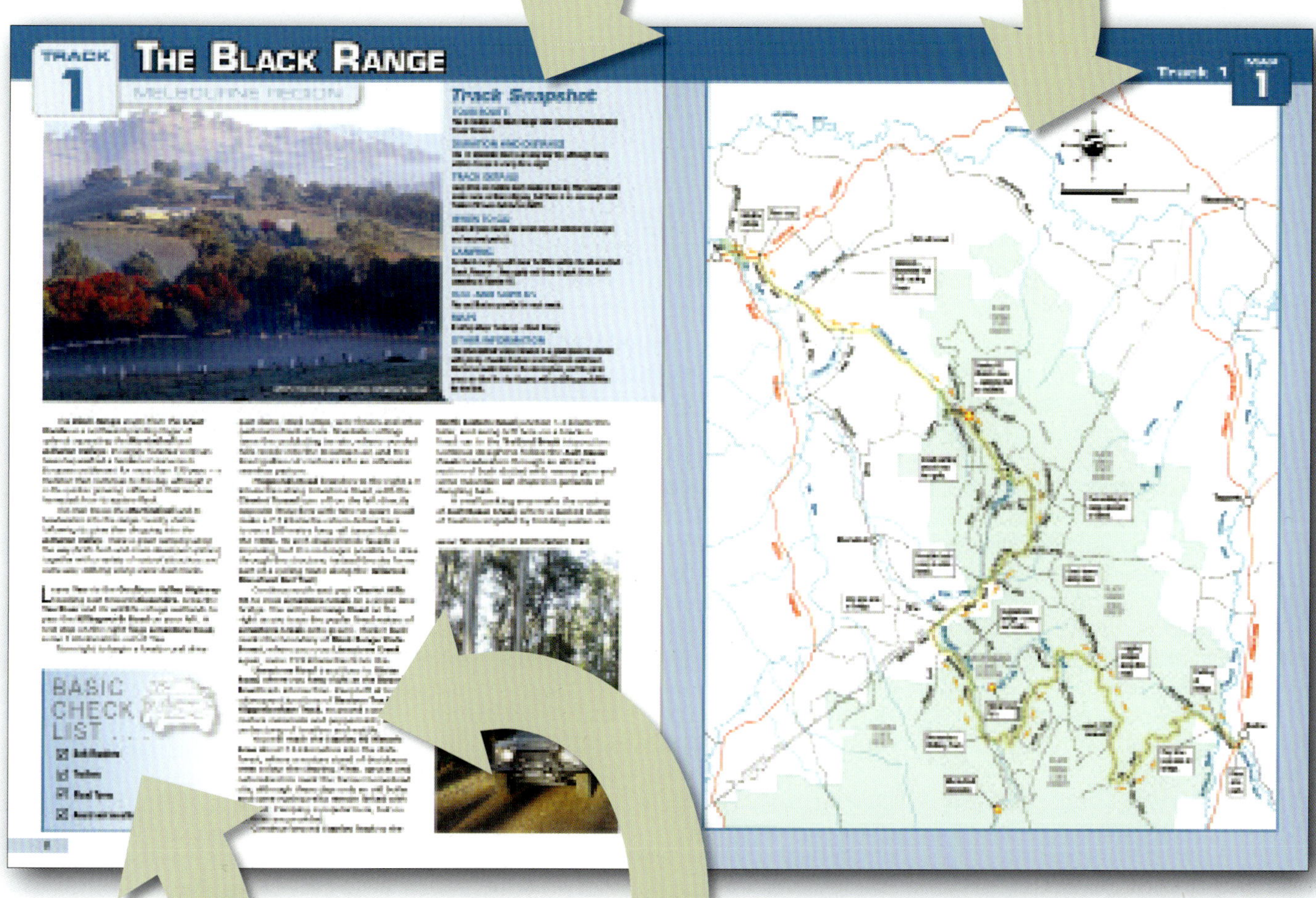

A "tick the box" list of tour hazards and basic requirements is included with Map 1 of each trek. This list cannot account for every combination of driver, vehicle and weather combination, but rather attempts to provide a guide for what is likely on that tour. For example a tick in the "Steep Climbs" box cannot indicate how steep the climbs are, but if there is a tick in the "Soft Roaders" box as well, then they are likely to be climbs that will not require low range.

Similarly, a tick in the "Water Crossings" box, but without one in the "Snorkel" box would indicate relatively shallow crossings (although it is customary for travellers to check out an unknown water crossing on foot before plunging in – with the exception of waterways that may be the habitat of salt water crocodiles).

The text follows the vehicles journey using landmarks and intersections as stepping stones through the trek. The intermediate distances mentioned can be compared with your own progress, but it will be necessary to read ahead through the text to identify the next "stepping stone". Those running a GPS unit within the vehicle will have an advantage here, as they can easily compare their position in relation to the maps provided. (A GPS is recommended on any tours where the "Navigation Skills" box has been ticked). In any case, try to keep a record of your odometer readings as you reach the various landmarks described in the text.

ATLAS

MAKE TRAX VICTORIA describes 33 of the best 4WD destinations and tours from across the state. From the north west desert country to shorter treks just out of Melbourne, there is no time frame that cannot be satisfied. We will travel to the jungles of far east Gippsland, explore the high country mountains and find some great camping locations right on Melbourne's doorstep.

Each trek is graded, allowing travellers to choose a suitable tour matching their experience and vehicle's capability. Camping details, together with practical notes, encourage you to plan your own itinerary, with one eye on the information presented here and another on making the trek a personal adventure.

THE PRACTICALITIES:
This book has been produced as a guide book and does not attempt to cover the technique of 4WDing in any detail. Some of the treks described require a little more knowledge than that to drive a conventional car, but others will require a much greater level of skill. It is important to understand that a novice is unlikely to drive their new 4WD up a rocky climb with any more "natural ability" than somebody reversing a trailer for the first time.

An experienced instructor can dramatically flatten the learning curve. Travel with such a person in the early days – or better still join a 4WD Club or undertake a commercial training course. It is an unfortunate irony that most newcomers underestimate what their vehicle is capable of, but overestimate their ability to reach that limit.

VEHICLE CHOICE:
These tours have been field checked in full sized conventional 4WDs, occasionally towing a trailer or boat, and regularly with a utility based camper outfit. I have also travelled to many of these destinations in soft roaders with reasonable success.

Ground clearance, rather than gearing would be the limiting factor for 4WDs on most of these tours, so tactical driving can compensate for some dimensional restrictions. Choosing a suitable line over rough sections will elevate the underbody of any vehicle, while robust tyres and traction control assist in the grip department.

Each of these tours indicate whether a full size 4WD (with low range gearing) is necessary, or whether a soft roader could undertake the journey. In some cases a well driven AWD will complete the tour routinely, but recent rain for example can scour troublesome ruts into what may have been an easy track.

Equally, full size 4WDs are not automatically guaranteed easy travel. Driving experience and track conditions are variable, so always drive within you and your vehicle's ability and turn back (or exit via an easier track) if the conditions demand.

NAVIGATION:
These trek notes and associated maps should be used in conjunction with a compass and preferably a vehicle mounted GPS. Our maps provide the essential information, but can be supplemented with the relevant 1:50K or 1:25K topographic maps if you need contour lines or more detail. A GPS is also invaluable for locating your position quickly and allowing it to be plotted on a paper map.

It should be noted that the accompanying maps indicate more tracks than may be accessible to the travelling public. Follow the described route for each tour and only use other tracks if they are known to be for general use, perhaps seeking local knowledge or permission.

The trek notes utilise fixed locations such as rivers, T-intersections, items of interest etc as the reference points for distances throughout the tour. By working with intermediate distances, rather than a cumulative distance from the trip start, a number of inaccuracies are reduced. Variables such as odometer changes due to worn or non-standard tyre sizes, or loose surface slippage can be significant, so follow the kilometre readings with a degree of caution and lookout for other defining features as described in the notes.

TRACK ACCESS:
Most of these tours follow public roads through national parks, state forests and past private land. Access is generally both free and unrestricted – providing you stay on the designated tracks and not venture onto private land or drive onto management vehicle only tracks, which are usually locked or clearly sign posted.

In all cases it is essential to behave in a respectful manner. Do not drive on closed or rain affected tracks, obey all road signs, leave gates as found and do not drive "off road" especially over vegetated sand dunes.

Seasonal road closures apply to large areas of Victoria during the wettest times of the year. The typical closure period is from just after the Queen's Birthday long weekend in June until just before the Melbourne Cup Weekend in November. Tracks affected will usually be locked off by a gate and have signage indicating their closure period. Sometimes the closure period can be longer than expected (because of fire danger or a wetter winter than usual for example), and some tracks routinely have a longer period of closure. Always abide by the current restrictions; they are there to protect you, the environment and to reduce track damage.

CAMPING:
Bush camping sites have been detailed in most of the treks and may be private, state forest or national park based. Private camping grounds have all of the usual facilities, while the state forest and national park options vary from just a plot of dirt, to more friendly campgrounds with some facilities.

Camping in National Parks (if permitted) usually attracts a fee that varies between parks and seasons. Ph 131963 or *www.parkweb.vic.gov.au* Prebooking is often essential for the more popular parks, especially over the school holiday period and for public holiday long weekends.

TRAILERS
Trailers can be successfully towed along many of the tours presented (check our TRACK SNAPSHOT for an overview), but will limit your progress in tight country (sharp creek crossings, overgrown tracks and obstacle bypasses etc) and are a particular burden on soft sand or muddy sections – while slippery descents and failed climbs can be disastrous.

If a trailer is considered essential, gain some experience on the easier treks, before undertaking a more difficult tour. Travel in company if possible, as vehicle recovery can be tedious when travelling solo and substantially more difficult with a trailer in tow. However it is sometimes possible to unhitch a bogged trailer / vehicle combination and continue to drive out without the additional weight hampering progress – it is a good idea to fit a skid plate underneath the trailer's leading "A" frame structural member to facilitate the subsequent trailer recovery.

It is very desirable to select a robust trailer with a similar track to the towing vehicle and preferably ride on the same wheel / tyre combination. An extended articulation coupling is essential and it is important to adjust the trailer tyre pressures in proportion to those needed by the towing vehicle. In soft sand for example, a typical front and rear pressure may be 18psi and 22psi in the vehicle, but the trailer may only require 16psi for the weight it is carrying.

SAFETY:
Touring by 4WD is not without risk in itself, so travellers should minimise any hazards within their control. Always travel in a roadworthy vehicle, on good tyres and at a speed consistent with the terrain ahead. Full size 4WDs tend to be more top heavy and require longer braking distances than a conventional car (or soft roaders), so drive conservatively, particularly on side slopes and on wet bitumen.

Secure any load within the vehicle, preferably behind a cargo barrier and use the roof rack for light weight items. **Keep a fire extinguisher and first aid kit handy, together with a satphone or new generation EPIRB.** A UHF radio is very desirable for convoy chatter, but can be a lifesaver in mountain country too. Regular bush travellers could consider fitting a HF radio for longer distance communications.

Recovery gear should always be carried, with shovel, axe and heavy duty jack being mandatory items. A snatch strap together with rated shackles and suitable anchor points (definitely NOT a tow ball or vehicle tie down point) may be useful when travelling in company. All items of recovery gear should only be used by experienced people, noting especially that snatch straps should not be joined together by any type of metal coupling.

Always carry adequate water, fuel and food on even the shortest of trips; a breakdown or accident can happen anywhere. On longer tours, top up with water and fuel wherever possible, as track closures can mean lengthy detours and rain can close tracks for days at a time.

Summer time presents another hazard in Victoria and that is potential bushfires. Do not travel into forested country if a bushfire is current and immediately drive away from any fire activity if it is safe to do so (travel cautiously and with your headlights on). Some areas of public land will be closed on days deemed as Code Red and bush users are not permitted to enter or remain within these prescribed areas. You will need to keep aware of current restrictions and advice by listening to the local ABC radio station, regularly monitoring the CFA website on *www.cfa.vic.gov.au* or phoning the Victoria Bushfire Information Hotline on 1800 240 667.

Obviously follow all fire regulations including Total Fire Ban protocols and keeping any campfire under constant supervision. Use fireplaces where provided and keep fires to the minimum needed for cooking or warmth and certainly no bigger than one square metre in size.

ABBREVIATIONS USED IN TEXT:
N.P. National Park
S.F. State Forest
H.S. Homestead
M.V.O. Management Vehicle Only

TOUR LISTINGS BY REGION:
MELBOURNE REGION
The Black Range, Rubicon State Forest, Marysville, Mount Disappointment, Otway, Brisbane Ranges, Lerderderg, Wombat State Forest

HIGH COUNTRY
Merrijig to Porepunkah, Wonnangatta, Donnellys Creek, King River, Davies High Plains, Dargo High Plains, Billy Goat Bluff, Moroka Range, Jamieson to Licola, Howitt High Plains, Dargo to Omeo, Buckland Valley, Grant Goldfields, Sheepyard Flat

WESTERN VICTORIA
Sunset Country, The Big Desert, East Wyperfeld, South Wyperfeld, Little Desert, Grampians/Gariwerd

EAST GIPPSLAND
Croajingolong, Errinundra, Yalmy River, Orbost to Buchan, Timbarra River.

CHANGING CONDITIONS:
Please be aware that track conditions, campsites, locations and many other aspects of access can change. It is the responsibility of individuals to ensure and enquire about the current status of these possible changes prior to departure.

DISCLAIMER:
The publisher and consultants cannot accept responsibility for any errors or omissions in this guide as track conditions can change overtime. Every effort has been made to ensure the information in this book was accurate at the time of publication. The representation of roads and tracks on maps is not evidence of right of way.

ABOUT THE CONSULTANTS

John and Anne Morton, have been four-wheel driving for over 30 years clocking up nearly 700,000 kilometres around Australia.

John is a qualified mechanic and an accredited member of the Australian Institute of Professional Photographers (video division). Anne is an editor and writer. Their knowledge of four-wheel driving tracks around Australia is comprehensive and in their home state of Victoria, they have pretty well covered every track and 4WD adventure.

In 1995 they started Lifestyle Video Productions, and produced their first video documenting their month-long adventure on the Canning Stock Route. Their videos now document the four-wheel driving, the route and track conditions, mud maps of daily travel, as well as the sights, history, landscapes, scenery and the camaraderie of travelling with others.

Over the years Lifestyle Video Productions has grown into an award-winning business. Together John and Anne have completed a multitude of 4WD adventures – they have travelled Cape York 4 times, Canning Stock Route 3 times, Simpson Desert 7 times, plus dozens of trips on tracks all over Australia and more recently trips in New Zealand and Africa.

They are currently planning further explorations in NSW and Queensland.

Chapter 1
MELBOURNE AREA

◀ *Bushfire has claimed some of the forest.*

TRACK 1

THE BLACK RANGE

MELBOURNE REGION

Misty morning scene along Limestone Road.

Track Snapshot

TOUR ROUTE

Yea to Buxton via Black Range State Forest and Murrindindi Scenic Reserve.

DURATION AND DISTANCE

The 75 kilometre tour is an easy day trip, although many visitors choose to camp for a night.

TRACK DETAILS

Easy drive on routine bush roads in the dry. Wet weather will make some sections slippery, but there is no real rough stuff. Trailers OK even behind an AWD.

WHEN TO GO

Open all year round, but avoid days of extreme fire danger and very wet periods.

CAMPING

Excellent camping with basic facilities within the Murrundindi Scenic Reserve – fees apply and busy at peak times. Bush camping at Stanley HS.

FUEL AND SUPPLIES

Yea and Buxton provide for most needs.

MAPS

Rooftop Maps: Toolangi – Black Range

OTHER INFORMATION

The Murrundindi Scenic Reserve is a great place to unwind with plenty of water features and temperate rainforest. Numerous walks take in the atmosphere, and the picnic areas are ideal for day trippers, with paddling possibilities for the kids.

*The **Black Range** erupts from the **Great Divide** as a northward pointing finger of uplands separating the **Murrindindi** and **Acheron Valleys**. Its largely forested contours have bequeathed a hardwood resource to European settlement for more than 150 years – a tradition that continues to this day, although it is the quicker growing softwoods that are now harvested from its eastern flank.*

*This trek traces the **Murrindindi** and its headwaters into the range country, before following its spine then dropping into the **Acheron Valley**. There is great camping along the way (both bush and more developed options), together with a variety of natural attractions and some easy 4WDing along scenic bush tracks.*

Leave **Yea** via the **Goulburn Valley Highway** heading east toward **Alexandra**. Cross the **Yea River** and its wildlife refuge wetlands to pass the **Killingworth Road** on your left. A rest stop on the right flags **Limestone Road**, some 2.4 kilometres out of Yea.

Turn right to begin a lovely rural drive past dams, stock ramps, wire fences and other pastoral infrastructure. Roadside cuttings tame the undulating terrain, where rounded hills recede into the mountain air, and tree lined gullies cut contours into an otherwise seamless pasture.

Frogponds Road branches to the right 2.9 kilometres along Limestone Road, with the **Cheviot Tunnel** turn off on the left directly opposite (travellers with time to spare could make a 7.2 kilometre return detour here to see a 200 metre long rail tunnel built in the 1880s. Its arch shaped brick facade is imposing, but it is no longer possible to drive through the structure; instead the site forms part of a cycling route along the **Tallarook – Mansfield Rail Trail**).

Continue south east past **Cheviot Hills HS** to cross **Limestone Creek** on a single lane bridge. You will pass **Langs Road** on the right as you trace the poplar lined waters of **Limestone Creek** onto gravel. Thicker bush marks the boundary of **Black Range State Forest**, where you cross **Limestone Creek** again, some 13.9 kilometres from Yea.

Limestone Road transitions to **Ginter Road**, where you keep right at the **Boundary Road** track intersection. Keep left at both the subsequent junctions of **Beatson Track** and **Higgenbotham Track**, to pound a path under mature messmate and peppermints, with an understorey of treefern and wattle.

You will reach the **Stanley HS Historic Area** about 2.6 kilometres into the state forest, where a mature stand of deciduous trees colour the clearing. Pines, spruces and naturalised iris mark the former homestead site, although these days only an old boiler and some rusting relics remain linked with the past. Camping is popular here, but no facilities are provided.

Continue beyond **Stanley Track** to the **North Eastern Road** junction 1.3 kilometres later, and swing left here on a bracken lined run to the **Tratford Break** intersection. Continue straight to follow the **Ault Beeac Creek** headwaters through an attractive section of bush dotted with manna gum and some mountain ash draped in garlands of dangling bark.

A small parking area marks the crossing of **Ault Beeac Creek**, where a packed clump of treefern irrigated by trickling waters can

BELOW: *Tall eucalypts on North Eastern Road.*

BASIC CHECK LIST . . .

- ☑ Soft Roaders
- ☑ Trailers
- ☑ Road Tyres
- ☑ Avoid wet weather

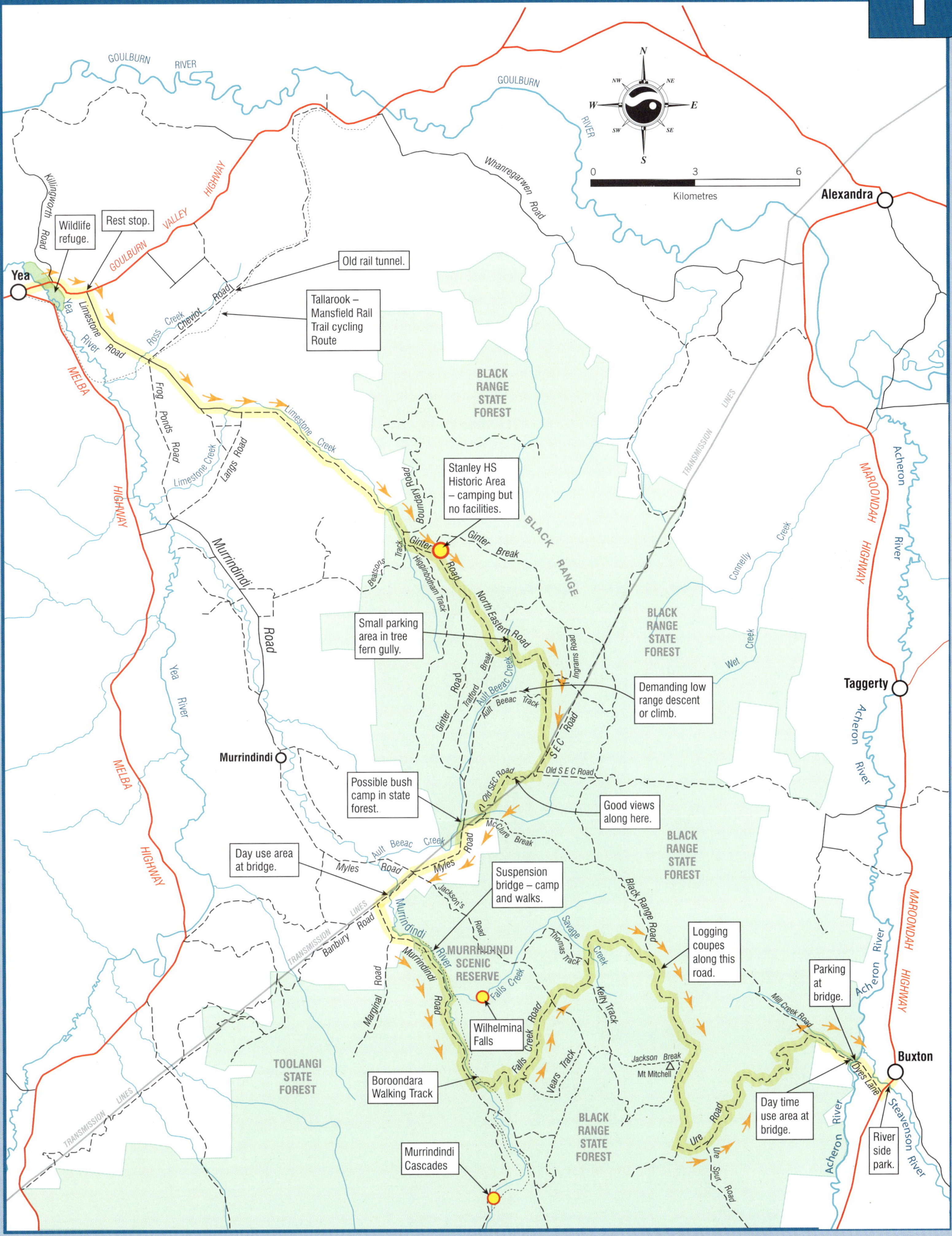
Wildlife refuge.
Rest stop.
Old rail tunnel.
Tallarook – Mansfield Rail Trail cycling Route
Stanley HS Historic Area – camping but no facilities.
Small parking area in tree fern gully.
Demanding low range descent or climb.
Possible bush camp in state forest.
Good views along here.
Day use area at bridge.
Suspension bridge – camp and walks.
Logging coupes along this road.
Parking at bridge.
Wilhelmina Falls
Boroondara Walking Track
Day time use area at bridge.
River side park.
Murrindindi Cascades
Yea
Alexandra
Taggerty
Murrindindi
Buxton
BLACK RANGE STATE FOREST
BLACK RANGE
MURRINDINDI SCENIC RESERVE
TOOLANGI STATE FOREST
GOULBURN RIVER
GOULBURN VALLEY HIGHWAY
MELBA HIGHWAY
MAROONDAH HIGHWAY
TRANSMISSION LINES
Whanregarwen Road
Killingworth Road
Limestone Road
Limestone Creek
Yea River
Ross Creek
Cheviot Road
Frog Ponds Road
Langs Road
Murrindindi Road
Boundary Road
Ginter Road
Ginter Break
Beatsons Track
Higinbotham Track
North Eastern Road
Ingrams Road
Connelly Creek
Wet Creek
Acheron River
Trafford Break
Ault Beeac Creek
Ault Beeac Track
SEC Road
Old SEC Road
Old S E C Road
McClure Break
Myles Road
Jackson's Road
Banbury Road
Murrindindi River
Marginal Road
Savage Creek
Thomas Track
Black Range Road
Falls Creek
Falls Creek Road
Kelly Track
Years Track
Jackson Break
Mt Mitchell
Mill Creek Road
Ure Road
Ure Spur Road
Dyes Lane
Steavenson River
Kilometres
0
3
6
N
NE
E
SE
S
SW
W
NW

be more closely appreciated from an informal walking track. The ferny gully continues as you drive to the **Ingrams Road** junction, and keep right to remain on **North East Road**.

You will pass an unsignposted track on the left and **Ault Beeac Falls Track** on the right (demanding low range rubble strewn descent), before reaching **SEC Road** and its dominating overhead power lines. Turn right here and follow the pylons with good views opening up from the crest of the **Black Range**. Avoid any side tracks to reach the **Old SEC Road** junction 600 metres later. Keep right at the turn and at the next junction about 500 metres later. Commanding views of the **Murrrindindi Valley** open up on a winding descent to **McClure Break**, about three kilometres from the **Old SEC Road** junction.

Keep right at the junction to reach a tee intersection back on **Ginter Road** at the site of an informal bush camp. Turn left here to follow the gathering waters of **Ault Beeac Creek** back into freehold land, and under the high voltage power lines again, to reach **Myles Road**.

Grazing cattle and pasture precedes **Jackson's Road** on the left, where you keep straight on the now sealed **Banbury Road**. Steel towers aplenty mark the power transmission lines as you cross the **Murrindindi River Bridge** and its small day use carpark on the west side.

Turn left 500 metres later onto **Murrindindi Road**, signposted "**Wilhelmina Falls**", and the recommencement of gravel. Keep left at the **Marginal Road** junction 1.1 kilometres later, to enter **Toolangi State Forest**. The **Murrindindi Scenic Reserve** begins 300 metres later at signposted "**Suspension Bridge**".

A number of camping areas, walking tracks and picnic areas are located along the next 11 or so kilometres of road, with access to the **Murrindindi River** being the common denominator. It is a popular destination for campers, caravanners, hikers and those simply looking to cool off on a hot day.

Basic facilities are provided at the camps, fees are payable and prebooking is required for some popular sites. Walks range from easy river strolls to strenuous options of 9 kilometres and more.

The 75 metre drop of **Wilhelmina Falls** is a popular hike destination, with historic timber milling sites accessible, and river cascades a major drawcard, as they race under a rainforest jungle of myrtle beech and sassafras.

We turn off **Murrindindi Road** at the **Falls Creek Road** junction, some 4.8 kilometres beyond **Suspension Bridge**. Head east crossing the **Murrindindi** on a concrete bridge, where **Boroondara Track** fans off left and right (walkers only – carpark at junction).

Keep straight past **Vears Track** on a gradual climb to the **Jackson Road** intersection. Continue on **Falls Creek Road** through wattle forest to **Kelty Track** on the right, about 6.7 kilometres from the bridge.

Continue ahead to pass **Thomas Track** on the left and cross **Salvage Creek** at a culvert, then reach a tee intersection on the **Black Range Road**. Turn right to follow the range's spine on better road. Logging coupes are evident on the drive south as you pass a couple on either side of this forestry arterial.

Jackson Break flags **Mount Mitchell** and a graveyard of burnt trees now thickening in a corridor of regrowth. Turn left onto **Ure Road** 6.4 kilometres beyond the **Falls Creek Road** tee, and begin a sustained drop off. Views of the knife like **Cathedral Range** define the **Acheron Valley** directly ahead as you pass **Ure Spur Track** and its neighbouring gully of treefern.

Winding road and numerous cuttings allow for easy travel, but don't forget that this is still a logging truck route, and other users including mountain bikers and trail bikers also frequent the area. A block of pine plantation marks the lower end of **Ure Road** with young patches forming a mosaic of green against the khaki native bushland.

Avoid side tracks until you reach a tee intersection on **Mill Creek Road,** where you turn right, keeping right again at the **Francis Road** junction. Follow **Mill Creek** into cleared land with stockyards and grazing cattle.

You will exit **Black Range State Forest** and cross **Mill Creek** at a bridge with some parking available for daytime users. The **Buxton Mountain Bike Park** is next on the left (day use, parking area, toilet, shelter shed), where you cross the **Acheron River** (day use parking both sides of the bridge).

Continue past **Steavenson Road** on the left to follow the **Little Steavenson River** along **Dyes Lane**. A patch of deciduous trees heralds the **Maroondah Highway**, where you turn left. Drive past the **Buxton Trout Farm** to cross the **Steavenson River** (toilet and park) and conclude the tour at **Buxton**.

RIGHT: *Suspension Bridge is just one feature on the Murrundindi River.*

BOTTOM RIGHT: *Side tracks like Ault Beeac Falls Track can be quite demanding.*

BELOW: *There are numerous cascades within the Murrindindi Scenic Reserve.*

Rubicon State Forest

TRACK 2

MELBOURNE REGION

TRACK SNAPSHOT

TOUR ROUTE
Snobs Creek to Thornton via the Rubicon Historic Area and Royston Range.

DURATION AND DISTANCE
This 60 kilometre trek will take a day, but it will be a long one if you undertake the hike to Mount Torbreck.

TRACK DETAILS
An easy forest drive suitable for all vehicles and trailers. The optional detour to Barnewall Plains will require a full size 4WD with low range gears.

WHEN TO GO
Seasonally closed gates on the Barnewall Plain and Rubicon Historic Area limit access to the warmer months between November and early June. Avoid wet weather and access may be restricted during periods of timber harvesting.

CAMPING
Nice bush camping at Barnewall Plain and more popular camps at Kendalls with basic facilities.

FUEL AND SUPPLIES
Thornton can cater for basic requirements, with more possibilities at the township of Eildon.

MAPS
Rooftop Maps: Lake Eildon

OTHER INFORMATION
Be prepared for wet weather at any time of the year, and possible snow at Mount Torbreck. Road tyres will be OK if the tracks are dry.trippers, with paddling possibilities for the kids.

Historic trestle bridge at Royston River Power Station.

*A variety of attractions make the **Rubicon State Forest** one of Victoria's most appealing pieces of bushland. Visitors intrigued by history or engineering feats will appreciate the isolated but still operational Rubicon hydro-electricity operations, while sightseers will enjoy waterfalls, sub alpine bushland and the occasional viewpoint.*

Hikers can find plenty of ways to expend their energy, while fishers can try their luck on some great waterways. Campers are well catered for with choices ranging from bush camps to caravan parks. Tracks within the state forest can be quite demanding, but this trek follows an easy route, with one optional detour if you feel like a challenge.

The trek begins at the hamlet of **Snobs Creek**, located on the **Goulburn Valley Highway**, where **Snobs Creek** joins the **Goulburn River**. Head south along **Snobs Creek Road** with the pub dominating the corner and a few houses making up the community. The local fish hatchery is a prominent industry here, but cattle grazing is also a way of life, with stockramps and other pastoral infrastructure marking the drive out.

You reach **Rubicon State Forest** after 2.7 kilometres and hit the gravel about 1 kilometre later. Follow the steady climb to signposted **"Snobs Creek Falls"**, 3 kilometres into state forest. Parking is available both sides of the walking track, which allows visitors to follow a short path to a couple of viewpoints overlooking the cascades and final 100 metre drop off.

One kilometre beyond the falls, **Dry Creek Road** peels off to the left, with **Herbs Road** branching right 500 metres later (access to **Morris Lookout** via seasonally closed track punctuated with erosion control mounds and sharp switchbacks). Mature eucalypts shade an understorey of fern and correa on the drive past **No 6 Track** on the right, then a crossing of **Snobs Creek Bridge** 300 metres later. Fire damage to the bush along Snobs Creek is minimal, making travel a visual pleasure despite the blackberry invasion.

You will reach **Conns Gap Road** on the left some 2.3 kilometres from the bridge where an optional detour can be made. The drive to **Barnewall Plains** is well worthwhile, but will require a vehicle with good clearance and low range gears.

Turn left if you feel confident and climb the 800 metres to **Conns Bridge**, where a nice gully backs up to a parking area. **Barnewall Plains Road** begins on the west side of the bridge, with a seasonally closed gate marking the entrance. It is a rough and steep beginning pocked with large holes and will require thoughtful wheel placement.

However the surface quality quickly improves to a plain earthen track following tree fern gully with just a few rocks jutting out to trap you. A couple of switchbacks ramp the climb into the **Mount Torbreck Scenic Reserve**, and the final 600 metres to **Barnewall Plain**. Although the plains area is relatively small, it is fringed with lovely wattle forest, and backed by tall mountain and alpine ash. Reedy tussock plants define a camping and picnic area with fireplace and table as the only facilities.

A 2.1 kilometre walking track leads to the 1516 metre peak of **Mount Torbreck**, taking

BASIC CHECK LIST . . .

- ☑ **Soft Roaders**
- ☑ **Trailers**
- ☑ **Avoid wet weather**

The hydro power stations in the Rubicon forest are still operating.

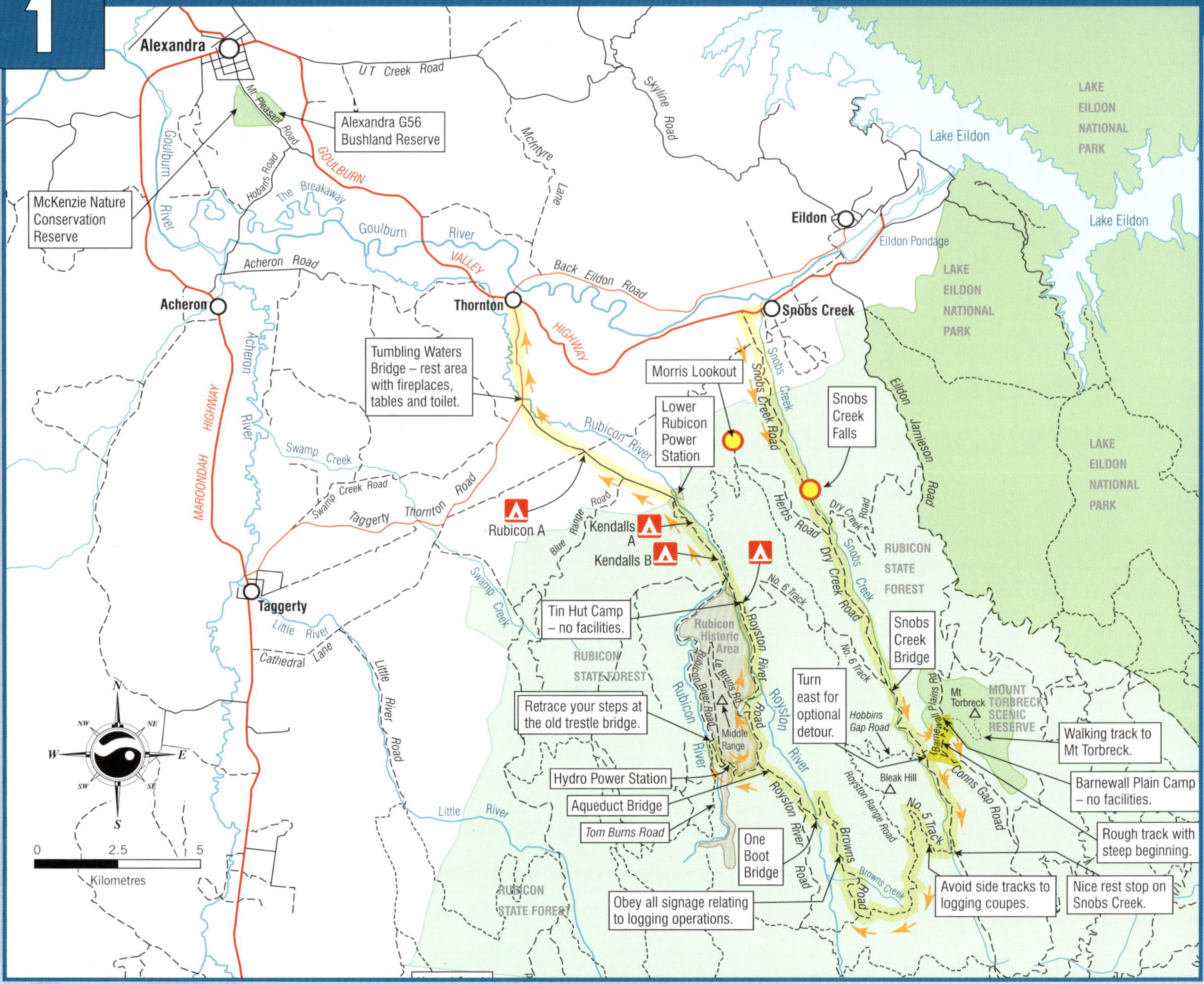

MAP 1 Track 2

Alexandra
Alexandra G56 Bushland Reserve
McKenzie Nature Conservation Reserve
UT Creek Road
Skyline Road
McIntyre Lane
Mt Pleasant Road
Hobans Road
The Breakaway
Goulburn River
GOULBURN VALLEY HIGHWAY
Lake Eildon
LAKE EILDON NATIONAL PARK
Eildon
Eildon Pondage
Back Eildon Road
Acheron Road
Acheron
Acheron River
MAROONDAH HIGHWAY
Thornton
Snobs Creek
Tumbling Waters Bridge – rest area with fireplaces, tables and toilet.
Morris Lookout
Lower Rubicon Power Station
Snobs Creek Falls
Snobs Creek Road
Jamieson Road
Rubicon River
Swamp Creek
Swamp Creek Road
Taggerty Thornton Road
Rubicon A
Kendalls A
Kendalls B
Blue Range Road
Herbs Road
Dry Creek Road
RUBICON STATE FOREST
No. 6 Track
Taggerty
Little River
Cathedral Lane
Little River Road
Tin Hut Camp – no facilities.
Rubicon Historic Area
Royston River Road
Le Bruns Rd
Rubicon River Road
Middle Range
Snobs Creek Bridge
Turn east for optional detour.
Hobbins Gap Road
Mt Torbreck
MOUNT TORBRECK SCENIC RESERVE
Barnewall Plains Rd
Walking track to Mt Torbreck.
Barnewall Plain Camp – no facilities.
Retrace your steps at the old trestle bridge.
Hydro Power Station
Aqueduct Bridge
Tom Burns Road
One Boot Bridge
Bleak Hill
Royston Range Road
Conns Gap Road
No. 5 Track
Rough track with steep beginning.
Browns Road
Browns Creek
Obey all signage relating to logging operations.
Avoid side tracks to logging coupes.
Nice rest stop on Snobs Creek.
0 2.5 5
Kilometres

LEFT: *View over Lake Eildon from Morris Lookout.*

hikers on a steep obstacle course to the roof of the **Torbreck Range** for views overlooking **Lake Eildon**. The well defined route is marked with orange triangles as it passes huge granite boulders, and reaches snowgums for the final push to a trig point and memorial on **Conn Ridge**.

Return from **Barnewall Plain** to the **Snobs Creek Road** junction and continue south past **Hobbins Gap Road** and a logged coupe on the side of **Bleak Hill**. You will reach **No 5 Track** on the right, 2.5 kilometres beyond the **Barnewall Plain** turn off.

Veer right at this junction to cross **Snobs Creek** and reach its adjacent parking area. This is an excellent spot to stop for lunch or to stretch your legs, with clear water bubbling under a verdant canopy of jungle. There are no facilities at this informal stop, but there is easy creek access and a nice grassy area on which to set up the chairs.

You will climb from **No 5 Bridge** past recent logging coupes (stay on the main

ABOVE: *Snobs Creek Falls are just off the access road.*

ABOVE: *There is good camping and a challenging walk on the Barnewall Plains.*

ABOVE: *Nice rest stop on No 5 Track at the bridge.*

road) to reach **Royston Range Road** on the right. Keep left at this junction and descend past other logging access tracks for a seamless transition onto **Browns Road**, some 7.3 kilometres from **No 5 Bridge**.

Logging has been associated with the **Rubicon** area for many years, most actively during the 1930s when eight spotmills sprang up to cut the harvested timber. Many of these sites were destroyed following the ravaging 1939 bushfires, but timber production remains a key industry to this day. Mountain and alpine ash are the prized species, but messmate and shining gum are also found in the area.

Travel heads in a northerly direction now, with excellent views over the **Middle Range** and its harvested coupe. You cross **Browns Creek** into what could be a logging area (obey all signs and follow any instructions which may include announcing your presence via UHF radio) then cross the **Royston River** on **One Boot Bridge**.

You will reach the **Royston River Road** at a tee intersection 700 metres later, where you turn right and continue to **Aqueduct Bridge** 1.4 kilometres beyond the tee. A formed concrete aqueduct passes under the bridge, channeling water from the **Royston River** to a nearby historic hydro-electric power station.

The **Rubicon Historic Area** is home to four such power stations having commenced production in 1927, and at one time supplying about a fifth of the state's power requirements. These days its output cannot provide even 1% of Victoria's needs, but the facility is still viable and well worth a look.

So drive a further 300 metres from **Aqueduct Bridge** to a tee intersection, with **Rubicon River Road** branching to the left. We will return to this junction to complete the trek, but for now turn hard left through a seasonally closed gate and past a MVO track on your left.

You will see the **Royston River** power station on your left not far from the junction, and although access is not permitted, the road side views are quite good, and from a distance you will hear the turbine whirring from beneath the iron clad building.

Continue westward to pass the **Rubicon Outdoor Centre** and a derelict power station building (no access to either), before reaching an impressive trestle bridge. The tramway is no longer used, but it is worth stopping to take a look at the site where other historic infrastructure lies as it was left.

Return from the trestle bridge to the **Royston River Road** junction and turn left past **Le Bruns Road** and over a culvert on **Icey Creek**. **Webbys Corner** flags numerous logging roads to the side (keep straight) as you closely follow the **Royston** with its mossy boulder strewn gully on the right.

Three Kilometre Bridge continues the practice of naming every possible feature on this drive, followed by The S's and Rock Wall (an engineered erosion containment device). **No 6 Track** enters from the right about 1 kilometre prior to a block of private property on the left (the historic old post office) and nearby **Tin Hut Camp** – a bush camping area with no facilities.

You cross the **Royston** here at a bridge to reach a tee intersection on the **Rubicon River Road**. Your exit will be on the right, but a short stretch of road on the left heads to other bush camping sites and an impressive view of the water tunnel feeding the **Rubicon Power Station**. Other items of interest can be seen locally, but there is no access beyond the fenceline.

Heading north you will find the formal camping areas of **Kendalls A** and **B**, with the turn offs beginning 500 metres beyond the bridge. These are popular campsites with bollards and fences restricting access to the river, but leaving a large area for tents and caravans. Toilets are located at the free camp, but bring your own firewood as there is not much within walking distance of camp.

Walking tracks link the two camps, together with the **Lower Rubicon Power Station**, chasing the river as it bubbles over cascades. **Kendalls Link Track** and **Cicada Circuit Trail** follow the river (using an elaborate footbridge over one gully) and sections of steeper pathway, on a lengthy ramble totaling 8.2 kilometres if done in its entirety.

Head north from **Kendalls** and cross **Skinny Bridge** into the widening valley with the **Lower Rubicon Power Station** on the right (a more recent addition to the hydro-power scheme). Grazing land and deciduous trees flag **Blue Range Road** on the left and the community of **Rubicon A** about one kilometre later.

You will reach a tee intersection on the **Taggerty – Thornton Road**, where you turn right to cross the **Rubicon River** at **Tumbling Waters Bridge**. A rest area here with fireplaces, tables and toilet makes a good stop, with the township of **Thornton** just 3 kilometres further on.

TRACK 3

MARYSVILLE

MELBOURNE REGION

ABOVE: *Deciduous trees still colour the main street of Marysville.*

TRACK SNAPSHOT

TOUR ROUTE
Marysville to Buxton via Keppel Falls and Lady Talbot Forest Drive.

DURATION AND DISTANCE
The 55 kilometre tour is easily done in a day.

TRACK DETAILS
Easy forest driving in the main, with a little rough stuff on Camerons Cascade Track and Keppel Hut Track. Generally OK for capable AWDs, and trailers no problem.

WHEN TO GO
The seasonal road closure on Camerons Cascade Track and Keppel Hut Track limits travel to the drier months between November and early June.

CAMPING
Bush camping with basic facilities at Keppel Hut and Keppel Creek.

FUEL AND SUPPLIES
Marysville and Buxton can cater for most requirements.

MAPS
Rooftop Maps: Marysville-Lake Eildon.

OTHER INFORMATION
Lady Talbot Forest Drive is open all year round, so if the link trails are closed it is still possible to enjoy the falls and jungle walks by taking Lady Talbot Forest Drive directly out of Marysville.

Following the devastating Black Saturday bushfires of 2009, ***Marysville*** *has literally risen from the ashes with a new commercial hub and a renewed grip of the tourist market – a vital piece of its economy. The surrounding bushland however bears enormous scars from the inferno; many of which will remain for years to come. But vast tracts of the land are recovering with noticeable regrowth and the return of wildlife.*

This tour takes in contrasting pieces of the landscape with apocalyptic views of the razed mountain ash, followed by gullies of verdant treefern and lyrebird habitat. The area's famous waterfalls and cascades still offer a visual feast, and this relatively easy forest drive will suit most visitors with some nice walks, picnic areas and bush camping if you feel the need.

Leave the main street of **Marysville** by turning south onto **Pack Street**, then veer left to follow **Falls Road**. Mostly new houses dot the road out, and despite the town being decimated by the fire, many deciduous trees still survive to colour the run up the **Steavenson Valley**.

You'll reach a parking bay at 1.8 kilometres where the challenging **Oxley Climb** begins (steep uphill trudge through burnt mountain ash to commanding viewpoints and optional return via **Steavenson Falls**). We will turn left 100 metres later onto unsealed **Yellow Dog Road** signposted "**Yellow Dog Picnic Area**".

However the bitumen ribbon of **Falls Road** continues uphill to a carpark from where a short walk reaches the iconic falls. First visited by tourists in the 1860s, the falls are now floodlit at night, as they tumble 84 metres over five steps. It is well worth making this detour, before returning to **Yellow Dog Road** and heading east over **Treefern Gully Track** (walking and cycling track following a lovely waterway studded with massive treeferns).

You will reach **Yellow Dog Picnic Area** 1.2 kilometres from **Falls Road** where table, seats and fireplace mark the **Steavenson River** crossing. **Treefern Gully Walking Trail** also meets here, with **Water Race Track** branching to the left.

Keep heading south east on a slow climb as you weave in and around the **Steavenson** headwaters, with a mass graveyard of burnt mountain ash dominating, especially to the south. Wattle regrowth is now encroaching on the towering needles of silver hardwood, with pea flowers dotting the understorey in yellow blotches.

Pfeiffer Falls trickles from **Robley Spur** and under a culvert as you follow the **Bicentennial National Trail** to **Olsen Road** on the right. Keep left at this junction as the track deteriorates a little with clay patches and possible fallen trees.

BASIC CHECK LIST . . .

- ☑ Soft Roaders
- ☑ Trailers
- ☑ Road Tyres
- ☑ Avoid wet weather

Forests of burnt mountain ash still stand after the devastating fire of 2009.

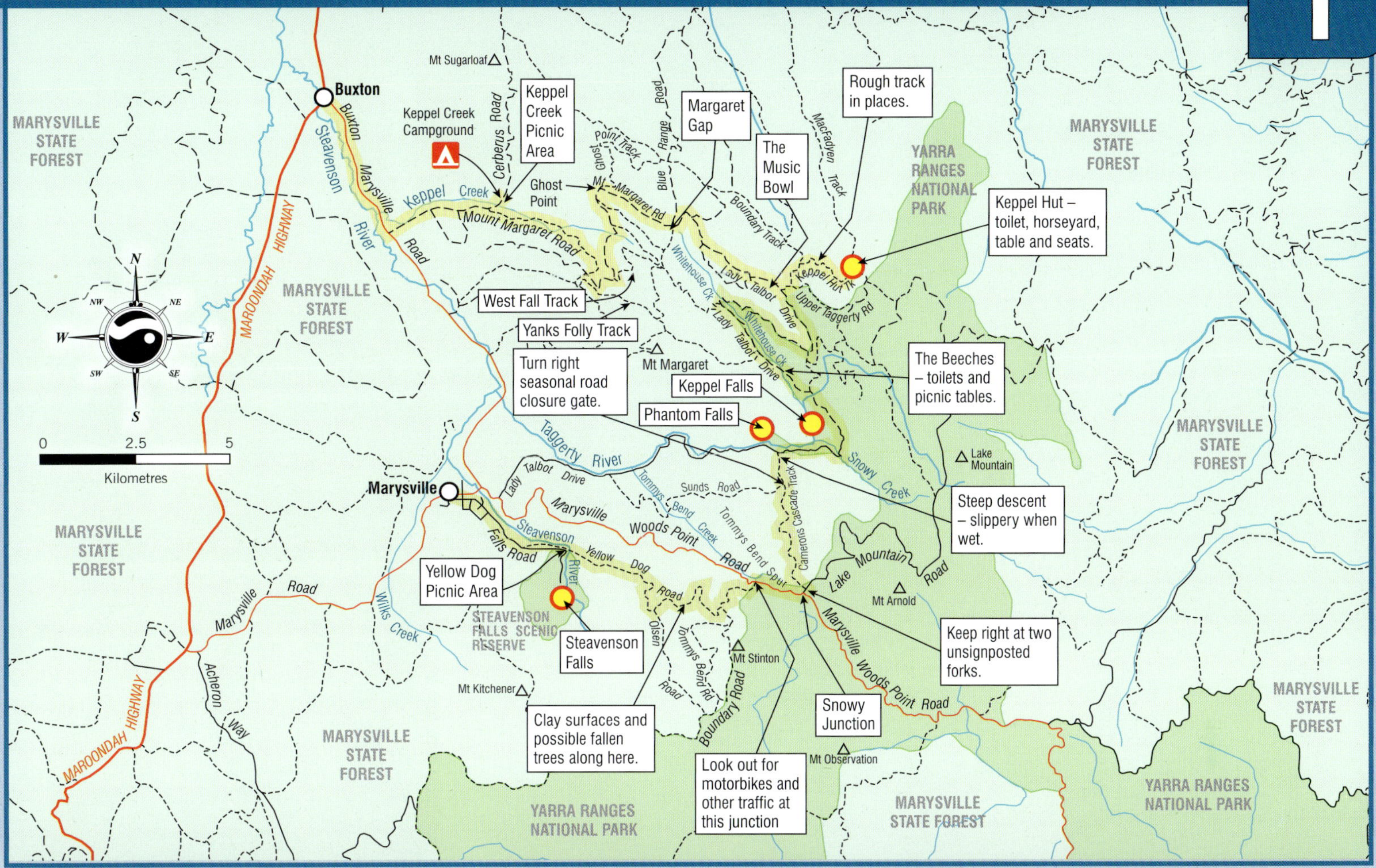

ABOVE: *The king parrot is home in the tall eucalypt forests around Marysville.*

RIGHT: *Camerons Cascade Track is probably the most testing section for AWD vehicles.*

You'll reach a tee intersection on **Tommys Bend Road** some 6.4 kilometres from **Yellow Dog Picnic Area**, where you turn left. Follow the logging road along the **Great Divide** and past **Mount Grant** to the **Marysville – Woodspoint Road** 1.4 kilometres later.

Turn right at the junction and follow the blacktop into **Yarra Ranges NP** (motorbikers have a particular liking for this winding strip of bitumen, so take particular care when turning). Swing left 1.2 kilometres later at **Snowy Junction**, taking the **Lake Mountain Road** into **Alpine Reserve**.

Yellow line markings indicate travel toward the winter snowline, but we turn left onto **Camerons Cascade Track** after only 100 metres. Keep right at the fork 100 metres later, and right again 300 metres beyond that at an unsignposted intersection. The winding forest drive heads northward past a myriad of rivulets trickling from **Tommys Bend Spur**.

You will reach the **Sunds Road** junction some 3 kilometres beyond the **Snowy Junction**, where you turn right through a seasonally closed gate for a sustained low range descent. This earthen track would be slippery in the wet, but when dry no problem for a full size 4WD on reasonable tyres, and even trafficable to a well driven and capable all wheel drive.

The drop off finishes at a tee intersection on **Lady Talbot Drive** where you turn right to continue the trek. However those interested in taking a peek at **Phantom Falls** can swing left to find a carpark 500 metres later. From here walkers can cross the **Taggerty River** and follow a steep 400 metre trail through nice treefern to a viewing platform overlooking the falls as they smother granite boulders on a tortuous race under myrtle beech and around mossy fallen branches.

Further east and 200 metres beyond the

ABOVE: *Keppels Hut offers camping possibilities nearby.*

LEFT: *Some of the eucalypt forest managed to survive the inferno.*

RIGHT *Steavenson Falls drop in spectacular style.*

Camerons Cascade Track junction is another carpark with a longer but easier standard walk (2 kilometres return) that takes in **Keppel Falls**. This impressive drop in the **Taggerty River** was named by European settlers in the 1880s, and can be appreciated from two viewing platforms along its length.

Beyond the walk carpark follow the drive 800 metres to a lookout taking in the falls (from a distance) and begin a climb along **Snowy Creek**. A backdrop of burnt out trees presents a monochromatic view of the landscape as you cross the **Taggerty River** at a one lane bridge.

A carpark and picnic area are located at the crossing, where hikers can undertake a four kilometre return circuit walk. Less energetic folk can follow a path past the **Taggerty River Falls** to the confluence of **Whitehouse Creek**. The circuit walk uses a series of bridges to trace **Whitehouse Creek** to **"The Beeches"** – it is a very pleasant stroll and well worthwhile, but **The Beeches** are also accessible by vehicle.

Follow **Lady Talbot Drive** north on a moister, more rutted path to a carpark at **The Beeches** 1.2 kilometres later. Toilets and picnic tables mark a crossing of **Whitehouse Creek** where a rainforest loop trail originates, and the longer circuit walk can also begin. Ancient myrtle beech trees feature on the trail (some over 300 years old) together with sassafras, blackwood and delicate greenery like mosses, lichen and kangaroo fern.

Continue past **The Beeches** to **Whitehouse Saddle**, where a fire line track heads toward the winter snow clad peak of **Mount Margaret**. Keep right at the junction to pass a dense stand of tree fern, reaching **East Fall Track** on the left. **Lady Talbot Drive** continues as you cross the trickling waters of **Whitehouse Creek** and swing back through jungle in a south easterly direction.

The climb heads back more northerly through burnt out bush to reach the **Upper Taggerty Road** on the right, some 7.2 kilometres from **The Beeches**. The trek will continue past this junction, but for now turn right through a seasonally closed gate to **Boundary Track** on the left, 200 metres later. Turn left here and climb for a further 700 metres to **Keppel Hut Track** on the right. Turn right at the fork to travel over some roughish road and around the switchback marking **Cameron Creek**.

You will arrive at a carpark adjacent to the hut, where **McFadyen Track** continues north. Access to the hut is walk in (20 metres), although it is a popular camp with toilet and horseyard. A stone weir on a nearby creek provides some water access and table and seats are provided. The original hut (itself rebuilt from a previous fire) was rather appealing with weatherboard walls, stone chimney and timber shingle roof. Unfortunately it succumbed to the 2009 blaze and has since been rebuilt around the iconic chimney – albeit in basic corrugated iron.

Return to **Lady Talbot Drive** and turn right past **The Music Bowl** on a gradual climb to **Mount Margaret Gap**. **Mount Margaret Gap Road** branches south here, with **Blue Range Road** heading north. Continue west on **Mount Margaret Road** to leave **Yarra Ranges NP** on improving road surface to **Ghost Point**.

You will pass **Ghost Point Track** on the right, with views of **Marysville** opening up on the descent. **West Fall Track** branches to the left with **Yanks Folly Track** not far after. A viewpoint on the right offers a clear view of the northern country, with **Mount Sugarloaf** and the **Cathedral Range** dominating the skyline. Continue the descent to a tee intersection, with **Cerberus Road** branching to the right.

We will turn left here to finish the trek, but those who turn right will reach **Keppel Creek Picnic Area** on the right 300 metres later. Table seats and fireplace allow visitors to stop for a break or to take a walk along the creek. **Keppel Creek Campground** is situated a further 200 metres away on the left for those who wish to linger a while.

Return to **Cerberus Road** junction and keep heading west to enter the **Steavenson Valley** with its lush pasture and farming infrastructure. Continue to another tee on the **Buxton – Marysville Road**, where you turn right, and reach the township of **Buxton** 4 kilometres later.

MOUNT DISAPPOINTMENT

TRACK 4

MELBOURNE REGION

TRACK SNAPSHOT

TOUR ROUTE
Wallan to Strath Creek via Mount Disappointment State Forest.

DURATION AND DISTANCE
The 90 kilometre run is easily done in a day.

TRACK DETAILS
Routine gravel and unsurfaced tracks in the main, with a sustained climb up Escreet Road. Suitable for AWDs and trailers. However be aware that many tracks fanning off the tour route are substantially harder to negotiate.

WHEN TO GO
Seasonal Road closure on Morrison Road at the Sunday Creek headwaters limits access to the warmer months between November and the start of June.

CAMPING
Popular camp at Andersons Garden with other options at Regular Camp and No 1 Camp. Regular Camp is usually quiet, while No 1 Camp has better access for vehicles and trailers. Basic facilities at each site.

FUEL AND SUPPLIES
Wallan and Strath Creek have fuel and basic supplies.

MAPS
Rooftop Maps: Toolangi-Macedon

OTHER INFORMATION
Although much of the state forest was ravaged by fire in 2009, rebuilt visitor facilities and forest regrowth have combined to again welcome bush enthusiasts.

Tree ferns and boulders dot the drive along Board Road.

Although the explorers Hume and Hovell were less than enthusiastic about this piece of the ***Great Dividing Range****, it is likely that you will leave here thanking them for their efforts. The intrepid duo (and party) combed a broad swathe of country from Geelong to Albury searching for productive grazing land. Along the way they did indeed identify much needed pasture, but felt somewhat melancholic with this area; naming its most lofty peak:* ***Mount Disappointment****.*

These days 4WDers can follow in the footsteps of Hume and Hovell to marvel at some quite inspiring range country, etched by creeks and dominated by the occasional lookout. Timber cutters did (and still do) make use of the forest's tree resource, and although fire has claimed some of the bushland, there are still some nice pockets to be found, and some excellent camps to be enjoyed.

The trek begins by following **Watson Street** east from the main shopping strip in **Wallan**, signposted "**Whittlesea**", with the peak of **Mount Disappointment** visible directly ahead. An overpass brings you beyond the **Hume Freeway** to a roundabout, where you keep straight to cross the rail line. Turn left at the tee intersection on the **Broadford Road**, signposted "**Wandong**", then right 200 metres later on the signposted "**Whittlesea Road**".

Begin a winding climb over **Cleve Hill** for a rural run past stockyards and hay sheds, to a sweeping right bend at **Upper Plenty**. You will pass the primary school and turn hard left onto **Mahadys Road** at a bus shelter. There is no signpost at the junction, but you will be about 8.6 kilometres from **Wallan**.

Gravel paves the way now as you cross **Bruces Creek** and pass a series of farmlets. Horse riders also use this road, so keep your speed down and pass **Stokes Road** on the right along an avenue of pines. Thick bushland flags **Lords Road** on the right 1.8 kilometres later, where you keep left and squeeze down a much narrower track.

Rutted passage continues to a triangulated intersection on **Cockpit Road** some 1.2 kilometres beyond Lords Road. Keep left here remaining on **Mill Range Road** to follow a descent over **Bruces Creek** and subsequent climb out. Occasional views take in lines of deciduous trees and a view over the hamlet of **Upper Plenty**.

A number of side tracks fan off into private property (follow the main road) as you enter **Mount Disappointment State Forest**. Minor forestry tracks break away from the sustained climb, and these together with most of the arterial tracks can be popular with trailbike riders especially on weekends – take particular care on bends and crests.

Hollowback Reservoir marks the end of **Mill Range Road** at a tee intersection on **Main Mountain Road**. There is no access to the dam, so turn left at the tee, then right 100 metres later, onto **Raynors Road**. You will drop off the crest of the **Great Divide** along a potentially slippery track, with some drainage lines built up with rubble. Continue the descent past side tracks to a tee on **Westcott Creek Road**. We will turn right here to continue the trek, but for now swing left to the camping area at **Andersons Garden**.

Located on **Boundary Road**, you will cross the **Sunday Creek** bridge to a pleasant camp with fireplaces, toilets and tables. Bollards restrict campers to walk-in arrangements, but there is good shade, and a 6 kilometre, 1.5 hour return walk to nearby **Sunday Creek Reservoir**.

BELOW: *Patches of burnt trees are found along Mount Disappointment Road.*

BASIC CHECK LIST . . .

- ☑ Soft Roaders
- ☑ Trailers
- ☑ Road Tyres
- ☑ Avoid wet weather
- ☑ Navigation Skills

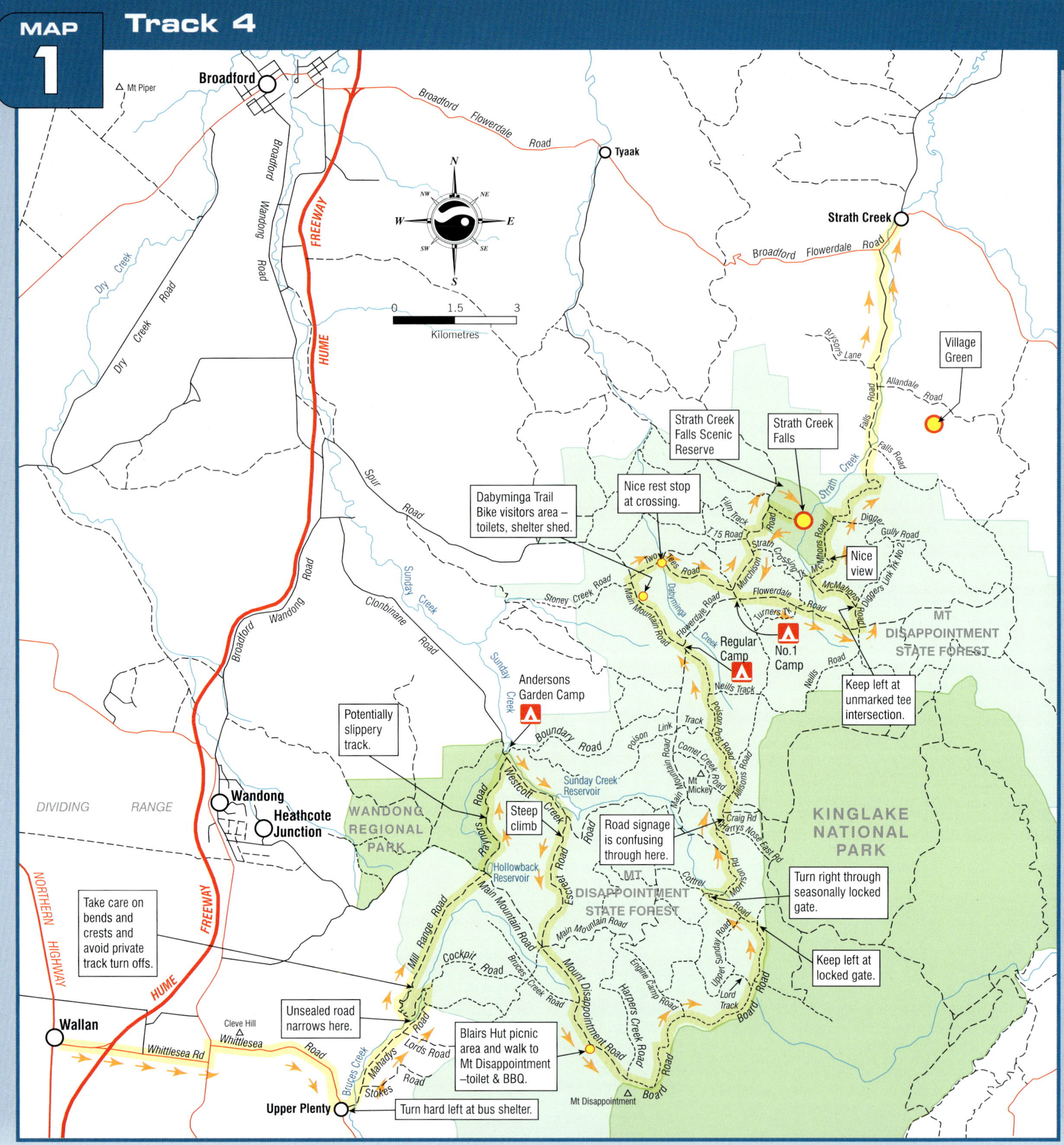

Continue the drive south east on **Westcott Creek Road** on a winding and corrugated climb, with views over the reservoir on your left. Tree ferns define the waterlogged gullies as you reach **Escreet Road** on the right, about 3.6 kilometres beyond **Andersons Garden**.

Keep right here and climb the unrelenting spur over erosion control mounds and past recently logged coupes. Some access restrictions may apply during times of timber harvesting, so follow all signage and instructions if required. Impressive views open up to the west through the logged terrain, before you reach a five way junction 3.8 kilometres from the turn.

The **Main Mountain Road** breaks away to your left and right, with the remaining fork veering right along **Lords Road**, and veering left on **Mount Disappointment Road**. We will take the latter option to follow a better road surface fringed with bracken.

Bruces Creek Road peels away on the right, flagging some tall timber country and a picnic area at **Blairs Hut**, some 2.9 kilometres from the five way junction. The old loggers hut no longer stands, but a BBQ, toilet and seating marks the pleasant site. A 3.5 kilometre return walk to the summit of **Mount Disappointment** begins here following good track. Walkers who make the 1.5 hour return hike in clear weather will be rewarded with good views over **Melbourne**.

Drive 1.2 kilometres beyond **Blairs Hut** to **Harpers Creek Road**, keeping right at this junction, then begin a more easterly run on signposted "**Board Road**". Follow this road as it traces the boundary of **Kinglake NP** with a backdrop of fire damaged skeletal trees.

New treefern growth and mossy boulders

colour the understorey as you pass some old side tracks on the right now closed off (access is not permitted into the prescribed water catchment area of **Kinglake NP**). You will pass **Engine Camp Road** on the left, as a stand of large eucalypts flag the successive junctions of **Lord Track** and **Cottrel Road**.

Swing left at **Cottrel Road** (a carpark at the turn is situated close to the **Flat Rock Lookout**, although a locked gate now prevents access). Continue past **Upper Sunday Road** on the left and reach the **Morrison Road** intersection, about 1.9 kilometres from **Board Road**.

Turn right through a seasonally closed gate here, then make your way through a firewood collection area and wetland marking the **Sunday Creek** headwaters. Another seasonally closed gate heralds the **Harrys Nose East Road** intersection, where you keep straight on signposted **"Comet Link Track"** (some maps show this as still being **Morrison Road**, and there are other inconsistencies between maps and signage around this area).

Craigs Road branches to the right 500 metres later, with the **Comet Creek Road** junction 400 metres after that (the **Comet Sawmill** operated on the slopes of **Mount Mickey** near here, with some sawdust piles and other relics gradually being reclaimed by the bush). Keep straight on **Allisons Road**, then turn left onto **Poison Post Road**. Follow this track past **Poison Link Track** on the left and Neills Track on the right to reach **Main Mountain Road** at the site of **Regular Camp**. Basic facilities are provided here with bollards restricting campers to carry-in camping.

Remain on **Main Mountain Road** to pass the Flowerdale Road before reaching the **Dabyminga Trail Bike Visitor Area** 2 kilometres later (parking area for trail bike groups with toilets and shelter shed). Beyond here, pass **Stony Creek Road** on the left, before reaching **Two Tees Road** on the right, 2.8 kilometres from **Regular Camp**.

Turn right here and follow powerlines to an elevated crossing of **Dabyminga Creek**. A small park on the west side of the crossing would make a nice rest stop with water flowing even in the drier months. Continue past **Murchison Spur Road** on the left to reach **Flowerdale Road** at **No. 1 Camp**.

Excellent camping opportunities are available here, with both walk in and drive in options. Toilets, fire rings and tables are provided across a large site, which once was home to 75 Italian POWs during WW2. In later years forestry workers were based here, with some remaining until the 1970s. Few relics remain from the bush settlement, although a prominent concrete slab does mark the **Flowerdale Road** junction. A horse riders camp is located diagonally opposite with similar facilities, together with holding yards.

Leave camp via **Murchison Spur Road**, veering right onto **Murchison Road** 200 metres later. Follow good gravel north east past **Strath Crossing Track** on the right, then **Tree 15 Road** and **Film Track** on the left in quick order. You will reach the turn off to **Strath Creek Falls**, some 3 kilometres from camp.

Turn right here and follow a one way loop trail to a parking area overlooking the falls. A viewing point and chairs are located near the carpark, but walkers who undertake the additional steep 500 metre hike will get an even closer view of the 50 metre drop.

Retrace your steps from here back to **No. 1 Camp** and follow the **Flowerdale Road** east past **Turners Track** and a one lane bridge over **Strath Creek**. You will reach **McMahons Road** on the left with **Neills Road** branching to the right, some 3.4 kilometres from **No. 1 Camp**.

Turn left here to pass **Diggers Link Track No. 2** on your left 1.2 kilometres later, then reach an unmarked tee intersection 400 metres beyond that. Turn left here and pass **Strath Creek Crossing Road** on your left 700 metres later, remaining on **McMahons Road**.

Elevated views take in the steeply dissected country dropping away in the west, and skyline views toward the **Brown Range**. Pass **Digger Track** on your right to reach a clearing close to **Tunnel Hill**. Self contained campers could set up a bush camp here near some broken views, although it is a rather exposed location.

The scree like descent from here follows **Strath Creek** past superb views over the northern aspect, before it swings to the east and exits state forest into **Digger Gully**. Colourful deciduous trees define the valley as fences and private property make a return.

Disturbed ground, blackberry and old fruit trees are tell tale reminders of this former gold mining area as you reach a tee intersection on **Falls Road**, 6.7 kilometres from the start of **McMahons Road**. Turn left to pass the **Allandale Road** on your right (access to the **Village Green** – a cafe and cricket ground with accommodation options), then **Brysons Lane** on your left. Broad views open up all around as you reach sealed road with a rather grand old farmhouse standing sentinel.

You reach the **Broadford – Flowerdale Road** at a major tee. Turn right onto the busy road to then cross **Rowans Bridge** and reach the lovely hamlet of **Strath Creek**. An historical tribute to the explorers Hume and Hovell stands at the town's gateway, with most supplies available and a lovely pub centred in the main street.

ABOVE: *Some side tracks are rutted and difficult to drive.*

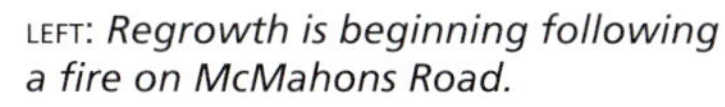

LEFT: *Regrowth is beginning following a fire on McMahons Road.*

TRACK 5

OTWAY

MELBOURNE REGION

TRACK SNAPSHOT

TOUR ROUTE

Anglesea to the Great Ocean Road near Glenaire via the Otway Range.

DURATION AND DISTANCE

The 170 kilometre main tour route can be done in a day, although two days would be better if a few of the highly recommended walks are to be undertaken. The optional detour will require another 21 kilometres of driving.

TRACK DETAILS

Easy driving in the main and suitable for all drivers and vehicles. The optional detour is slightly more demanding, but usually no problem in the dry, even for AWDs.

WHEN TO GO

All year round is possible for the main route, although very wet weather should be avoided. The optional detour is subject to seasonal closure from June to November. The waterfalls run harder after local rain and are quite impressive. The summer holiday period is busy across the Otway.

CAMPING

Designated camps at Hammonds Road, Sharps Track (no facilities or fires), Beauchamps Falls and Aire Crossing. Plenty of commercial options along the Great Ocean Road.

FUEL AND SUPPLIES

Anglesea and Deans Marsh can cater for your needs.

MAPS

Meridian: The Otways

OTHER INFORMATION

A substantial part of this tour follows one of Parks Victoria's Iconic Drives. Check out *www.iconic4wd.com.au*

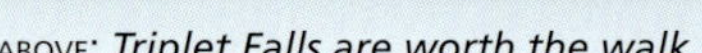

ABOVE: *Triplet Falls are worth the walk.*

*The **Great Ocean Road** follows a grand section of Victoria's coastline, hugging the Southern Ocean's wave break from Anglesea to Peterborough. Just inland from this surf action lies the **Great Otway NP**; more than 100 000 hectares of densely forested range, thick with a ferny understorey. Wet rainforest dominates the higher reaches of this park, but open heathland and more diverse drier woodland is also part of the package.*

*This tour visits the heart of the **Otway Ranges**, where a multiplicity of waterfalls and cascades tumble from a verdant backdrop of vine festooned jungle. Access is via arterial tracks and roads linking national park with forest park and blocks of freehold land. There is an optional 4WD loop trail (subject to seasonal road closure) that visits several of the waterfalls near Lorne.*

Our journey starts at **Anglesea**, where you follow **Noble Street** away from the coast, on the west side of the **Anglesea River** bridge. Continue a steady climb through town heading to the transmission towers on **Mount Ingoldsby**. Veer right onto **Mount Ingoldsby Road** 2 kilometres into the tour, before passing the towers 600 metres later, when the road narrows to gravel, as you enter **Anglesea Heath Natural Heritage Area**.

Vistors may spot warblers or honey eaters

BASIC CHECK LIST . . .

- ☑ Soft Roaders
- ☑ Trailers
- ☑ Road Tyres
- ☑ Avoid wet weather

BELOW: *Most of the arterial tracks have stone topping.*

darting around the heath here, with parrots and cockatoos more likely to make their presence felt reeling around the tree tops further into the ranges. More than 150 bird species call the Otway home, including the larger species like eagles and albatross.

Veer left away from **Messmate Track** as you follow the power lines with ocean views on the left. Keep right at a fork 700 metres beyond **Messmate Track** to remain on **Mount Ingoldsby Road**. Follow fencelines for another 1.6 kilometres to a tee intersection on **No. 2 Road**.

Turn left here, and keep right at **Distillery Creek Road** 200 metres later for a potentially slippery run through heathland coloured with cream and red flowers in season. You will enter **Great Otway NP** at the **Batson Track** junction, where you swing right for a winding and undulating drive over **Pinchgut Hill**. Trail bikers use the tracks through here regularly, so keep an eye out for other road users, and leave your headlights on.

You will arrive at a four way junction 4 kilometres beyond **Batson Track**, with the sealed **Bambra Road** heading left to **Aireys Inlet**, and **Breakfast Creek Road** peeling off to **Wensleydale** on the right. We keep straight on the gravel heading toward **Bambra**. Some taller timber marks the transition out of heathland and past a trig point to **Hammonds Road** on the right, some 3 kilometres from the four way junction.

We will continue straight at this junction, but **Hammonds Road Camping Area** lies just 150 metres away on the right. Basic facilities are provided with larger vehicle access and pleasant shady sites, although bookings are required.

Head west past the **Old Telegraph Road** and fire tower on **Peters Hill** (no access), keeping right at the **Retreat Road** junction. Follow the main road past pine plantation and some logging activity to enjoy excellent views over the rolling hills toward **Wensleydale**. Grazing lands at **Jinda Park Station** merge into the **Bambra Bushland Reserve**, and a tee intersection on the **Deans Marsh Winchelsea Road**.

Turn left onto sealed road here to cross **Retreat Creek** and follow winding bitumen past a lovely weatherboard shearing shed into the community of **Deans Marsh**. Keep straight in the town centre to pass the **Birregurra Road** on your right, and find cafe, bar and fuel supplies. Keep left at **Pennyroyal Valley Road** as you exit town and climb quickly for superb views of this undulating country with its patchwork of pasture and forestry blocks.

Previously logged forest is a feature of this area and plank notches are readily spotted on numerous trees across the **Otway** – many of impressive sizes. Indeed some stumps were attributed with almost mythical dimensions – one giant at the **Beech Forest Racecourse** reputedly covered an area large enough on which to build the 1800s grandstand.

You will enter **Great Otway NP** 7 kilometres beyond **Deans Marsh** to have the rural views replaced by native bushland,

Jungle view.

Lavers Hill
Otway Fly
Youngs Creek
Phillips Track
Youngs Creek Tk
Triplet Falls
Aire Crossing Camp
Aire Crossing Track
Aire River
Wait - a - While Road
Aire Settlement Road
Bennett Track
Great Ocean Road
Glenaire
Sand Road
Aire River Camp (East)
Aire River Camp (West)
Cape Otway Lighthouse

as you wind your way to the locality of **Benwerrin**. Look out for a sweeping right hand bend with **Big Hill Track** fanning off to the left (possible bush camping area at junction), before you swing right onto **Mount Sabine Road** just after that. (The sealed **Deans Marsh – Lorne Road** is often busy and the traffic travels quickly, so take particular care at this turn.)

You are back on gravel immediately for a scenic run through tall timber and pockets of majestic mountain ash draped in garlands of bark. Follow the crest of the **Otway Range** past a farmhouse and old sawmill, to **Pennyroyal Track** on the right (walkers only). **Norman Track** flags the locality of **Wymbooliel** where mature pines and colourful deciduous trees mark another block of private property.

Three kilometres later, the substantial **Erskine Falls Road** peels off to the left, with **Delaneys Road** on the right, 3 kilometres after that. You will reach **Garvey Track** some 1.4 kilometres beyond **Delaneys**, where an optional loop drive can be made. In dry weather it is a relatively easy run and suited to most vehicles and drivers, although conditions can change, so be prepared to turn back if it becomes too slippery or rutted.

Turn left onto **Garvey Track**, signposted '**Mount Cowley**' to reach a junction 1.2 kilometres later (**Mount Cowley** tower is 100 metres to the right, but there is no access or views). Keep left here and head through a seasonally closed gate to find a verdant forest between here and **Garvey Clearing**, about 1 kilometre further on.

Keep left at the clearing to follow **Sharps Track** on a sustained descent. This largely clay based road has some rock, but would be slippery in wet weather. You will make your way through narrow gaps between tall trees on a rutted surface at the headwaters of **Sheoak Creek**. Follow Telstra cable markers through a seasonally closed gate and into **Sharps Track Camp** – a lovely bush camp of 6 sites that cannot be reserved or booked. No facilities are provided and no fires are permitted.

Just beyond the camp is a carpark from where walks to **Henderson** and **Won Wondah Falls** can be made; both are easily accessed, but are potentially busy given their close proximity to the seaside holiday town of **Lorne**. Continue through another seasonally closed gate to reach a tee intersection on **Garvey Track**, where you turn right to the **Sheoak Picnic Area** (electric BBQ, tables and seats, rotunda) for more walking options along disused timber tramways.

(Timber was often milled on site in the forest here and then transported on narrow gauge tramway to **Beech Forest** or elsewhere for distribution. Grades of one in 25 were achievable climbs by rail, which used a track width of only 760 mm – a width chosen to reduce the onerous task of track cutting in the hilly terrain.)

Proceed through a seasonally closed gate and climb along **Garvey Track** through blue gums and some more open forest to an informal parking area. Short walks to the verdant fern lined gorge of Upper and Lower **Kalimna Falls** originate here, albeit via a steepish route. Follow a sustained climb over potentially slippery ruts through lovely ash forest back to **Garvey Clearing**. Retrace your steps from here to the **Mount Sabine Road** and turn left for a serpentine drive past several side tracks including **Gail Clearing** (once the location of an old timber trolley track) and **Curtis Clearing** where naturalised jonquils mark the site of a pioneering homestead.

You will reach the **Kaanglang Road** turn off 9.4 kilometres beyond **Mount Cowley Track** (access to **Lake Elizabeth** for basic camping, but a nice walk and some mountain biking options). The ridge top drive continues south west through some impressive forest passing **Grey River Road** and reaching **Sunnyside Road** 2.7 kilometres later (left turn here leads 1.5 kilometres to picnic area and 3.6 kilometre walk to **Sabine Falls**).

Keep right on **Sunnyside Road** to pass the old **Mount Sabine** fire tower (no longer standing) to arrive at a tee intersection on the sealed **Forrest – Apollo Bay Road**. Turn left and follow a 4 kilometre descent to **Haines Junction**, where you swing right onto signposted '**Turtons Road**'. The junction here is one of the wettest locations in the state. Back in 1952 nearby **Tanybryn** was drenched in three days with over 500 mm of rain.

Now sealed and with a 40 kph speed limit, **Turtons Road** meanders through some special forest with abundant tree ferns and rainforest timbers festooned with moss. A couple of parking areas are found along the mostly narrow road corridor, where you can stop and get out to appreciate this wet jungle. Many of Turton's massive mountain ash trees have fallen to loggers over the years, and although it can take up to 150 years for these trees to reach maturity, the young saplings grow fairly quickly. These juvenile kings of the forest may reach two storeys high in just four years and top 15 storeys high within 20 years. The regrowth here is impressive, with vines and wiry vegetation hanging like a veil from the dizzy

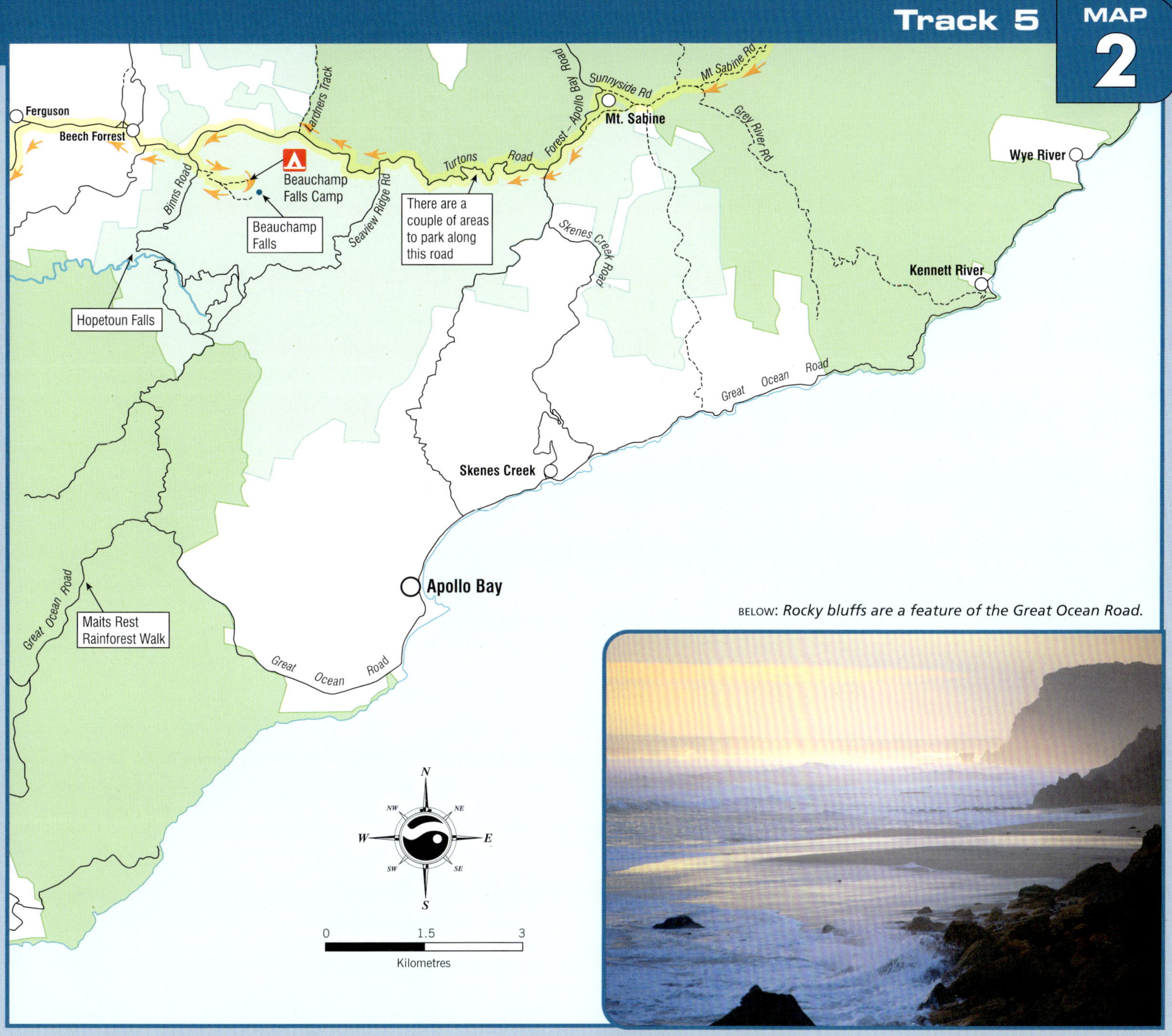

BELOW: *Rocky bluffs are a feature of the Great Ocean Road.*

canopy.

Keep straight at the **Seaview Ridge Road** junction and at **Lardners Track** 3.6 kilometres later. You will reach **Binns Road** 3.8 kilometres beyond that, where signposted **'Beauchamps'** and **'Hopetoun Falls'** can be visited. (Turn left, veering left 600 metres later and reaching **Beauchamps Falls Camping Area** 2.4 kilometres beyond that. Basic facilities and a pleasant (but steep) walk are found at the camp.)

Keep heading west through the community of **Beech Forest** (hotel, rail trail and picnic facilities) to pass great views and the ridge line property of **Buchanan**. **Phillips Track** branches to the left some 4 kilometres beyond the **Beech Forest Hotel**, where you turn south toward the signposted **'Otway Fly'**. (Those looking for a feed can continue 300 metres further west on the main road to a quirky cafe and museum at **Ferguson**).

Follow **Phillips Track** past the **Otway Fly** (popular tree top walk and visitor facilities) before gravel returns on a descent through dairy country. You will reach **Youngs Creek Track** some 3 kilometres beyond the **Otway Fly**, and we will turn right here to continue this tour, but for now keep straight to arrive at a carpark 400 metres later. From here a 2 kilometre walk follows a well constructed trail to viewpoints taking in the three separate drops of Triplet Falls. There is no access to the water on this walk, but the remains of an old sawmill steam engine can be inspected.

Beyond the falls follow **Youngs Creek Track** on a winding descent to a bridge over **Youngs Creek** (limited parking at bridge), before reaching a tee intersection on **Aire Crossing Track**. The tour continues by turning right at this junction, but if you turn hard left you will follow a sustained descent to the **Aire Crossing Campground** 1.6 kilometres later.

There is nice camping on a terrace above the **Aire River**, with toilet and flying fox over the waterway. It is a lovely place to cool off at over the warmer summer months. **Halls Ridge Road** continues beyond the river, but it can be a slippery experience, so retrace your steps to **Youngs Creek Road**, and continue past the junction.

One kilometre later you will reach another tee intersection on **Wait-a-While Road**, where you turn left. Trace a winding route into **Otway Forest Park** to make a seamless transition onto **Aire Settlement Road** 6 kilometres later, at the **Bennetts Track** junction.

Pockets of cleared private land continue south over the **Aire River's West Branch**, before you reach sealed road again just prior to the busy **Great Ocean Road**. From here **Princetown** and the **12 Apostles** lie to the west, or you could follow the **Great Ocean Road** east back to **Anglesea** for one of this country's most spectacular coastal drives.

TRACK 6 BRISBANE RANGES

MELBOURNE REGION

TRACK SNAPSHOT

TOUR ROUTE
Anakie to Bacchus Marsh via Steiglitz and the Brisbane Ranges.

DURATION AND DISTANCE
This 70 kilometre run is an easy day trip.

TRACK DETAILS
Routine unsealed roads in the main; suitable for all drivers and vehicles.

WHEN TO GO
All year round is OK, but avoid very wet periods. Spring is a great time to see the wildflower display.

CAMPING
Designated sites at Fridays Camp and Boar Gully Camp. Bookings are essential; ph 13 1963

FUEL AND SUPPLIES
Basic supplies at Anakie and all services at Bacchus Marsh.

MAPS
1:100K Bacchus Marsh 7722

OTHER INFORMATION
With only 70 easy kilometres to travel in a day, there will be plenty of time to undertake one or more of the marked walks. Distances and standards vary, but there will be at least one to suit your requirements.

ABOVE: *Grass trees are common in the Brisbane Ranges.*

RIGHT: *Aboriginal people have gathered at the Brisbane Ranges for millenia.*

*Geological action along the **Rowsley Fault** has pushed the **Brisbane Ranges** well above the mostly flat country seen between **Bacchus Marsh** and **Geelong**. These ranges have formed a mostly dry forest of stringybark and grass trees, etched with gullies and minor creek lines.*

*Many plant and animal species have adapted to life here, making the destination a magnet for amateur botanists and naturalists. The tour described through here is easy and quite suitable for a day or weekend trip out of Melbourne. Walks of various grades weave through the landscape, with the old gold mining village of **Steiglitz** bringing substance and life to its historic park.*

Kick off the journey by heading south from the **Anakie General Store**, turning right onto **DeMotts Road**, signposted 'Steiglitz', 500 metres later. Pass the **Anakie Reserve** to follow single lane bitumen under an avenue of trees and past a gravel side street 1.5 kilometres later. Keep straight to begin an abrupt climb overlooking pastoral holdings to pockets of private land hidden in the bush, that is now recovering from a serious fire.

Wider road is reached beyond the **Clarkes Road** intersection as you begin an equally sudden drop off on a winding run around tight corners. A floodway marks the **Sutherlands Creek** crossing as you enter lovely forest where some of the Brisbane Range's 50 orchid species may be seen, and begin a climb past a gravel pit to Butchers Road, 1.6 kilometres later.

Turn right at this tee intersection to reach another tee 100 metres later on the Steiglitz – **Maude Road**. The historic **Steiglitz Cemetery** lies directly ahead at this junction (turn left to its access gate) but we will turn right at the tee to enter **Steiglitz Historic Park**.

You will pass **Brick Track** on the right then reach **South Steiglitz Road** on the left shortly after (access to the **Bert Boardman Recreation Area** with shelter shed, seats, tables, fireplaces and toilets). Continue past here into the community of **Steiglitz** where mullock heaps and old rusting relics hark back to the area's gold mining heritage of the 1860s.

Some private residences, including the **Peppercorn Place** cafe, dot the old town, with **St Pauls Church** propped up on the right in Regent Street. The more substantial brick court house is a good place to park for a walking exploration of this town.

Leave **Steiglitz** on the **Meredith Road** heading west, remaining on bitumen to cross **Grahams Creek** and pass the c1868 **Roman Catholic Church**. The climb passes Hut Road on the right and the Steiglitz – Sheoaks Road on the left. **Eclipse Road** is reached 300 metres later where you turn right onto unsealed road, with **Cooks Walking Track** beginning at the junction.

Follow a corridor between private grazing land and the historic park on the right to the other end of **Cooks Track** 900 metres later, and **Grahams Creek Road**, 800 metres beyond that. Turn right here into **Brisbane Ranges NP** to pass **Box Track** (walkers only) 300 metres later. Follow a descent over the next kilometre to a crossing of **Grahams Creek** and its adjoining picnic area. Fireplace, table and seats are provided here, with a nice outlook and some tree cover making it a pleasant stop.

Continue east past **Hazel Track** (walkers only) and a rocky outcrop, to a triangulated

BASIC CHECK LIST . . .

- ☑ Soft Roaders
- ☑ Trailers
- ☑ Water Crossings
- ☑ Avoid wet weather
- ☑ Navigation Skills

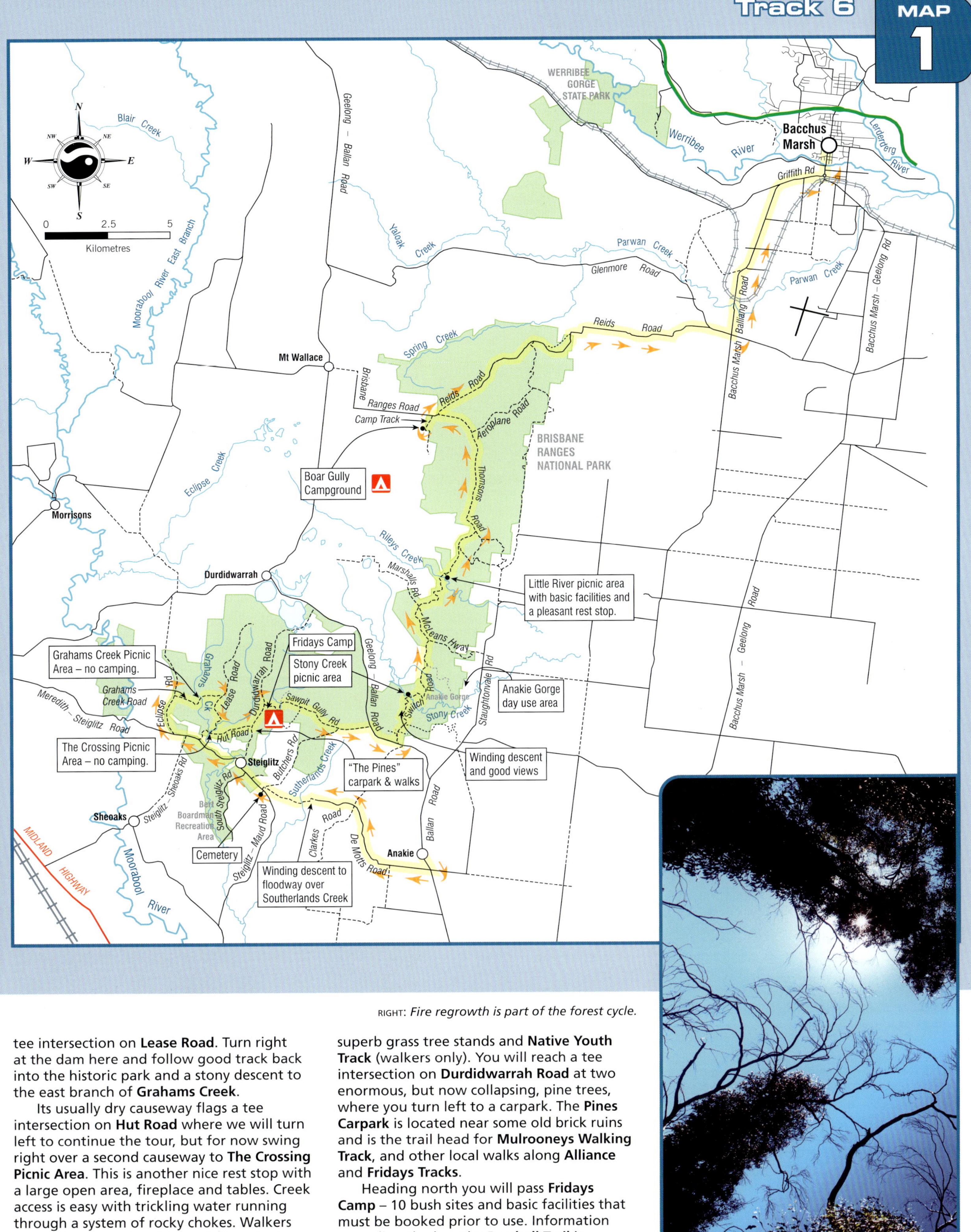

RIGHT: *Fire regrowth is part of the forest cycle.*

tee intersection on **Lease Road**. Turn right at the dam here and follow good track back into the historic park and a stony descent to the east branch of **Grahams Creek**.

Its usually dry causeway flags a tee intersection on **Hut Road** where we will turn left to continue the tour, but for now swing right over a second causeway to **The Crossing Picnic Area**. This is another nice rest stop with a large open area, fireplace and tables. Creek access is easy with trickling water running through a system of rocky chokes. Walkers can undertake a circuit hike via **Box Track** from here, although as with **Grahams Creek Picnic Area**, no camping is permitted.

Head east along **Hut Road** to climb past superb grass tree stands and **Native Youth Track** (walkers only). You will reach a tee intersection on **Durdidwarrah Road** at two enormous, but now collapsing, pine trees, where you turn left to a carpark. The **Pines Carpark** is located near some old brick ruins and is the trail head for **Mulrooneys Walking Track**, and other local walks along **Alliance** and **Fridays Tracks**.

Heading north you will pass **Fridays Camp** – 10 bush sites and basic facilities that must be booked prior to use. Information regarding the lengthy **Burchell Trail** is available here detailing the 40 kilometre three day hike that criss crosses the **Brisbane Ranges**.

LEFT: *Some buildings remain from the goldrush days at Steiglitz.*

Turn right onto **Sawpit Gully Road** just beyond the camp to follow a winding descent to reach **Pine Track** on the left 900 metres later (walkers only). Cross **Sutherlands Creek** on a culvert at this junction and follow fenceline past **Friday Track** on the right (MVO). You reach a tee intersection on **Butchers Road** where you turn left past cleared land to another tee intersection on the **Geelong – Ballan Road** 1.1 kilometres later. Turn right onto this potentially busy sealed road, then drive south for 1.3 kilometres before turning left onto **Switch Road.**

Head back into national park on gravel, following a serpentine drop off past **Red Beak Track** on the left and crossing a causeway at the same point. **Aquaduct Track** branches to the right as you climb past **Nelson Track** for broken views to the north. A winding descent offers a scenic journey through some fire damaged forest (the result of a large fire in 2006) before several subsequent tight switchbacks flag the **Stony Creek Picnic Area**, some 2.1 kilometres from the turn off. Picnic facilities and toilets are provided here, with some pleasant walks to suit all tastes. The **Reservoir Walk** to **Lower Stony Creek** will cover just 800 metres, while the **Ted Errey Nature Circuit** requires a three hour investment for the difficult 8.3 kilometre hike.

The **Anakie Gorge Walk** of 3 kilometres and one hour one way is a beauty, following **Stony Creek** on an easy meander along the route of the first aqueduct that supplied water to the **Geelong** region. The aqueduct was originally constructed with wooden tubes around 1890, before being replaced by a steel pipeline that can be seen crossing the creek today. Some rock hopping is required, but there are strategically placed seats along the way, and walkers could do just a one way hike, to be picked up by vehicle at the **Anakie Gorge Picnic Ground** on **Staughtonvale Road**.

Switch Road continues beyond **Stony Creek** crossing the waterway at a culvert, before following a steep climb out. Golden wattle and roof high bracken form a corridor along the winding path which would be slippery if wet. You will reach a parking area on a switchback, 1 kilometre beyond the picnic area where views take in **Anakie Gorge,** extending to the background **You Yangs.**

Proceed past the **Burchell Walking Trail** and **Shaft Track** on the right to reach a tee intersection on **McLeans Highway**, 2.4 kilometres from the lookout. Turn left here, keeping straight at the **Marshall Road** junction for elevated views through creamy trunked eucalypts.

A steep and winding descent follows uneven switchbacks and some rocky eroded sections to a fording over **Reillys Creek**. You will reach the **Little River Picnic Area** 300 metres later, to find basic facilities and a pleasant rest stop. Climb from here through roadside cuttings along the boundary of national park and past several MVO tracks to a tee intersection on **Thomson Road.**

Turn left here past some big grass trees, keeping right at an unmarked track 600 metres later. **Thomson Road** runs parallel to what is known as the **Rowsley Fault** – a geological fault line attributable to volcanic activity millions of years ago, and now defining the national park's eastern boundary. It is also a good area to look out for the **Brisbane Ranges** grevillea along here, found only in this national park. You will pass several other MVO tracks before you reach **Aeroplane Road** about four kilometres beyond **McLean Highway**. Keep left at this junction to remain on **Thomson Road** for a further 1.5 kilometres before reaching a tee intersection on **Reids Road**.

We will turn right at this junction, but those looking to camp will find **Boar Gully Campground** on the left, 200 metres to the west, and located at the end of **Camp Track**. Seven sites with basic facilities are found near a dam fringed with stringybarks, although bookings are essential. **Reids Road** heads north east along good gravel and past a number of MVO tracks to the other end of **Aeroplane Road**. Keep left here to follow a slow and winding descent marked with broken views.

Heather Track defines the boundary of national park as you reach sealed road and cottages on private property. Turn right at a quarry 900 metres beyond **Heather Track** to pass shearing sheds and grazing stock. You will reach a tee intersection 4.7 kilometres beyond the quarry where you turn right toward signposted ' **Bacchus Marsh**'.

A newly planted strip of pencil pines marks the **Rowsley Avenue of Honour**, as you arrive at a roundabout and turn left. Cross **Parwan Creek** at a bridge, and head under the **Ballarat – Melbourne Rail** bridge to reach the **Bacchus Marsh CBD** about 8 kilometres later.

RIGHT: *Old water pipe on Anakie Gorge walk.*

LERDERDERG

MELBOURNE REGION

TRACK SNAPSHOT

TOUR ROUTE
Bacchus Marsh to Blackwood via Lerderderg State Park.

DURATION AND DISTANCE
This 80 kilometre route can be comfortably done as a day trip out of Melbourne.

TRACK DETAILS
Mostly routine unsealed forestry tracks, with some slippery low range descents and climbs over the waterways. The very demanding optional detour through Goodmans Creek will require good clearances and considerable experience. Trailers are not recommended, especially through Goodmans Creek, but could be a burden on the other creek access tracks as well if they are slippery.

WHEN TO GO
Seasonally closed sections limit travel to the warmer months between November and June. Avoid wet weather regardless as the tracks will be slippery and the water crossings can be deep.

CAMPING
Camping is popular at O'Briens Crossing (conventional vehicle access), but the water crossings on both XL Track and Amblers Lane offer other bush camping options. Various other possibilities marked on map.

FUEL AND SUPPLIES
Bacchus Marsh has all supplies and services, while Blackwood offers basic supplies.

MAPS
Meridian: Wombat State Forest covers most of this touring route.

OTHER INFORMATION
This trek links up with our Wombat State Forest tour for an easy run into Daylesford.

Lerderderg River at O'Briens Crossing.

Largely seen as a trail bike destination, the ***Lerderderg State Forest*** *is also a pleasant day or weekend trip for 4WDers. The centrepiece* ***Lerderderg River*** *usually runs at not much more than a trickle over the warmer months, but it is a welcome refuge nonetheless.*

This tour follows a combination of routine forestry tracks and some low range work linking them. There is an optional (very difficult) detour for those travellers with a panel beater in the family! Very civilized camping is possible at ***O'Briens Crossing****, while self contained groups will find any number of bush sites elsewhere along the route.*

Begin by leaving **Bacchus Marsh** heading north on the Gisborne Road. You will pass over the **Western Freeway**, then cross the **Lerderderg River** at **Darley**, 2.6 kilometres from **Bacchus Marsh**. Turn left 400 metres later onto **Lerderderg Gorge Road**, signposted **'MacKenzies Flat'**. Apple orchards front the river flats as you cross **Goodmans Creek** and reach **Camerons Road** 600 metres later on the right.

We will turn right here, but for now keep left to follow the sealed road into a picnic area at **MacKenzies Flat** with basic facilities and electric BBQs. This is a popular day use area on the river, especially over the warmer months when swimmers cool off in the pleasant waters, and walkers follow the scenic river to **Grahams Dam**.

Return to **Camerons Road** and turn north to head uphill through rural country with vineyards, stockramps and old fences. A marker recognising the WW2 military camp at **Darley** is found 900 metres along this road, with red brick footings to be seen in the paddock opposite.

A patchwork of bushland and cleared farmland continues to **Seereys Road**, where you turn right onto gravel following a netting fence on the left. The road surface is good, but narrow, so turn your headlights on to be seen more readily. The winding drive continues to **Blue Gum Creek**, 1.7 kilometres later where two causeways cross the creek.

It is quite a pretty area with reeds and reflections under a canopy of mature trees. The drive swings more northerly now, to another water crossing where spear grasses mark a lagoon on **Goodmans Creek**. The road climbs now offering excellent views toward the range's spine on the right.

You will enter **Lerderderg State Forest** 2 kilometres beyond the last crossing to find a gravel pit on the left and numerous other tracks fanning off in both directions. Grass trees usher the way to a major intersection, some 2.7 kilometres into the **State Park**.

Turn right here through a seasonally closed gate onto **Bluegum Track** to pass Holts Road on the right and pine plantation on the left. Numerous tracks fan off left and right with many being dedicated motor bike trails. **Blue Gum Track** becomes rutted in places now as some steeper grades pull you back a gear or two.

Keep right at **West No 5 Track** to follow the boundary of **Conservation Area** past a number of other side tracks, where smaller bluegums have taken hold. You will reach **Nuggety Track** on the right (SRC) about 3.6 kilometres beyond **West No 5 Track** for great views to the north of **Mount Bullengarook**.

Follow **Blue Gum Track** for a further 1.6 kilometres to reach **Ratcliffe Track** where an optional detour follows this track to a very difficult creek crossing. All other travellers can keep heading north on **Blue Gum Track** to pass **O'Briens Road** and reach a tee intersection on Firth Road. You will then turn left here to pick up the notes later in this text.

Those keen for a challenge will turn right through a seasonally closed gate to begin a slow descent over a narrow and rough road. The track swings more northerly 2.4 kilometres later at a left bend, where a sign post indicates its former name of **No 1 Firebreak Trail**.

Drive past a potential camping flat among the trees for a rocky descent to **Goodmans Creek**. In season, the roar of cicadas seems amplified within **Scotties Gully** as you negotiate a sudden drop off staged over several erosion control mounds.

You will round a switchback and reach the

BASIC CHECK LIST . . .

- ☑ Steep Climbs
- ☑ Water Crossings
- ☑ Good Clearance Needed
- ☑ Avoid wet weather

MAP 1 Track 7

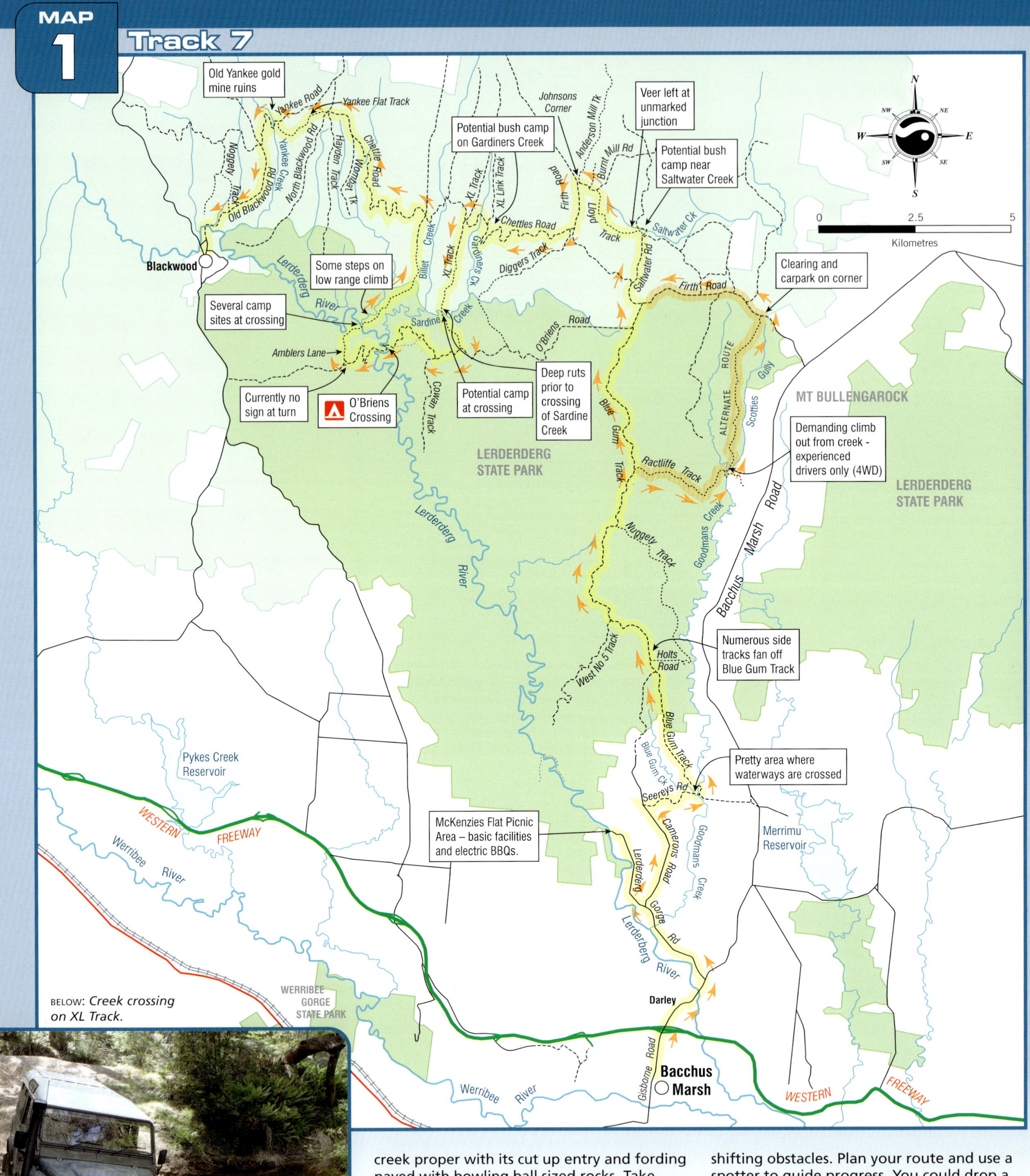

BELOW: *Creek crossing on XL Track.*

creek proper with its cut up entry and fording paved with bowling ball sized rocks. Take your time negotiating this obstacle, and take a good look at your exit on the eastern bank – it is very demanding.

The steep grade is one thing, but gouged rock with loose stones and a slalom course to be navigated, all conspire to make the climb a technically challenging one. Be prepared to do some track work with ramping rocks and shifting obstacles. Plan your route and use a spotter to guide progress. You could drop a little air from your tyres to help with traction, although this will also reduce your effective ground clearance.

Most of the nasties are dealt with early in the climb, with the track returning to high range standard within 800 metres. Some side tracks and a large clearing marks the finish of **Ratcliffe Track** as you reach a seasonally

ABOVE: *Some descents can be slippery.*

closed gate and tee intersection on **Firth Road**, 5 kilometres beyond the creek.

Turn left to trace a path on bluemetal past numerous marked and unmarked side tracks to **O'Briens Road** on the left, 3.7 kilometres beyond **Ratcliffe Track**. Veer right on the main road here (and those who have chosen to bypass **Ratcliffe** will turn left here) to follow **Firth Road** for a further 900 metres.

Swing right onto **Saltwater Road** for a rutted and possibly slippery descent to the **Lloyd Track** junction 1.4 kilometres later. We will veer left here, but for now keep right for 100 metres to arrive at a potential camp site on **Salt Water Creek** next to a bridge. Mature eucalypts shade a ferny jungle here where a concrete weir holds back some of the inky waters, just metres from the carpark.

Return to **Lloyd Track** and swing north through the seasonally closed gate and descend to the creek following the trickling rivulet past other potential bush camps. Veer left at an unmarked junction (despite a painted arrow in a tree indicating otherwise) and cruise through nice forest which has seen a light burn in recent years.

A seasonally closed gate flags **Burnt Mill Road** at a tee intersection, where you turn left past nesting boxes to **Johnsons Corner** 600 metres later. Turn left here, keeping left 100 metres later back onto **Firth Road**. You will pass a couple of tracks on the right where tree stumps mark an old logging site, before reaching **Chettle Road** 1.3 kilometres from **Johnsons Corner**.

Turn right here to follow good gravel past **Diggers Track** and several other side tracks heading into **Wombat State Forest**. You will reach a clearing on the right about 3 kilometres from **Firth Road** where a small camp could be made at a shady site on **Gardiner Creek**.

Proceed from here past **XL Link Track** on the right and a gully of fishbone ferns at the head of **Gardiners Creek** to **XL Track**, 1.2 kilometres beyond **XL Link Track**. Turn left here through a seasonally closed gate to pass a track on the right 600 metres later (access track to old **XL Mine** overlooking **Billet Creek**).

Continue south over rutted sections for a climb to broken views through native pine. More sections of rough track slow travel past some ugly eroded motorbike trails on the right. You will head downhill from here over deeply scoured ruts to cross **Sardine Creek** and reach **Lerderderg State Park**.

A nearby ruin marks a nice camp on the south bank, as you begin a climb over rough and eroded country. Try to pick the most friendly line over some exposed rock shelves to pass through another seasonally closed gate, reaching a tee intersection on **O'Briens Road**, 1.3 kilometres beyond the ford.

Turn right onto this forest arterial to pass **Cowan** and **Trout Tracks** (both MVO) to wind your way westward well above **Sardine Creek**. You will pass **Short Cut Track** (now walkers only) to reach **O'Briens Crossing** four kilometres beyond **XL Track**.

Camping is popular at this causeway over the **Lerderderg River**, where basic facilities including flushing toilets are found. Parking and campsites are limited however, so consider the bush options found just prior to the crossing, which drop down from **O'Briens Road** via a steep access track. Fires are only permitted in the fireplaces provided however, so get here early on weekends if you require that luxury.

Head further beyond the crossing to reach **Amblers Lane** 2.6 kilometres later. Currently no signpost marks the turn where you swing right through a seasonally closed gate as the road hooks back on **O'Briens** and begins the descent past a walking track.

You will reach a small camping flat 1.4 kilometres later, with a larger option on the left 100 metres beyond that. Neither of these informal sites have permanent fireplaces, or any other facilities, but their outlook over the river may be reward enough. The main camp is reached 200 metres later where you ford the Lerderderg and find several sites together with fireplaces under some nice eucalypts.

Continue along **XL Track** to cross the river for a low range exit through blackberry, and a gnarly climb over a rocky section of track. Pick your line to clear some minor steps, as you progress up the spur to broken views on either side.

Keep straight at a four way intersection marking the return to **Wombat SF**, and an uneventful return to **Chettle Road**, 2 kilometres later. Turn left here and follow the gravel to a tight bend 1.6 kilometres later, where a potential camping area can be found at a bridge (no facilities).

The winding route continues past **Wombat Track** to what is effectively a tee intersection 1.1 kilometres later, with **Chettle Road** meeting the substantial **North Blackwood Road**. **Hayden Track** peels away hard left at this junction, while our route out is via **Yankee Flat Track**, just offset to the left directly ahead.

The unsignposted track pushes west through dry sclerophyll forest, with branches and wind thrown vegetation littering the trail. A potentially wet and rutted area flags an old timber tram line to the right, before you descend to a tee intersection on **Yankee Road** 2 kilometres later.

Turn left here to overlook the old **Yankee Gold Mine** directly ahead. Some unfenced mining shafts make the area potentially hazardous, but there is much to see along the picturesque **Yankee Creek**. Smaller relics are gradually disappearing to the bush, although concrete footings and some timber structures remain relatively sound. A large hot riveted tube lies rusting where it was abandoned, after probably serving as an air vent for the once productive mine.

Continue along **Yankee Road** to cross the bridge over **Yankee Creek**, then swing back to the north past a couple of potential camp clearings. You will reach a four way intersection on the **Old Blackwood Road**, where you turn left onto a recently improved track. Drainage works and surface topping contributes to easy passage past **Nuggety Track** on the right.

Follow the deep gully of **Nuggety Creek** past private land holdings on the outskirts of **Blackwood**. Cross a stone causeway under thick forest to a low level bridge spanning the **Lerderderg River**. Cross the river to a tee intersection and keep right past a couple of clearings on the river. Continue past a cluster of cottages onto sealed road and the town centre of **Blackwood**. A pub and cafes define the main street, but a mineral springs and picnic area at **Shaws Lake** are popular local attractions.

BELOW: *Lerderderg bushland.*

TRACK 8

WOMBAT STATE FOREST

MELBOURNE REGION

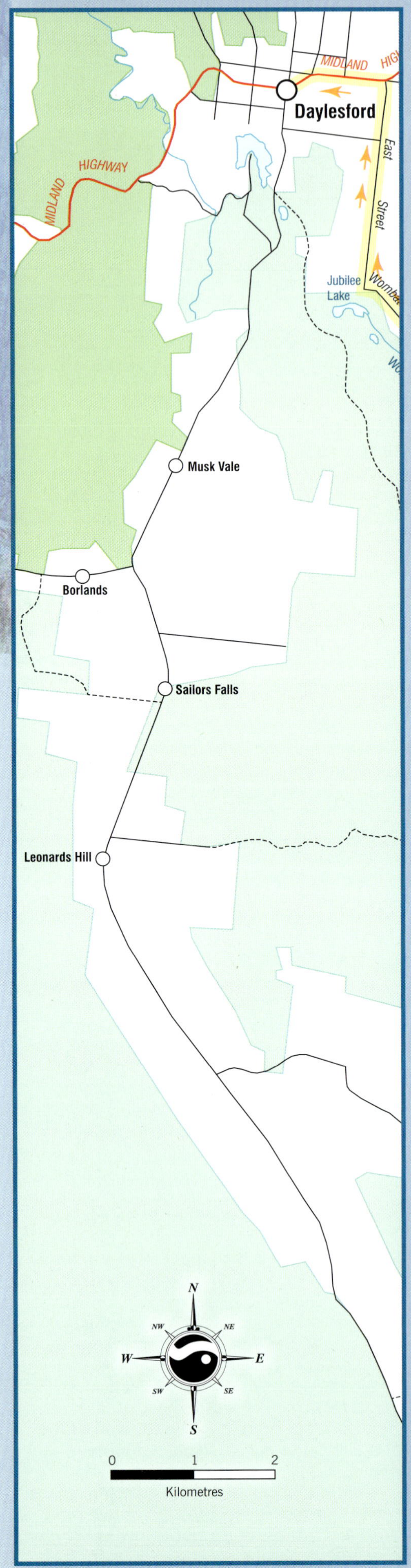

ABOVE: *Misty morning in the Wombat Forest.*

*This drive from **Blackwood** to **Daylesford** is an ideal day trip for newcomers to the bush touring scene. Mostly gravel roads pave a scenic route into lovely forest, where occasional stops allow visitors to enjoy a piece of the **Central Highlands**. The verdant riverine forest delineating the **Lerderderg River's** flow is a highlight of the tour, with the first section of the drive following this corridor. Informal bush camps and defined walks are possible along the **Lerderderg**, while more intrepid groups could explore further into the state forest.*

You will leave **Blackwood** by heading west on **Simmons Reef Road** at the CFA station. Follow the blacktop around a sweeping bend to reach the **Lerderderg Road** on your right some 2 kilometres beyond the town centre. (The popular **Garden of St Erth** lies directly ahead, where visitors can wander through a secluded park first established in the 1860s by an anonymous Cornish settler. The site was named in honour of his Celtic birthplace and features Australian native plants together with exotic specimens, some of which date from the late 1800s. The gardens offer a cafe and quiet retreat now that would have been unthinkable during the bustling gold rush days when 13 000 prospectors rushed to the area.)

Head west on the gravel of **Lerderderg Road**, signposted '**Wombat Forest Drive**', to cross the **Lerderderg Heritage River Walk** – a section of the much longer **Great Dividing Trail**. You will reach a four way junction 1 kilometre later, with **Easter Monday Track** and **New Sultan Road** branching to the left. Keep right on the main road through some lovely manna and yellow gum forest to reach **New Sultan Mine Track** on the right 900 metres

TRACK SNAPSHOT

TOUR ROUTE
Blackwood to Daylesford via the Lerderderg River and Wombat State Forest.

DURATION AND DISTANCE
This 30 kilometre route is an easy half day run.

TRACK DETAILS
Routine state forest roads suitable for all vehicles and drivers.

WHEN TO GO
All year round, but avoid very wet weather. Plenty of shade and easy water access make it a pleasant summer trip.

CAMPING
Formal caravan parks at both Blackwood and Daylesford, but no designated camping en route. Bush camps possible in the state forest and at crossings of the Lerderderg River.

FUEL AND SUPPLIES
Daylesford and Blackwood can provide for most needs.

MAPS
Meridian: Wombat State Forest.

OTHER INFORMATION
Plenty of side tracks can be explored along this route, but be warned that many are narrow, rutted and not regularly used.

BASIC CHECK LIST . . .

- ☑ Soft Roaders
- ☑ Trailers
- ☑ Road Tyres
- ☑ Avoid wet weather

LEFT: *Blackwood Hotel.*

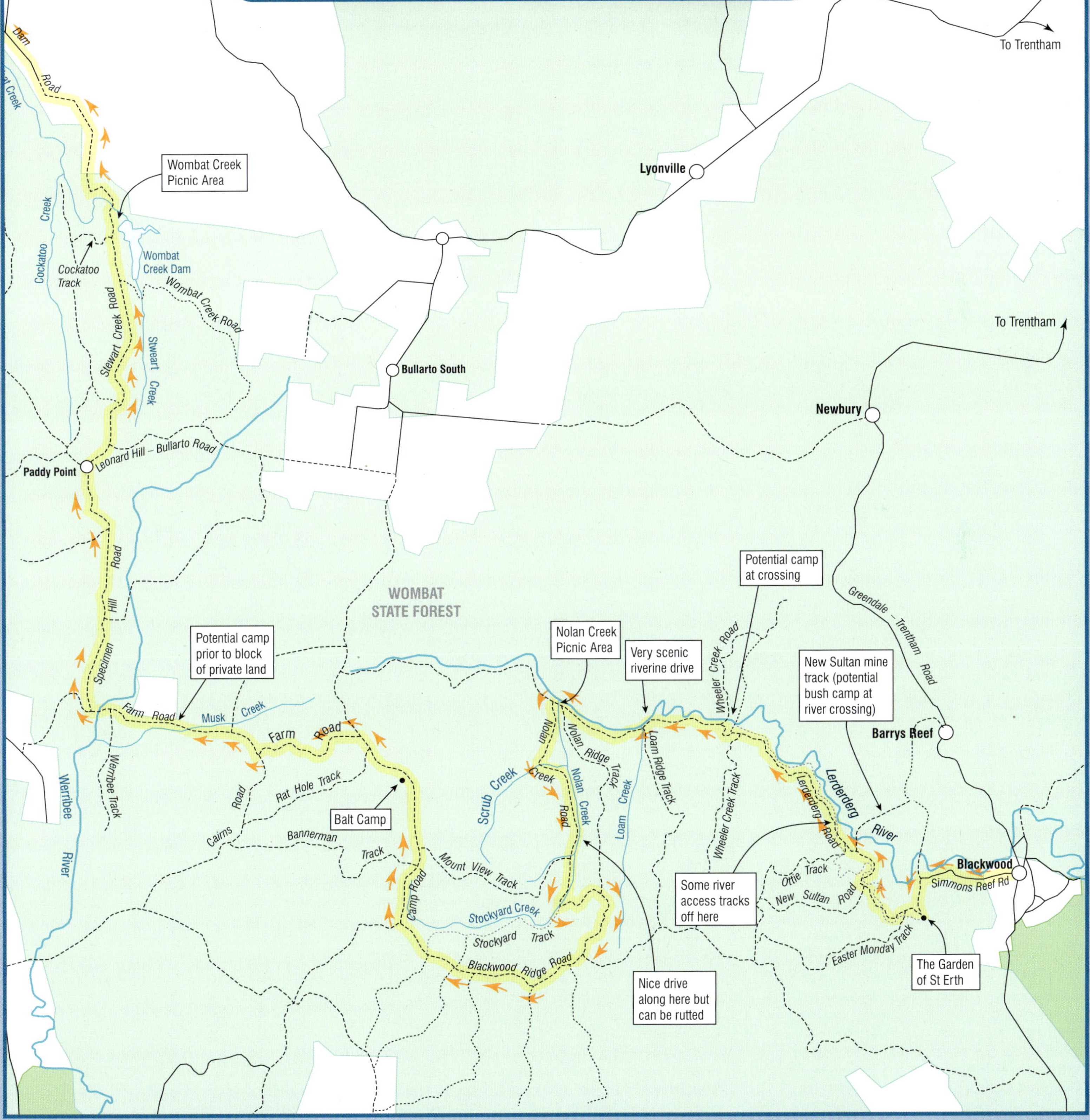

RIGHT: *Balt Camp dates back to the 1950s.*

BELOW: *Crossing the Lerderderg at a low level bridge.*

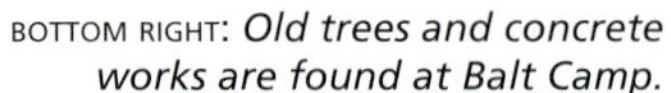

BOTTOM RIGHT: *Old trees and concrete works are found at Balt Camp.*

later. (There is a potential bush camp at the Lerderderg crossing just a couple of hundred metres along this track).

We will keep straight to pass a link track on the left with native pines, grevilleas and trigger plants delineating the **Lerderderg's** serpentine passage. Pass **Ottie Track** (river access on right here) and another river access track 600 metres later (again a potential bush camp with rocky ford, fishbone ferns and shady clearing on the other side of river).

Continue north west over a tree fern gully to climb through moss cloaked forest along the path of an old timber milling tramline. Old tramways became commonplace following widespread manual handling of logs in the late 1800s. Messmate, stringybark and peppermint were the prized species, with some specimens growing to 30 metres in height. The tramway would then transport the cut timber from spotmills in the bush back to the main road.

You will reach **Wheeler Creek Track** on the left and **Wheeler Creek Road** 400 metres later on the right (another nice camp at a causeway 300 metres off the main road). **Lerderderg Road** hugs the river closely now, sometimes with elevated views and at other times guiding you to within metres of water races and mini cascades, where mossy boulders and verdant forest call out for attention. Wallabies and rosellas are never far away as you reach a picnic area on the **Nolan Creek** confluence, 2.8 kilometres from **Wheelers Road**.

A rotunda, tables and fireplaces (but no toilet) are found here, with local walking opportunities under the gaze of neighbouring **Mount Wilson**. We swing left onto **Nolan Creek Road** just beyond the carpark and head south before a dogleg turn at **Scrub Creek** ushers you onto the **Nolan Creek** basin, just beyond the **Day Track** junction.

You will cross a culvert for a verdant drive through a fern gully and past **Mountview Track** on the right. Some ruts and plenty of leaf litter pave the way to **Stockyard Track** on the left (walkers only) and a sharp hairpin turn to **Nolans Ridge Track** 500 metres later. Continue straight through spiky tussock grasses to reach a tee intersection on **Blackwood Ridge Road** 1.1 kilometres later. Turn right onto this forestry arterial to pass numerous side tracks, reaching a tee intersection on **Camp Road** 2.8 kilometres later.

Swing right onto the bluemetal to pass more forestry tracks on a push north to **Balt Camp**, 1.7 kilometres later. The twin chimneys and building ruins here mark a post WW2 camp used by displaced Northern European forestry workers. A lovely spruce tree and some other exotics shade a potential bush camp, just west of the ruins.

Continue north west past **Rat Hole Track**, turning left onto **Farm Road** 200 metres beyond that. Follow a steady descent to the **Cairns Road** junction 1.7 kilometres later, where you keep right to pass **Farm Track** and enter a forest of tall timber smothered by a blanket of bracken. The descent continues to the crossing of **Musk Creek**, with a clearing and potential camp on the right, 100 metres prior to a private land holding. Old fenceline defines this block of pasture, with an isolated pine tree looking over a hayshed, bee boxes and an old steel stockyard.

Superb eucalypts mark the return to state forest as you pass **Werribee Track** and a bridge over the modest beginnings of the **Werribee River** 100 metres later. Turn right onto **Specimen Hill Road** just after the crossing and follow good gravel north past several side tracks. You will reach **Paddy Point** at a tee intersection 3.5 kilometres later, where you turn right onto the signposted '**Leonard Hill – Bullarto Road**'. Veer left onto **Stewart Creek Road** 400 metres later to again pass some unmarked tracks on either side.

Cockatoo Track flags broken views of **Wombat Creek Dam**, where you turn right 100 metres later to a carpark overlooking the dam wall. Boats are not permitted on this domestic water supply, but fishing is allowed with a permit from *Central Highlands Water* (ph 03 53203100). Continue north past the **Wombat Creek Picnic Area** 500 metres later (BBQ, table and seats, and local walk), turning left over a bridge.

A corridor of pea flowers compensate for some blackberry as you reach sealed road with cleared land and superb views over the **Cockatoo Creek** gully. Rural properties punctuate **Wombat Dam Road** as you look over **Jubilee Lake** on the left. Keep right on **East Street** to reach the **Midland Highway** at the **Farmers Arms Hotel**. From here the town centre of **Daylesford** lies just 2 kilometres away to the left.

Chapter 2

HIGH COUNTRY

◀ *Looking east at sunset from Bluff Hill.*

TRACK 9

Merrijig to Porepunkah

HIGH COUNTRY

Lake Cobbler dawn.

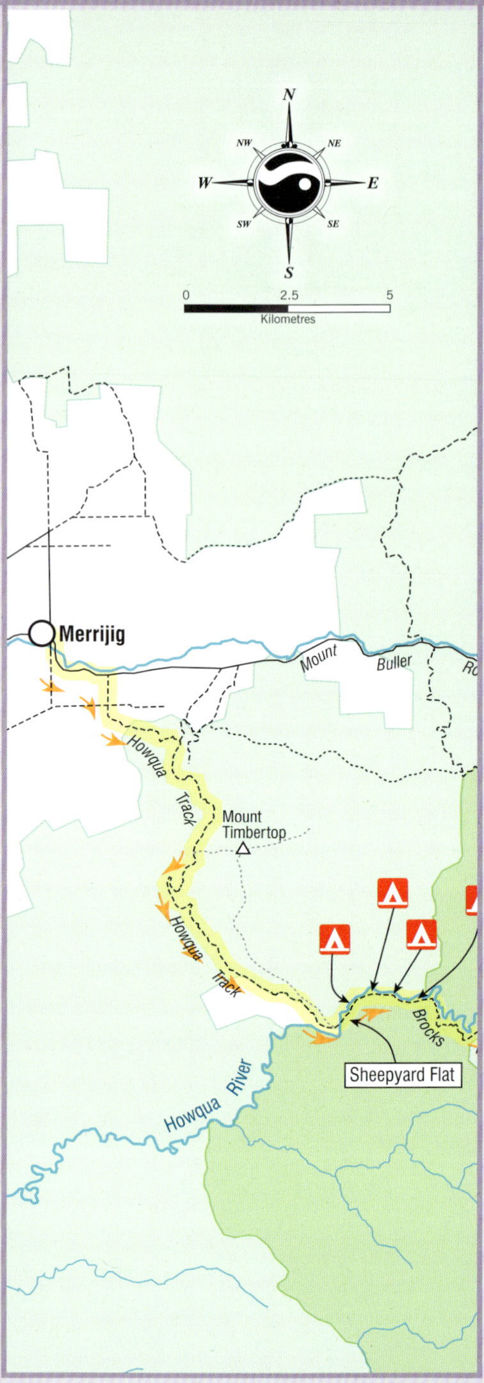

TRACK SNAPSHOT

TOUR ROUTE

Merrijig to Porepunkah via The Bluff, Bindaree Falls, Lake Cobbler and the Buffalo River.

DURATION AND DISTANCE

This 180 kilometre trek is best done over a two or three day period to get a good feel for Victoria's High Country.

TRACK DETAILS

Mostly medium standard 4WD tracks with low range and good clearances required.

WHEN TO GO

The warmer months are best, with seasonal road closures applying to parts of the tour. Access is from November to June.

CAMPING

Camping with basic facilities at Sheepyard Flat, Bluff Hut, Pikes Flat, Upper Howqua Camp, Lake Cobbler and Buffalo River camps. Other bush camps possible.

FUEL AND SUPPLIES

Mansfield, Porepunkah and Bright have services and supplies.

MAPS

Rooftops: Mansfield – Mount Howitt, Bright – Mansfield

OTHER INFORMATION

Nearby Mount Buffalo NP is well worth a visit at the end of this trek. A sealed access road winds around scenic bends, climbing to the lovely old chalet near The Hump. A number of bushwalks are possible around the peak, and there is great camping at Lake Catani.

*Victoria's **Alpine NP** protects a large portion of this state's highest peaks and their life sustaining waterways. Its tentacles follow **High Country** ridges and valleys, clinging to the underlying bones like a sprawling organic blanket.*

*This trek roams across the **Alps** on a scenic ramble along the winter snowline to some impressive mountains and iconic rivers. Regal stands of mountain ash and sprawling snowgum survivors shelter the more delicate understorey of ferns and seasonal wildflowers. Two lofty waterfalls and a sometimes mist shrouded lake combine with weather beaten **High Country** huts, to make this a journey with plenty of interest.*

Leave **Merrijig** taking the **Howqua Track** south on winding gravel past **Mount Timbertop** and its walking track. Keep left on the narrow trail to pass a couple of side tracks and reach **Sheepyard Flat** over the **Howqua River** bridge. Turn left here to follow the bubbling waters east past a sizable camping area and basic facilities. The valley drive follows a series of river flats reputedly used as a stock route in the 1840s.

You will continue up the **Howqua** to pass a number of other river flat camps – most with basic facilities and plenty of shade. **Brocks Road** follows a serpentine path with an elevated outlook over the river to **Seven Mile Flat**, before leaving the waterway to begin a sustained climb.

Corrugated gravel paves the way to **Eight Mile Gap** and the left turn onto **Bluff Link Road**. Head east here on narrower road for a lumpy drive with good views of **The Bluff**. Dusty daisy bushes dripping with white flowers colour the drive to a clearing at **Refrigerator Gap**, some 4.7 kilometres from **Eight Mile Gap**. Keep left at **Refrigerator Gap Track** to enter national park and **The Bluff Walking Track** 700 metres later.

Dedicated walkers can climb to the 1726 metre alpine peak from here for broad views toward **Mount Buller** and beyond. It is a very steep and potentially slippery climb that will humble the fittest of walkers over the next two hours or so. The walking track is wet in places, and even in summer water trickles down the slope to irrigate delicate moss and fern gardens. For the energetic, a further 2 kilometres of walking will bring them to '**The Blowhole**' – a sharp break in the ridge where the prevailing wind is funneled up and over the summit (another option to reach **The Bluff** summit is via the longer, but much less demanding ridge climb from **Bluff Hut**, to be visited by vehicle shortly).

So head further east along **Bluff Link Road** over the twin gullies of **14 Mile Creek** to **Bluff Track**, 4.3 kilometres later. We will

BASIC CHECK LIST . . .

- ☑ Trailers with care
- ☑ Steep Climbs
- ☑ Water Crossings
- ☑ Good Clearance Needed
- ☑ Avoid Wet Weather

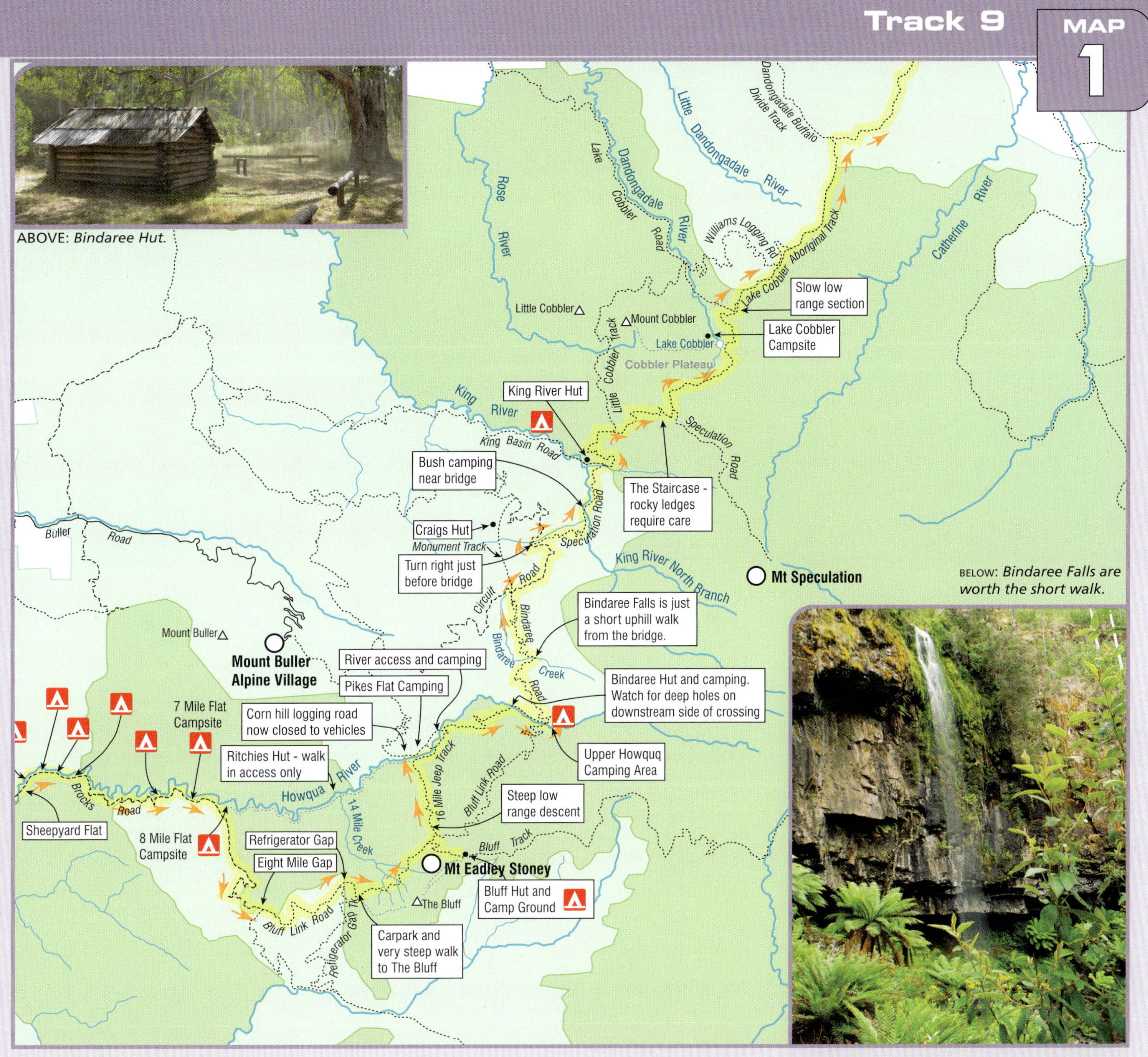

ABOVE: *Bindaree Hut.*

BELOW: *Bindaree Falls are worth the short walk.*

keep left here to continue the trek, but for now swing right to begin the climb up **Mount Eadley Stoney**. Patches of loose rock and a seasonally closed gate usher a 2 kilometre journey to **Bluff Hut**, located on a ridgeline with superb views of **Mount Buller** and beyond.

Bluff Hut is large, having been extended over the years. Corrugated iron is used to clad the multi-roomed structure, where an open fire and two slow combustion stoves provide useful warmth. The adjacent campground is popular, offering basic facilities and some shelter from the wind. As mentioned previously, you can walk from here through snow daisies, mint bush and rice flowers to **The Bluff** summit for a lofty outlook.

Return from the hut to **Bluff Link Road** and swing right through a seasonally closed gate where burnt alpine ash looks over an understorey of black wattle. Turn left onto **16 Mile Jeep Track**, 400 metres from the gate at a clearing, before beginning a steep low range descent. Fallen branches and leaf litter top the earthen track, with ruts gouged into the lower section, where **16 Mile Creek** gathers its surface run off.

Ferns dominate the moist landscape as the track heads east, away from the **Howqua Feeder Walking Track** on your left, some 3.5 kilometres from **Bluff Link Road**. (It is a 3.2 kilometre walk from here to **Ritchies Hut** – a picturesque hut on the **Howqua River** and popular with serious trout fishers). Continue along **16 Mile Jeep Track** to ford **16 Mile Creek** and follow the **Howqua** upstream within metres of its bubbling waters. Elevated views showcase some natural spa pools, as you reach the first of two river side camping flats, 900 metres from the creek crossing.

The first turn off leads to a large grassy area at **Pikes Flat** with a tin shed, fenced off sections and basic facilities. **Cornhill Logging Road** once forded the **Howqua** here, but it has been closed for some time, although walkers can cross the river to see a bush shelter built with resourceful construction techniques.

The next turn off is found 500 metres further along **16 Mile Jeep Track**, with camping opportunities on a pleasant section of the **Howqua**. You will break away from the river here for an undulating drive to **Bindaree Hut** 4.5 kilometres later.

Vehicles cross the **Howqua** here, keeping right away from some deep holes on the downstream side to reach some better road and a return to high range driving. You will pass **Bluff Link Road** 1.4 kilometres later, keeping left to reach **Bindaree Road** 400

ABOVE: *Bog hole on Abbeyard Lake Cobbler Track.*

ABOVE: *The Dandongadale Falls drop off the Cobbler escarpment.*

metres beyond that. We will turn left here to continue the trek, but for now keep straight to cross the **Howqua** on a concrete bridge into the **Upper Howqua Camping Area**, where potential sites and basic facilities are spread along a lovely stretch of river. There is a superb 6 kilometre day walk from here to **Howitt Spur**, that would be of interest to many bush enthusiasts.

Beyond the camp, head north on **Bindaree Road** for a winding drive through **Mansfield SF** to a timber bridge spanning **Bindaree Creek**. There is parking at the bridge and a short uphill walk to the amazing **Bindaree Falls**. Those visiting in the warmer months will probably choose to admire the view from just in front of the 30 metre drop, before pressing on for a cooling experience from behind the wall of water.

Follow **Bindaree Road** north for 4.7 kilometres to reach a four way intersection on **Circuit Road** with the much rougher **Monument Track** continuing directly ahead. Turn right here for nice range views over burnt bushland as you reach a concrete bridge some 3.5 kilometres later. Swing right onto **Speculation Road** just prior to the bridge, to follow the gully on a descent for 2.5 kilometres. Keep left at an unmarked junction (right turn to bush camp at seasonally closed gate), and follow the **King River** to an elevated bridge 900 metres later. There is nice camping under big eucalypts just after the crossing, with fishing possibilities aplenty.

Rocky sections of road continue to pave the way north as you enter national park at another bridge 2 kilometres beyond the last. We will continue straight at this point, but for now turn left onto **King Basin Road**, 50 metres beyond the bridge for a short run to **King Hut** and some shady camping areas. **King Hut** was originally built in 1957 as a weatherboard structure, but was rebuilt in iron with pine lining in 2011, following bushfire damage.

Return to **Speculation Road** and veer left past a gate and old fenceline to reach **Little Cobbler Track** on the left, 3.1 kilometres later. Keep right to follow a lumpy track eastward with the **Cobbler Plateau** looming ahead. A timber bridge and an especially scenic stretch of fern gully precede the once notorious **'Staircase'** – a rocky obstacle that begins a few kilometres east of **Little Cobbler Track**.

Although not as rugged as it once was, the obstacle is subject to heavy use and can deteriorate. The track was graded in 2012-2013 and the rocks were removed.

A series of switchbacks ramp up to a snowgum plateau, with **Cobbler Lake Track** fanning off to the north. Turn left here onto better road (**Speculation Road** continues directly ahead on a rugged and rocky path to a bush camp and locked gate at the foot of **Mount Speculation**). Undulations punctuate a gradual descent over erosion control mounds to a seasonally closed gate and tee intersection on **Cobbler Lake Road**.

Turn left here to cross the outlet creek of **Cobbler Lake**, and reach a camping area near the hut. Basic facilities are provided and the lake is just a stone's throw away. Although **Lake Cobbler** is man made, its glassy waters and tree reflections are quite scenic. Snow melt and water drainage from the plateau drain into the lake, maintaining its level, before the excess spills over a sandstone escarpment as the **Dandongadale Falls**. This graceful white ribbon of water can be safely seen from **Cobbler Lake Road**, although adventurous walkers can reach its origins via a nearby walking track – but supervise children on the short hike, and don't get too close to the sheer drop off. Other walks from **Lake Cobbler** include the more demanding trek to nearby **Mount Cobbler**.

Head east from **Lake Cobbler**, exiting via **Cobbler Lake Road** to follow good gravel past views of the **Dandongadale Falls** on your left (there is a small parking area about 2 kilometres drive from the hut). Broken views toward **Mount Hotham** appear at the **Abbeyard** turn off, 3 kilometres from **Cobbler Hut**, where we keep right away from the main road.

Drop back to low range for a scrambling climb, especially notable about 1 kilometre from the turn. Passengers will admire exceptional views extending from the **Barry Mountains** and **Howitt High Plains** to **Mount Buffalo**, while the driver will be kept busy dealing with some rock steps.

The track improves a little beyond the **Williams Logging Road** turn off as you follow an undulating drive past a helipad with views of **Razorback** to the west. You will reach a tee intersection 6.7 kilometres beyond **Williams Logging Road**, where you turn right away from **Dandongadale Buffalo Divide Track**. This section of track is notoriously full of bogholes and ruts, so take care especially when cresting erosion control mounds, to be sure where you are pointing the wheels. The slipping and sliding ends at a tee intersection on the **Abbeyard Road**, where you turn left under the shadow of **Mount Angus**.

Wider road and gravel topping paves the way northward past a series of small grassy flats, some with camping and fishing possibilities. **MacIvors** and **Abbeyard Picnic Areas** have fireplaces and tables set amongst the manna gums, and mark the upper reaches of the **Buffalo River**. Stockyards and cattle ramps are common along the road, but so too are some of our native wildlife. Wood ducks, currawongs and herons make their home around the flats, while kookaburras are never far away. A bridge over **Brandy Creek** and the **Abbeyard Stockyard** flag views of **Sugarloaf Hill** and the pyramid structure of **Mount Buggery**.

Abbeyard Road becomes more winding beyond the **Worseldine Track** junction on the left, with travellers getting good river views from the elevated road. **Mannagum Camp** is reached 8 kilometres later, with sheltered camping options and basic facilities provided.

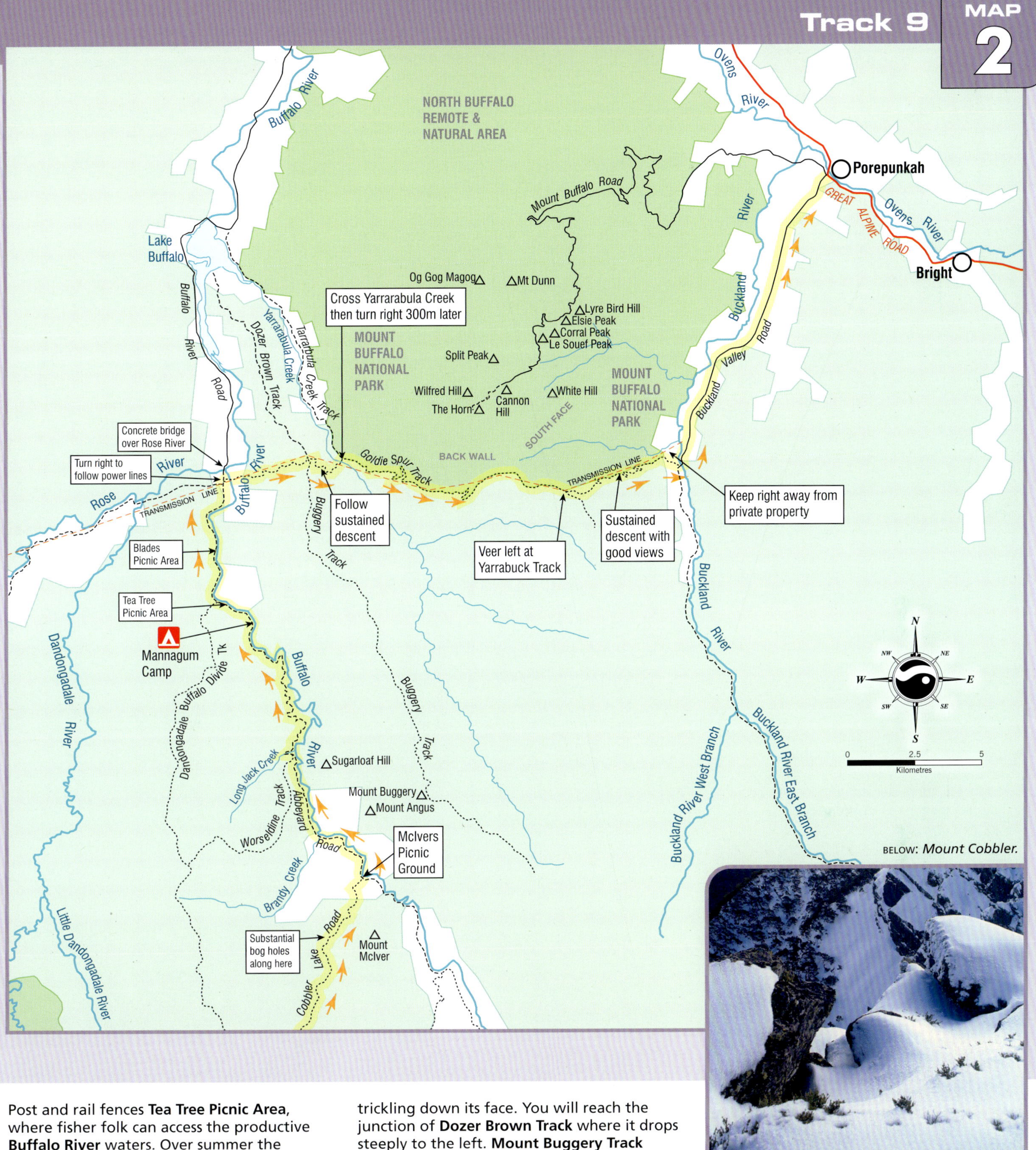

BELOW: *Mount Cobbler.*

Post and rail fences **Tea Tree Picnic Area**, where fisher folk can access the productive **Buffalo River** waters. Over summer the roadside tea tree will be laden with gleaming white flowers, but look out for wild roses, also common along the **Buffalo**.

Continue past the **Dandongadale Buffalo Divide Track** 400 metres later, then **Blades Picnic Area** following that. Cleared private land flags the locality of **Dandongadale**, where a lofty concrete bridge spans the **Rose River** and its confluence with the Buffalo.

We will turn right 500 metres prior to the bridge, following power lines on a climb toward **Mount Buffalo**. The narrow winding road offers views of **The Horn** and water trickling down its face. You will reach the junction of **Dozer Brown Track** where it drops steeply to the left. **Mount Buggery Track** peels away to the right, but we remain on the main road for a sustained descent.

You will reach a junction on the boundary of national park about 2 kilometres later, where you turn left to cross the south branch of **Yarrarabula Creek** at a rocky ford. Turn right at a tee intersection 300 metres later, at a clearing surrounded by blackberry. Follow a signpost pointing the way to '**Goldie Spur**', before you pass a power line track on the left 6.9 kilometres after that.

Keep straight to reach **Yarrabuck Track** on the right, 4.7 kilometres later. Veer left at this junction for a sustained descent along **Goldie Spur Track** with great views opening up over the **Buckland Valley**. Keep right, away from private property, 5.8 kilometres beyond the junction, to see ribbons of water dropping from the southern side of **Mount Buffalo**.

Huts and tobacco drying sheds flag the **Buckland Valley Road** shortly after (see **Buckland Valley** tour for details), where we turn left. Follow sealed road from here into **Porepunkah** and the conclusion of this trek.

TRACK 10 WONNANGATTA

HIGH COUNTRY

Wonnangatta Valley at the Myrtleford turn off.

*The **Wonnangatta Valley** is a popular destination with 4WDers for all of the usual reasons. It requires an adventurous drive to get there, there is excellent dispersed camping along a lovely river, and its history makes for some fascinating reading.*

*This trek drops into the valley from **Howitt Plains**, tracing the lazy **Wonnangatta River** for a while, then heads skyward again over **Mount Von Guerard**. There are great camping opportunities at **Wonnangatta** and **Talbotville**, and plenty of old gold mining sites to explore within the **Grant Historic Area**.*

The rough road action begins as you swing north onto **Zeka Spur Track** from the almost mile high **Howitt High Plains**, to drive through a seasonally closed gate and begin a gradual winding descent. Contorted snowgums usher the way as the descent gathers grade, crossing a creek 6 kilometres from the **Howitt Road**.

A superb fern garden irrigated by dripping water is reached 2.4 kilometres later, with a nice stand of alpine ash heralding a staircase section of track. Ledges and loose piles of smashed rock pave a low range drop off past a potential bush camp and the track swinging more to the south east.

You will cross a creek to find flax lilies and bluebells as you reach **Wonnangatta Track** at a tee intersection 21 kilometres from the **Howitt Road**. Keep right at the junction (left track is exit to **Myrtleford**) to follow the **Wonnangatta River** downstream as the valley begins to broaden.

Cross **Dry River** at a double fording,

TRACK SNAPSHOT

TOUR ROUTE

Howitt High Plains to Dargo via Wonnangatta Valley.

DURATION AND DISTANCE

This 110 kilometre trek is best done over at least two days to better appreciate this superb country.

TRACK DETAILS

Low range and high clearances are needed to negotiate the numerous rocky steps and steep grades. Water crossings can be deep, and trailers are not recommended.

WHEN TO GO

Enjoy the Wonnangatta over the warmer months between November and June when the seasonal track closures are lifted.

CAMPING

Great camping in the Wonnangatta Valley, Talbotville and Grant. Other bush sites possible.

FUEL AND SUPPLIES

Take on fuel and supplies at Heyfield or Licola and replenish at Dargo. There is nothing else en route.

MAPS

Rooftops: Dargo – Howitt Plains

OTHER INFORMATION

This tour takes in some highlights of Parks Victoria's iconic Wonnangatta Drive. See *www.iconic4wd.com.au* Other sections of this drive are detailed in our Howitt High Plains, Moroka Range and Billy Goat Bluff treks.

BASIC CHECK LIST . . .

- ☑  Steep Climbs
- ☑ Water Crossings
- ☑ Good Clearance Needed
- ☑ Snorkel Recommended
- ☑ Avoid Wet Weather

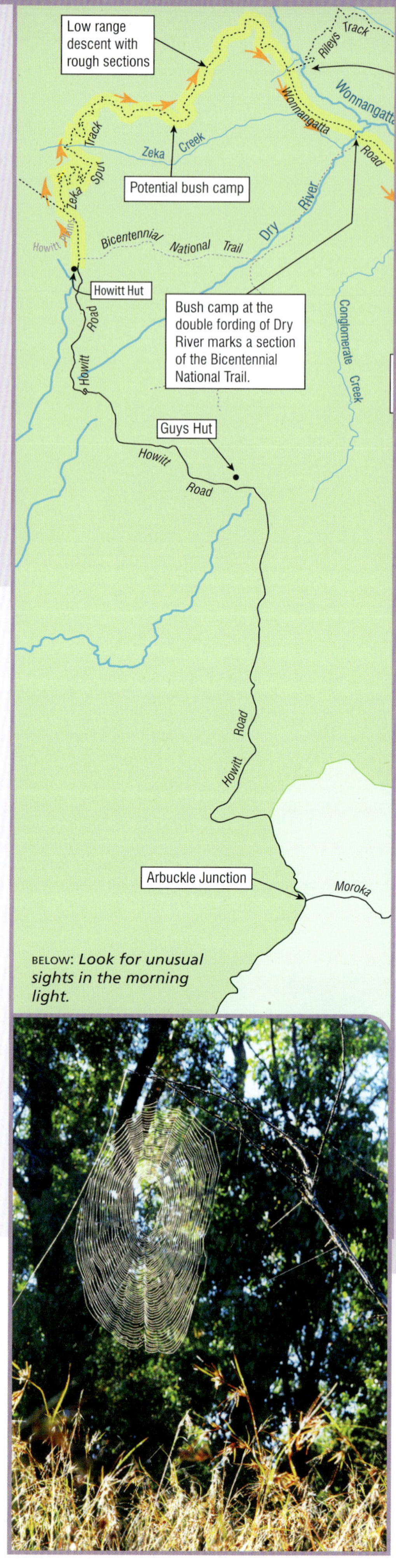

BELOW: *Look for unusual sights in the morning light.*

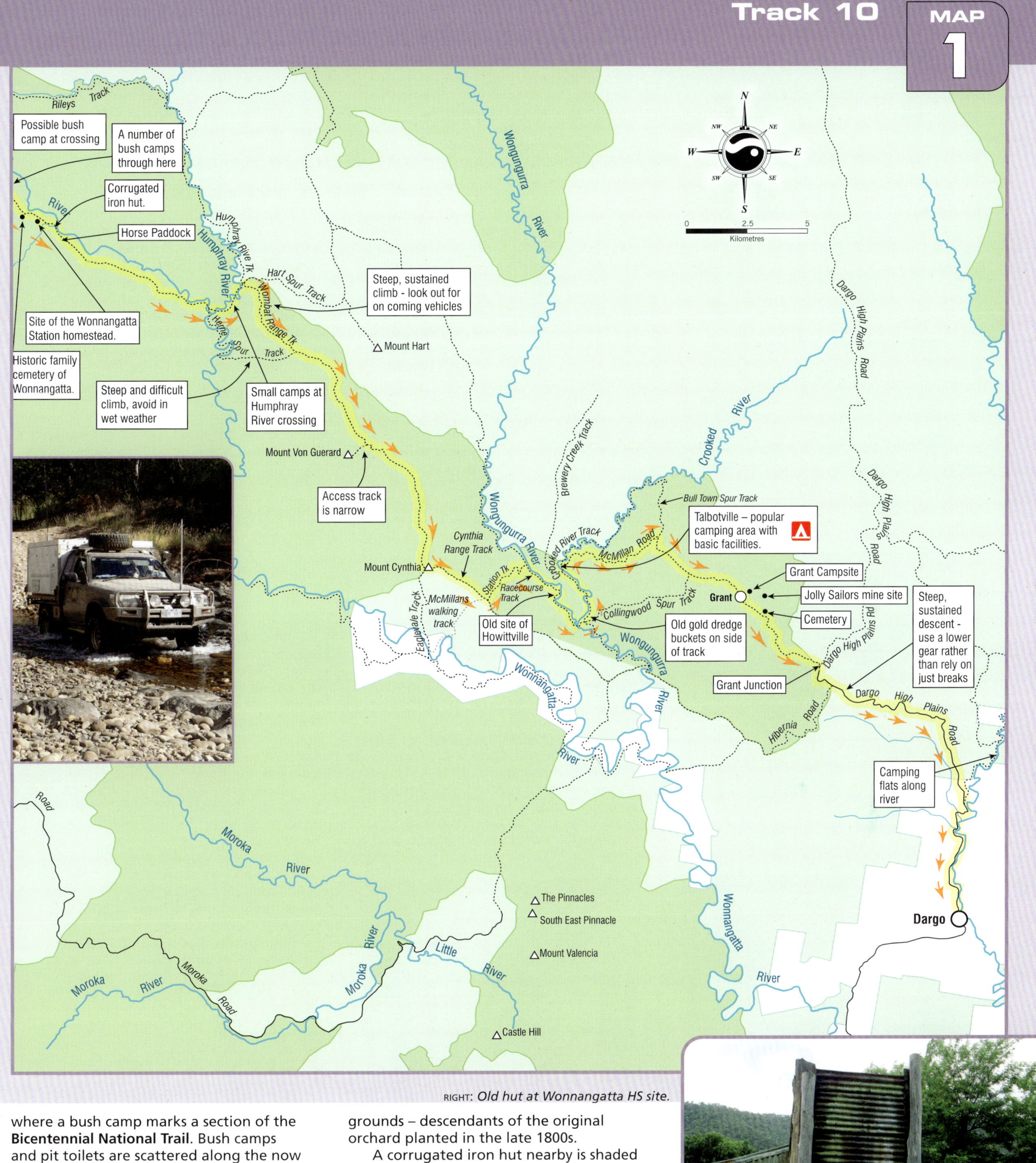

RIGHT: *Old hut at Wonnangatta HS site.*

where a bush camp marks a section of the **Bicentennial National Trail**. Bush camps and pit toilets are scattered along the now cleared and grassy valley with plenty of options even for large groups.

You will reach the historic family cemetery of **Wonnangatta**, shaded by conifers, then the site of the isolated homestead. River stones arranged to outline the house plan give visitors an idea of the original building's layout before it burnt to the ground in 1957. Plums, quince and other exotic tree species can still be seen around the homestead grounds – descendants of the original orchard planted in the late 1800s.

A corrugated iron hut nearby is shaded by pseudo acacia, and marks the crossing of **Conglomerate Creek**. **Horse Paddock** is reached 400 metres later – with an old fence line and large oak trees harking back to an earlier time.

Wonnangatta Track traces the river closely now, with several side tracks radiating to water side camps, before the valley narrows a little. A winding and undulating drive weaves around gullies, climbing away from the river to lofty views over some rapids and stony beaches.

You will cross the **Wonnangatta** at a wide ford, scrambling for traction on the exit, with mud and loose stones often gouged out with heavy track usage. Keep left at **Herne Spur Track** (difficult and steep climb to the **Wombat Range**), just after the crossing, to ford the **Humphray River** twice in quick succession (potential small camp at each crossing).

Turn right onto **Wombat Range Track** 200 metres from the second crossing, then keep right on a sharp switchback through a seasonally closed gate past **Harts Spur Track** on the left. Select your lowest gear to begin the climb over sections of rubble and off camber obstacles. The low range haul continues over erosion control mounds and past **Little Baldy**. Pay particular attention to any oncoming vehicles on this climb as passing opportunities are limited and will need to be planned. You will pass the other end of **Herne Spur Track** on the right, after a relentless lug of some 3 kilometres.

BELOW: *There are steep sections on Wombat Range Track.*

The climb moderates considerably now and you will have time to enjoy the valley views before reaching the turn off to **Mount Von Guerard**, 4.6 kilometres beyond Herne Spur Track. (This unmarked track pierces overgrown bushland and snowgum clumps to a helipad ringed with buttercups and broken views over the **Mount Darling / Snowy Bluff Wilderness**).

Continue the undulating drive along **Wombat Spur** to pass another section of **Bicentennial National Trail** and begin the steep climb to **Mount Cynthia**. You will reach the prominent peak 7 kilometres from the **Mount Von Guerard** turn off where you turn left (right turn to **Eaglevale** and **Wonnangatta River**).

Follow the mountain spine past side tracks, with good views over the **Wonnangatta** and **Wongungarra Valleys**. You will reach a four way junction 2.9 kilometres later with **McMillans Walking Track** peeling off to the right, and **Cynthia Range Track** continuing staight to separate the two major valleys.

We will turn left here though onto **Station Track** for a steep low range descent over erosion contol mounds with para hebes providing splashes of blue under some cypress pines. You will reach a tee intersection on **Racecourse Track**, where you leave national park and turn right to follow the **Wongungarra River** downstream (there is a nice bush camp at this location – the site of the former **Pioneer Racecourse** – with table seats and fireplace).

Continue past **McMillans Walking Track** and a gate to pass a private land holding with shed, yards and new fencing. The old town site of **Howittville** is marked with disturbed ground and building footings on a sharp river bend. Pass another private cottage and grid before crossing the **Wongungarra River** at a potentially deep ford, and turning left onto **Crooked River Track**, passing **Collingwood Spur Track** on the right. Two kilometres later you will pass an old section of dredge and reach **Brewery Creek Road** beyond that. Turn right to cross the river and arrive at an open area at the site of **Talbotville**.

LEFT: *Wonnangatta River at dawn.*

BELOW: *Lovely forest and afternoon light.*

Talbotville was once a small commercial hub for local mining activity, with dwellings and support services maintaining the goldfield. In latter years, as the gold became depleted, the population drifted away, leaving just market gardens to carry Talbotville's flag. However the remote location and freezing winters soon saw the end of even these endeavours, reducing the community to all but a memory.

Camping is popular here with easy access via **McMillans Road** and basic facilities. There is some shade and plenty of grassy sites along the river frontage. Mine ruins dot the area, so keep a close watch on children here – many shafts are left open and unguarded.

Leave the camping area at **Talbotville**, keeping right at the **Crooked River Track** to follow **McMillans Road** on a climb to the north east. Keep right at the Bulltown Spur Track junction 5 kilometres later, and left at the other end of **Collingwood Spur Track** some 3 kilometres beyond that.

The corrugated gravel passes several side tracks before arriving at a camping area at **Grant**. Today, little remains of this once bustling township which boasted of hotels, banks, and a variety of stores, but the cemetery is worth a visit. Engraved headstones recount some of the hardships of the goldfields, while eerie unnamed graves dot the surrounding bushland. The **Jolly Sailor Mine** lies nearby and can be reached via a walking track.

Follow **Grant Road** now for 5 kilometres to **Grant Junction** on the **Dargo High Plains Road**. Ruins from the old **Bandicoot Arms Hotel** mark the tee intersection, where you swing right onto sealed road. The **Freda Family Tree Reserve** protects a section of alpine ash and tree fern bush here, although much has been lost to recent bushfires.

Pass **Hibernia Road** on the right to continue a steep and sustained descent around a series of switchbacks. Avoid the temptation to ride your brakes on the descent, as it is a punishing ordeal for any vehicle – especially one with an automatic transmission. Hold a lower gear and let your engine do most of the work.

Follow the descent for views of the **Dargo Valley** and the **Upper Dargo Road** on your left, about 11.3 kilometres from **Grant Junction** (there are numerous camping possibilities at a series of river flats along here). Continue along the walnut tree lined run into **Dargo**, just 6 kilometres away.

Donnellys Creek

High Country

TRACK 11

TRACK SNAPSHOT

TOUR ROUTE
Heyfield to Matlock via Donnellys Creek goldfields.

DURATION AND DISTANCE
This 130 kilometre journey is best done over a weekend, although a day trip is also possible.

TRACK DETAILS
Medium standard 4WDing along Donnellys Creek and down Victor Spur into the Jordan Valley, with low range called for at times, and some water crossings.

WHEN TO GO
Most of this trek can be done all year round, but 4WD access into the Jordan Valley has an extended closure from May 1st until 30th November.

CAMPING
Nice camping along Donnellys Creek Road at various river access locations. Other options at Andersons, with bush camping at The Springs. No vehicle based camping permitted in the Jordon Valley as it is part of the Thomson Catchment Area.

FUEL AND SUPPLIES
Heyfield can provide for all needs at the start of this trek, but Matlock at the conclusion has no services. Nearby Woods Point can cater for basic needs.

MAPS
Rooftops: Walhalla – Woods Point

OTHER INFORMATION
Although there is an extended seasonal track closure into the Jordan Valley, visitors can still enjoy most of this trek at other times of the year by avoiding Victor Spur Road, and remaining on the Walhalla Road to reach Matlock. However take care on the water crossings after rain.

Sunset through fire damaged trees.

LEFT: *Old mining relics can be found in the bush.*

*The former gold mining towns around **Donnellys Creek** have largely vanished over the last 130 years or so, but 4WDers interested in history can still piece together some clues as to this area's recent past. Although most of the old shanties have been lost entirely to the bush, there are still some mine workings and other relics that can be reached by vehicle or on foot at various stages of this tour.*

*This route from **Heywood** to **Matlock** follows state forests into the **Thomson Reservoir Water** catchment along a sometimes moderately challenging track network. There are plenty of bush camping opportunities along **Donnellys Creek**, and some interesting walks to various locations relevent to the 19th century mining boom period.*

Leave **Heyfield** via the south part of town, turning west onto the **Seaton Road** just prior to the **Thomson River** bridge, signposted **'Dawson'**. Keep right on the **Seaton Road** to pass grazing land and nice views of the alpine foothills. Keep straight at the **Cowarr** and **Seymour Road** junctions, before passing the **Seaton Reserve** at a rest stop.

A string of letterboxes and scattered houses marks the start of a climb as you hit gravel at the **Glenmaggie Road**. Bush blocks and driveways mark the community of **Seaton** (first known as **Bald Hills** in the gold rush days). This tour follows in the footsteps of those early prospectors as you deal with corrugations along a log truck route following **McEvoys Track**; also known as **Springs Road** (keep your headlights on and stay on top of any truck movements by monitoring UHF channel 40).

Several tracks fan off the main arterial, before you reach **Back Creek Track**, some 7 kilometres beyond the **Seaton Reserve**. You will find the first of many historical markers here, erected to shed light on the local gold rush communities of the mid 1800s located between here and Jamieson. This particular site marked a c1863 hotel and nearby shanty, although parking is rather awkward at this junction, especially for a group of vehicles.

Continue past **Hugs Road** on the right for a steady climb through fire damaged forest and scotch thistle. A marker for the old **Viewpoint Hotel** and nearby grave is reached 5.3 kilometres beyond **Back Creek Track** where indigofera is growing with its wattle like leaf and pink flowers in summer.

Follow the spine of the **Great Divide** with views of **Mount Baw Baw**. You will pass **East – West Divide Track** to find a cluster of old shanty sites just prior to **Murderers Hill**. The site of **Porters Boarding House** flags a major road junction at **Binns Corner**, where you turn right away from the **Walhalla Road**.

Continue north past a stand of black wattle that marks the passing of **Dawes Hotel**, and the old **Bark Hut Boarding House** with views toward **Mount Useful**. Pass **Glenmaggie Creek Track** on the right to arrive at **The Springs** 2.2 kilometres after that.

Camping is possible at this cleared site, surrounded by native bush and some exotic trees. **The Springs** was a small settlement in the 1860s catering for travellers heading to the nearby goldfields. Three hotels served the increasing demand, while a market garden was established using natural spring waters.

Turn left onto **Donnelly Creek Road**, 2 kilometres further north, for a rough drive past **Edwards Reef Cemetery**. Sharp gutters and drainage lines cut the track at regular intervals, while switchbacks ramp a descent into the rocky country, where you will be in and out of low range. You will pass a potential camp site clearing just prior to a child's grave, and reach the reef gold mining area at **Edwards Hill**, 3.5 kilometres into the drive.

Further sharp bends around **Concord Gully** afford some views of the valley, as you descend to the old **Store Point** township site. Once home to 1200 people with a post office and police station, **Store Point** began with a rush in 1862, before fading away 60 years later. A renovated hut stands at a camping area (basic facilities), while nearby walks take in some of the local country and various mining relics.

Cross the creek just west of the hut to drive under chestnut and oak trees near one of several blocks of private land. You will pass a character rich hut at **Lloyds** 200 metres later, with the **Morning Star Track** on the right leading to a small but very pleasant creekside camp – and the beginning of a walking track to the **Morning Star Water Wheel** site. Continue west to pass **Middle Star Track** on the right for elevated creek views

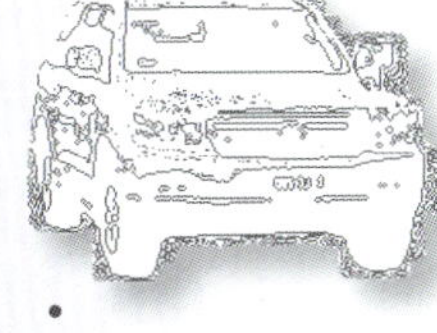

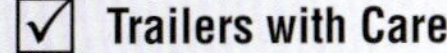

BASIC CHECK LIST . . .

- ☑ Trailers with Care
- ☑ Steep Climbs
- ☑ Water Crossings
- ☑ Good Clearance Needed
- ☑ Avoid Wet Weather

DONNELLYS CREEK

and several side tracks, reaching the turn off to **O'Tooles Flats** 7 kilometres beyond **Lloyds Hut**.

There is a large camping area at **Connaughtons Flat** on the creek here, with a grassed area, rotunda and basic facilities. Bollards restrict some access, but large groups can still remain together. Further downsteam you pass **Flats Track** on the left and **Little O'Tooles Camp** on the right (basic facilities). **White Star Track** peels off 300 metres later, with an especially nice creek camp reached 1.7 kilometres beyond that (no facilities).

You will cross **Donnellys Creek** shortly after to arrive at **Jorgenson** for basic facilities and an elaborate hut. Further on, an historic dog's grave precedes **Junction Track** on the left (access to camping at **Merringtons**), where you keep right on **Donnelly Creek Road**. Pass **Jorgensons Track** on the right to reach an enormous mullock heap 2.8 kilometres later at the site of **Toombon**.

The **Toombon Historic Walk** originates at a carpark near here, taking hikers on a 2.5 kilometre ramble to an impressive steel chimney and numerous other mining relics. You will see a replica of the original **Toombon Hotel** (private property), while those wishing to visit the historic cemetery can do so from this carpark too; as there is no parking at the access steps 800 metres further along the main road.

Continue along **Donnellys Creek Road** past the cemetery and **Smoko Point** to **Andersons Camp** about 3 kilometres beyond the mullock pile (pleasant riverside camping with basic facilities). Cross the **Aberfeldy River** at a bridge to arrive at **Codes Flat** and the **Aberfeldy Cabins**. This patch of private land contains a number of buildings – some of which date back to the original settlement. Look out for a lovely sedimentary stone hut, roofed in iron, that is visible as you veer left uphill away from the flat.

There is a steep climb from **Codes Flat** to the **Walhalla Road** that is unrelenting over several kilometres. You will reach the wider gravel at a tee intersection and swing right for views of **Mount Useful** from the locality of **Toner**.

Continue on to arrive at **Aberfeldy** to find a telephone box and a heritage walk, but no visitor facilities or services. Originally known as **Mount Lookout**, the community once boasted of several hotels and a shopping precinct. These days some private houses and exotic trees mark the locality, as you head north past the cemetery and **Pluto Track**.

You will swing eastward at a tree fern gully on the right, before heading northward again along **Spud Spur**. **Ash Road** branches to the right, 2 kilometres later where an historic water trough has been cut int the rock on the west side of the **Walhalla Road**. Trigger plants colour the bush here, and the permanent water supply was probably used to water pack horses in the pioneering days.

You will pass **Mount Selma Road** on the right and a 1926 survey party memorial 600 metres later. The remains of a corrugated iron hut will be seen 1.3 kilometres beyond that, as you near the summit of **Mount Victor**. **Victor Spur Track** branches left, some 4 kilometres from the **Survey Party** marker as a skyline view opens up on the right.

Turn left through a seasonally closed gate for a smooth and gradual descent through sheltered snowgums marking the boundary of the **Thomson Water Supply Catchment**. You will follow a section of **Alpine Walking Track** past **Dry Creek Track** and around rutted corners. Moss covered cuttings mark the lower section of **Victor Spur** as it follows **Red Jacket Creek** to a bridge spanning the **Jordan River**.

We will turn right just over the bridge to continue the tour, but for now swing left onto **Red Jacket Track** at the former outpost of **Red Jacket** itself. Little remains of the rugged mining town as you pass the school site to neighbouring **Blue Jacket** some 1.7 kilometres further down the **Jordan Valley**. Relics are being reclaimed by the bush all along the valley, but interpretive signs paint a picture of life on these remote goldfields. You can continue south from here past **Casper Creek Track**, to the site of **Violet Town** about 1.2 kilometres later. This cleared part of the valley was once a market garden with vegetables and fruit trees grown to feed hundreds of hungry miners.

Retrace your steps to **Victor Spur Road** and continue north west along the Jordan past the **Red Jacket Cemetery**, and keeping left away from **Red Jacket Spur Track**. A tree fern gully lines the gravel banked river under a canopy of tall eucalypts where water race depressions can still be traced. Stone footings and mullock heaps are visible from the track as you arrive at the old township site of **Jericho**, where many hopeful miners possessed by gold fever once lived and worked.

You will reach a tee intersection with **Poole Road** heading south and **Jericho Track** continuing north. Turn right at the junction to reach a picnic area on **BB Creek** where a river diversion tunnel has been chiseled through solid rock. This is a nice spot to take a break, however vehicle based camping is not permitted within the **Thomson Catchment Zone**.

Follow **Jericho Track** past the historic cemetery and a significant oak tree on a ramping climb past **Red Jacket Spur Track**. Erosion control mounds punctuate a steady climb back to the **Walhalla Road** at **Roberts**, where you turn left for the final few kilometres drive into **Matlock**.

Originally known as **Emerald Hill**, **Matlock** was, at 1200 metres, once the highest inhabited town in Victoria with two banks and 13 hotels. Today only a few houses stand on the ridge, but its rotunda and grassy area makes a nice rest stop. Travellers can follow the **Warburton – Woods Point Road** west from here to reach **Marysville**, or swing right to **Woods Point** for more unsealed driving along the **Woods Point – Jamieson Road**, with great bush camping at **Gaffneys Creek** or along the **Goulburn River**.

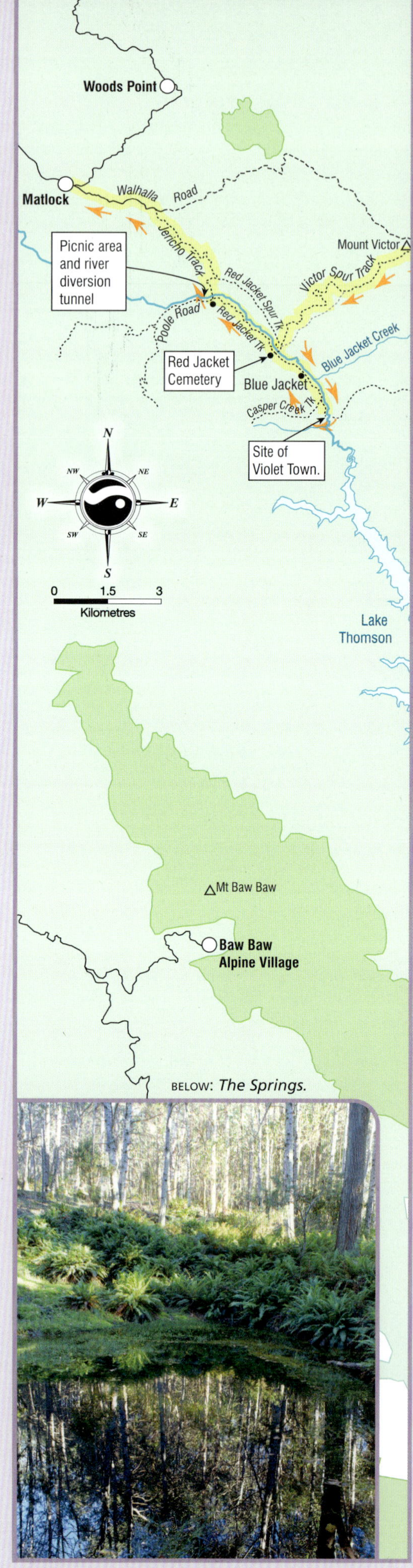

BELOW: *The Springs.*

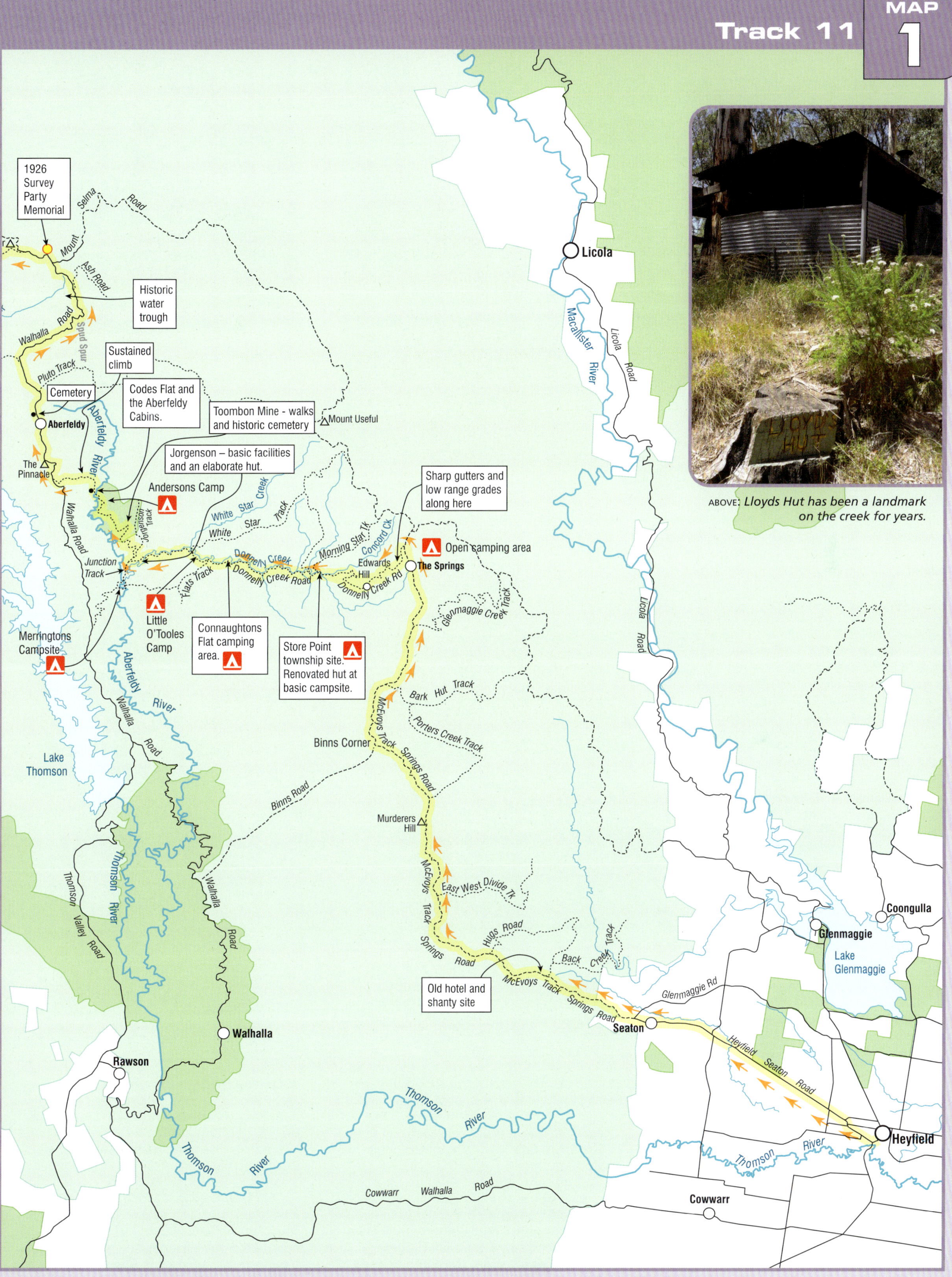

ABOVE: *Lloyds Hut has been a landmark on the creek for years.*

TRACK 12

KING RIVER

HIGH COUNTRY

King River crossing.

*Travelling into the **King River** valley is certainly one of the highlights of exploring **Victoria's High Country**, with great scenery, mountain huts and the possibility of pulling in a trout for dinner. This iconic waterway is popular with 4WDers especially along the alpine reaches upstream of **Lake William Hovell**. The crumpled mountainscape around **Burnt Top Hill** offers great 4WDing and views into the heart of the alps.*

*Drivers will grapple with steep mountain country, water crossings and the occasional boghole on a rewarding circuit drive around the **King**. Several huts provide interest for visitors, and there is excellent camping at riverside settings on **Sandy** and **Pineapple Flats**.*

Leave **Mansfield** via the **Mount Buller Road**, following good bitumen past the **Woods Point Road** turn off. Keep heading east through grazing country to reach **Buttercup Road**, some 14 kilometres from the town centre.

Veer left here between an avenue of poplar trees to drive by a platoon of roadside letterboxes. The sealed road turns to gravel as you pass **School** and **Gonza Roads**, keeping right at **Murphys Lane**. A winding section of road becomes tighter at the locality of **Buttercup**, where a cluster of houses are shaded under chestnut and pines. It is a pleasant valley view as you reach a crossing of **Buttercup Creek**, 8.7 kilometres from town.

A signpost indicating 4WD access guards the rough and rocky causeway as you enter **Mansfield SF** passing pockets of private land. The track hugs the creek where bracken and blackberry grow rampantly. Some informal camping areas have been closed and rehabilitated along here, as you reach **Buttercup No.2** – a designated camping area. Basic facilities are provided here, with easy creek access. You will reach the bigger camping area at **Buttercup No.3**, 1.6 kilometres later, again with basic facilities. **Buttercup No.4** is just 200 metres further on, also with toilet, fireplace and some shade.

Carters Road is reached 2 kilometres later where you turn left to pass **Buttercup Jeep Track** on the left, 300 metres further on. Follow the waterway past a jungle of thick tree fern gullies to **Plain Creek Track** on the right. Keep straight here to climb through tall

TRACK SNAPSHOT

TOUR ROUTE

Mansfield and return via Lake William Hovell, the King River and Wabonga Plateau.

DURATION AND DISTANCE

This 160 kilometre trek could be done in a day, but 2-3 would be much better.

TRACK DETAILS

Steep grades and water crossings limit this tour to full size 4WDs with low range gears. Take particular care at the King River crossing downstream of Lake William Hovell – deep and fast flowing water should not be forded. Off road trailers for experienced drivers only.

WHEN TO GO

Seasonal road closures limit this trek to the warmer months from November until early June. Some national park areas will be closed on days of catastrophic fire danger.

CAMPING

Good camping on the King at Pineapple Flat, Sandy Flat and Top Crossing Hut. Other possibilities are found along Buttercup Creek and several bush options – see map and text for details.

FUEL AND SUPPLIES

Mansfield can provide for all requirements.

MAPS

Rooftop: Bright – Mansfield

OTHER INFORMATION

The King River is a very popular destination – try to visit outside of the usual holiday periods, or mid week if possible.

BASIC CHECK LIST . . .

- ☑ Trailers with Care
- ☑ Steep Climbs
- ☑ Water Crossings
- ☑ Good Clearance Needed
- ☑ Avoid Wet Weather

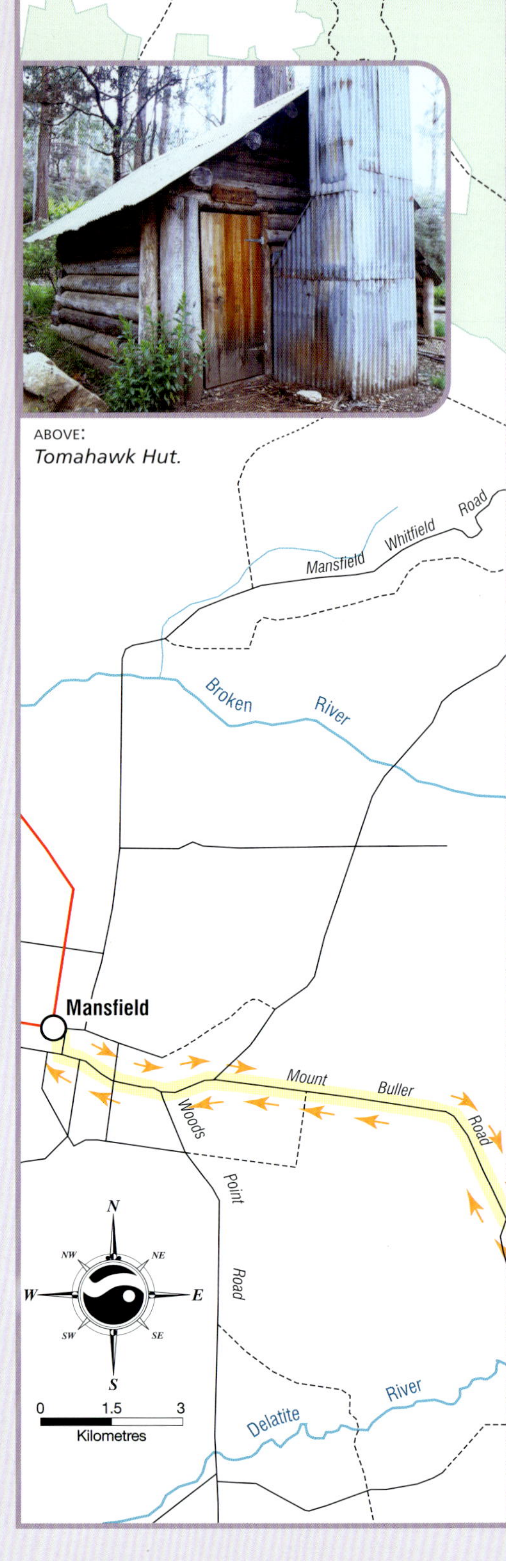

ABOVE: *Tomahawk Hut.*

MAP 1

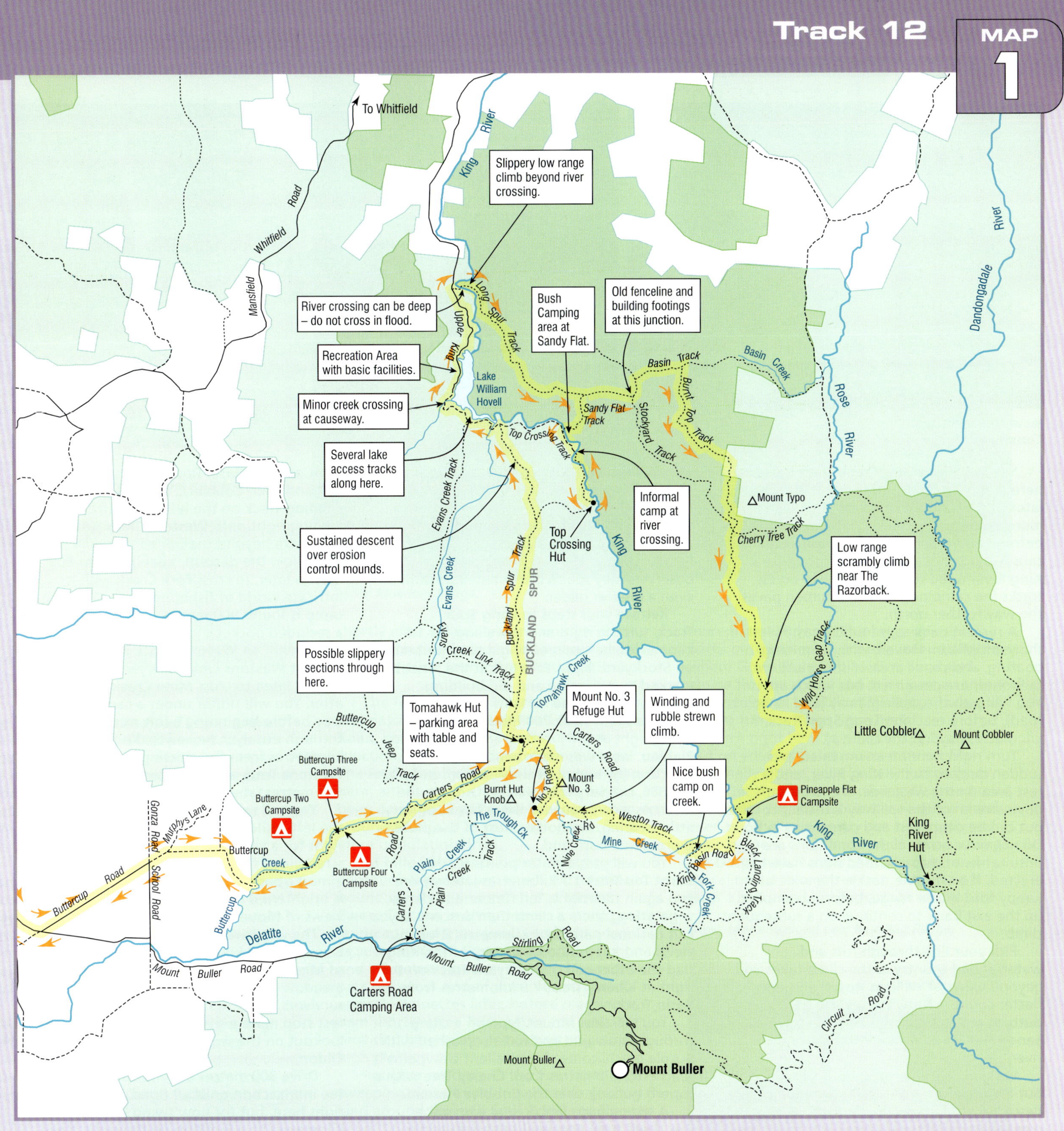

timber, with glimpses of **Burnt Hut Knob** on the right.

Pass **Evans Divide Track** on the left for a colourful run through wattle with dusty daisy bush and flowering clematis. Veer left onto **Buckland Spur Track** some 5.7 kilometres from the **Carters Road** turn, to enter alpine ash regrowth, now 20 years old. (Take note of this junction, as you will return here at the trek's conclusion.)

You will reach **Tomahawk Hut** 500 metres from the turn to find a chock log constructed hut, roofed in iron and featuring a character fireplace. A parking area together with table and seats make it a pleasant stop for travellers.

Continue through a seasonally closed gate to witness the transition to snowgums and broken views over the **King Valley**. Pass **Evans Creek Link Track** on the left, for a potentially slippery and waterlogged run past yellow daisies and trigger plants. Erosion control mounds punctuate the descent along the **Buckland Spur**, as views open up of **Mount Typo** in the distance, surrounded by a crumpled mountainscape. Further into the descent you will be greeted with views of **Lake William Hovell**, before undertaking the lumpy and tortuous final drop off.

A seasonally closed gate marks the **Top Crossing Track** junction at a tee intersection, where you turn left to follow the **King River** as it widens into the dammed body of **Lake William Hovell**. A short access track leads to the lake edge shortly after, where clumps of native iris fringe a nice rest stop. Anglers can try their luck here, among submerged and dead trees reflecting into the deep aquamarine colour of the lake.

ABOVE: *A grassy plain is all that remains of the old mining town of Mayford.*

LEFT: *The Wongungarra River marks the end of Blue Rag Range Track.*

forest spared from fire damage.

You follow the escarpment on a slow drive eastward, before dropping into low range for the descent, about 8 kilometres into the drive. The next 3 kilometres follow a sustained drop off ramping down via a series of switchbacks and slippery earthen sections. This is not the place to be after wet weather, especially around the rocky ledge section at the beginning of the drop off.

The track swings northward to follow the river for the last few hundred metres, before a final steep pinch delivers you to the water's edge. Some bogholes see the track split into optional pathways so check out their condition on foot if necessary, before committing your vehicle to a particular route.

Follow the track in a north westerly direction now as it crosses and recrosses the **Dargo** with a tight switchback and some pebbly, slippery exits. Taller bushland fringes a rather picturesque valley as you pass a small informal camp on the right, before entering the valley proper, where the township of **Mayford** once stood.

Like most other mining towns, little remains of this one, but some building footings and smaller relics can be found by those who have time to look around. The track ends at possibly the best camp in the valley, with shade and easy river access. Fly fishing can be productive here, but the site is equally appreciated by those just looking to get away from it all for a while.

You must retrace your steps from here, as there is no vehicle access to the **Dinner Plain Track** further east. Once back on the **Dargo High Plains Road**, turn right to cross **Lankey Plain** and reach a small carpark 3.5 kilometres later. Tables, chairs and BBQ are located here with excellent views toward **Mount Hotham** and **Hotham Heights**.

The turn off to **Mt Blue Rag** is reached 2.5 kilometres later at a parking area and water point on the left. Low range is required immediately to deal with a steep beginning that evolves into a rocky journey though snowgum woodland. Keep right 500 metres later (left track heads toward summit of **Mount Blue Rag**, but stops short at a potential camp clearing), and right again at the **Blue Rag Range Track** junction 3.5 kilometres beyond the **High Plains Road** turn off.

Continue through a seasonally closed gate to follow an undulating ridge past some panoramic viewpoints. In many sections the track shoulders drop steeply from both sides exposing a broad bushland view to as far as **Mount Buffalo**. Masses of shrubs and wildflowers colour the trackside verges, extending over the ridge to carpet the valleys. The snow daisies and orange alpine everlastings are particularly attractive in early summer. Unfortunately the alpine ash forests which once covered much of the valleys suffered greatly during serious bushfires in 2003.

The final climb to an exposed trig point is especially steep, and drivers must negotiate rocky steps forming the track surface, although it is rather less testing than once was the case. There is a carpark at the trig marker which makes a great spot to get out and appreciate this vantage point. From an altitude of around 1700 metres, views extend in every direction, making this one of the High County's most talked about lookouts.

Blue Rag Range Track continues to the Wongungarra River directly ahead, but it is a sustained drop off, clipping more than 1000 vertical metres from beneath your wheels and is not often used. For those looking for a remote camp or fishing spot under pleasant messmate forest it may tick all of the boxes, but otherwise, retrace your steps to the **High Plains Road** and turn left over **Mount Freezeout** to an intersection on the **Great Alpine Road** at **Mount St Bernard**. From here sealed road heads east to **Omeo**, or north to **Bright**.

BOTTOM RIGHT: *Gows Hotel site.*

CENTRE: *Little Womans Grave.*

BELOW: *Rock and steep grades keep you in low range off the High Plains Road.*

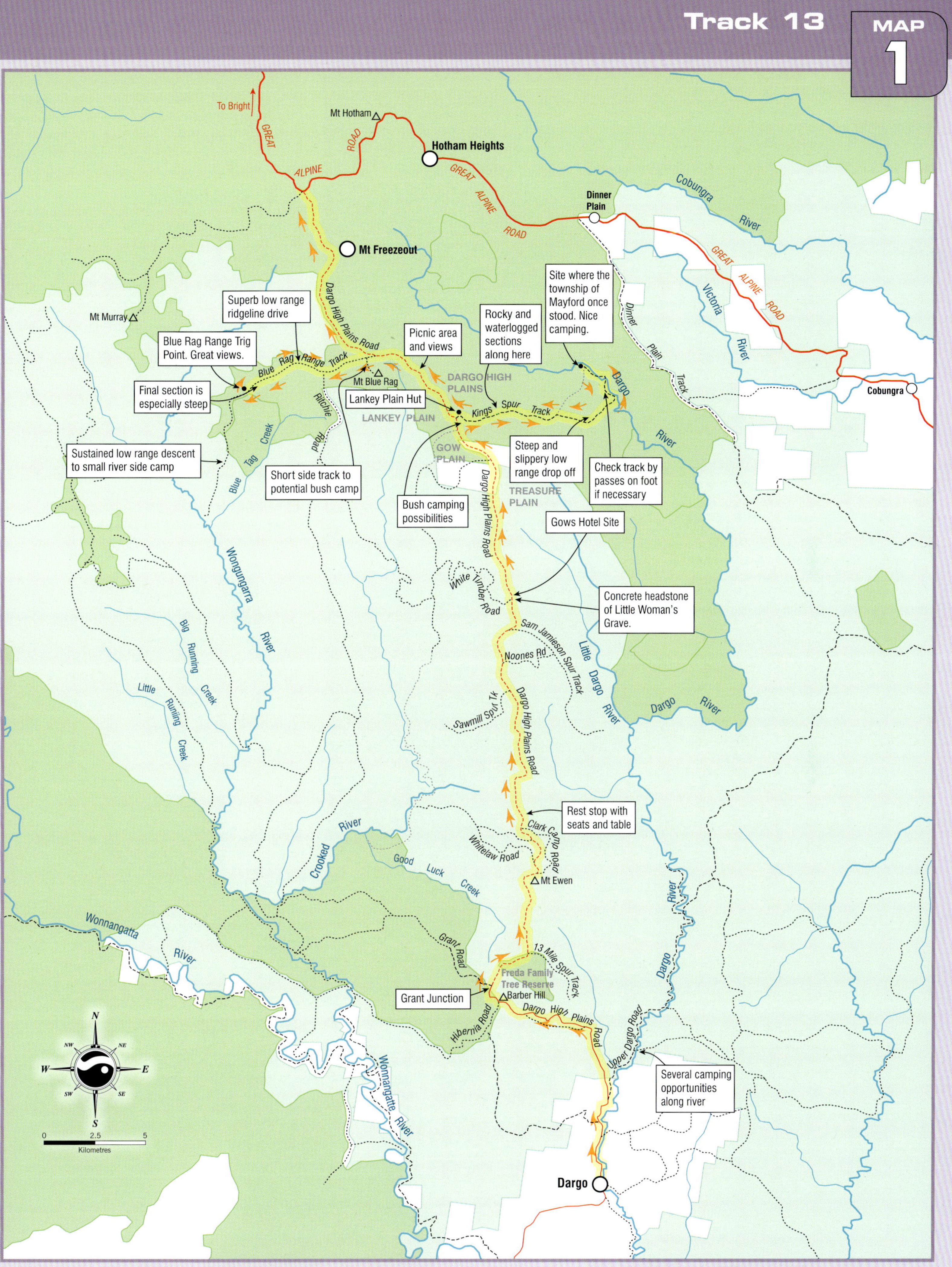
To Bright
GREAT ALPINE ROAD
Mt Hotham
Hotham Heights
Dinner Plain
Cobungra River
Mt Freezeout
Victoria River
Cobungra
Mt Murray
Superb low range ridgeline drive
Blue Rag Range Trig Point. Great views.
Final section is especially steep
Picnic area and views
Rocky and waterlogged sections along here
Site where the township of Mayford once stood. Nice camping.
Dargo High Plains Road
Blue Rag Range Track
Mt Blue Rag
Lankey Plain Hut
DARGO HIGH PLAINS
LANKEY PLAIN
Kings Spur Track
Dinner Plain Track
Dargo River
Ritchie Road
Blue Tag Creek
Sustained low range descent to small river side camp
Short side track to potential bush camp
GOW PLAIN
Steep and slippery low range drop off
Check track by passes on foot if necessary
TREASURE PLAIN
Bush camping possibilities
Gows Hotel Site
Wongungarra River
White Timber Road
Concrete headstone of Little Woman's Grave.
Sam Jamieson Spur Track
Noones Rd
Little Dargo River
Big Running Creek
Little Running Creek
Sawmill Spur Tk
Rest stop with seats and table
Clark Camp Road
Whitelaw Road
Crooked River
Good Luck Creek
Mt Ewen
Wonnangatta River
Grant Road
13 Mile Spur Track
Freda Family Tree Reserve
Barber Hill
Grant Junction
Hibernia Road
Dargo High Plains Road
Upper Dargo Road
Several camping opportunities along river
Wonnangatta River
N
NE
E
SE
S
SW
W
NW
0
2.5
5
Kilometres
Dargo

TRACK 14 DAVIES HIGH PLAINS

HIGH COUNTRY

ABOVE: *Murray River at Tom Groggin.*

BASIC CHECK LIST . . .

- ☑ Trailers with Care
- ☑ Steep Climbs
- ☑ Water Crossings
- ☑ Good Clearance Needed
- ☑ Snorkel Recommended
- ☑ Avoid Wet Weather
- ☑ Navigation Skills

*Although the **Davies High Plains** are perhaps the highlight of this trek, there is so much more to enjoy on this loop drive. The outstanding views from **Mount Gibbo** and the remote camping opportunities are matched by some picturesque country along **Limestone Creek**, and great access to the **Murray River** at **Tom Groggin** and **The Poplars**.*

*Driving conditions vary from routine and scenic rural legs, to some serious low range lugs and potentially slippery sections. The remote ridge country around **Davies Plains** is especially fragile and subject to a longer seasonal road closure than is usual for the **High Country**. Sometimes the tracks around here remain closed even beyond these additional restrictions, so plan your trip accordingly and get current advice from Parks Victoria if you are heading up here early in the season.*

Follow **Livingstone Creek** north from **Omeo** on the **Omeo Highway**, turning right 4 kilometres later onto the winding **Benambra Road**. The narrow bitumen climbs to **McMillans Lookout** 5 kilometres later (good views over the **Mitta Mitta Valley**), before following a rural path past the historic **Strathalbyn HS**. You will pass the

LEFT: *Rural view near Benambra.*

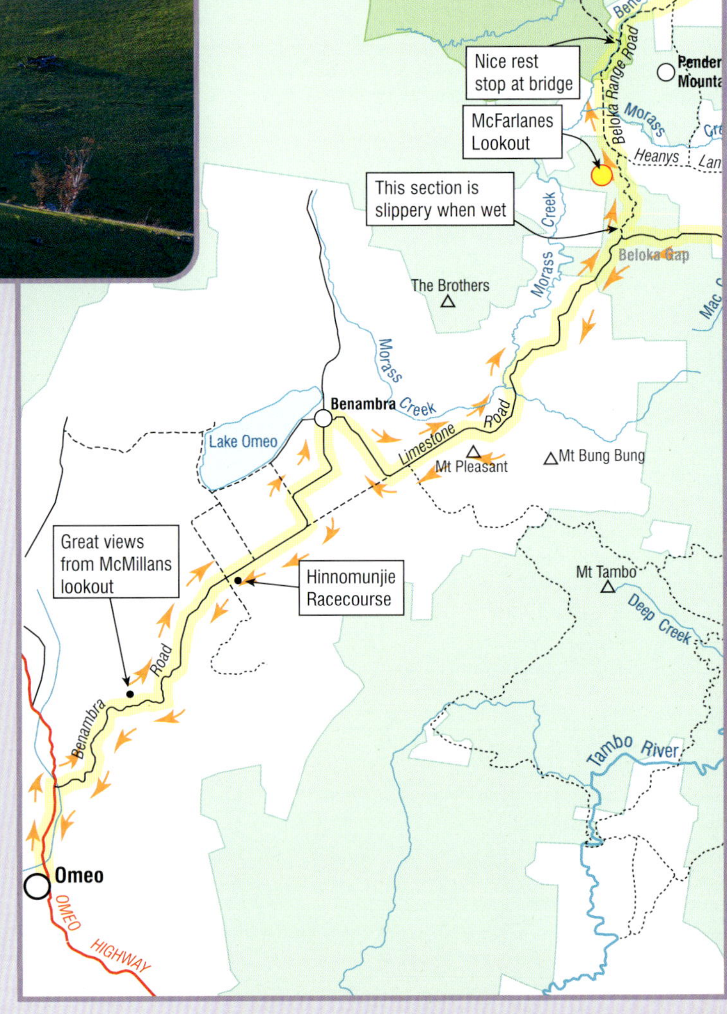

TRACK SNAPSHOT

TOUR ROUTE

Omeo and return via Mount Gibbo, Tom Groggin and the Upper Murray River.

DURATION AND DISTANCE

Allow at least two days for 250 kilometres of bush driving.

TRACK DETAILS

Some serious climbs, descents and water crossings will warrant a full size 4WD with low range gearing. Slippery sections would be difficult on standard road tyres, and those wanting to tow an off road trailer will need considerable experience.

WHEN TO GO

Seasonal road closures limit this trek to between December 1st and May 1st. Avoid wet weather outside of this period and note that days of catastrophic fire danger will see some areas of national park closed to visitors.

CAMPING

Excellent camping on the Murray River at The Poplars and Dogmans Hut. Other options include Buenba Flat, Limestone Creek, Davies High Plains, and Charlies Creek.

FUEL AND SUPPLIES

Benambra offers fuel and basic supplies, but Omeo will have a wider range.

MAPS

Rooftop: Corryong – Omeo – Thredbo

OTHER INFORMATION

Although the Murray River can be forded near Dogmans Hut at certain times of the year, it will definitely pay to check its depth on foot first. This waterway can be deep and fast flowing.

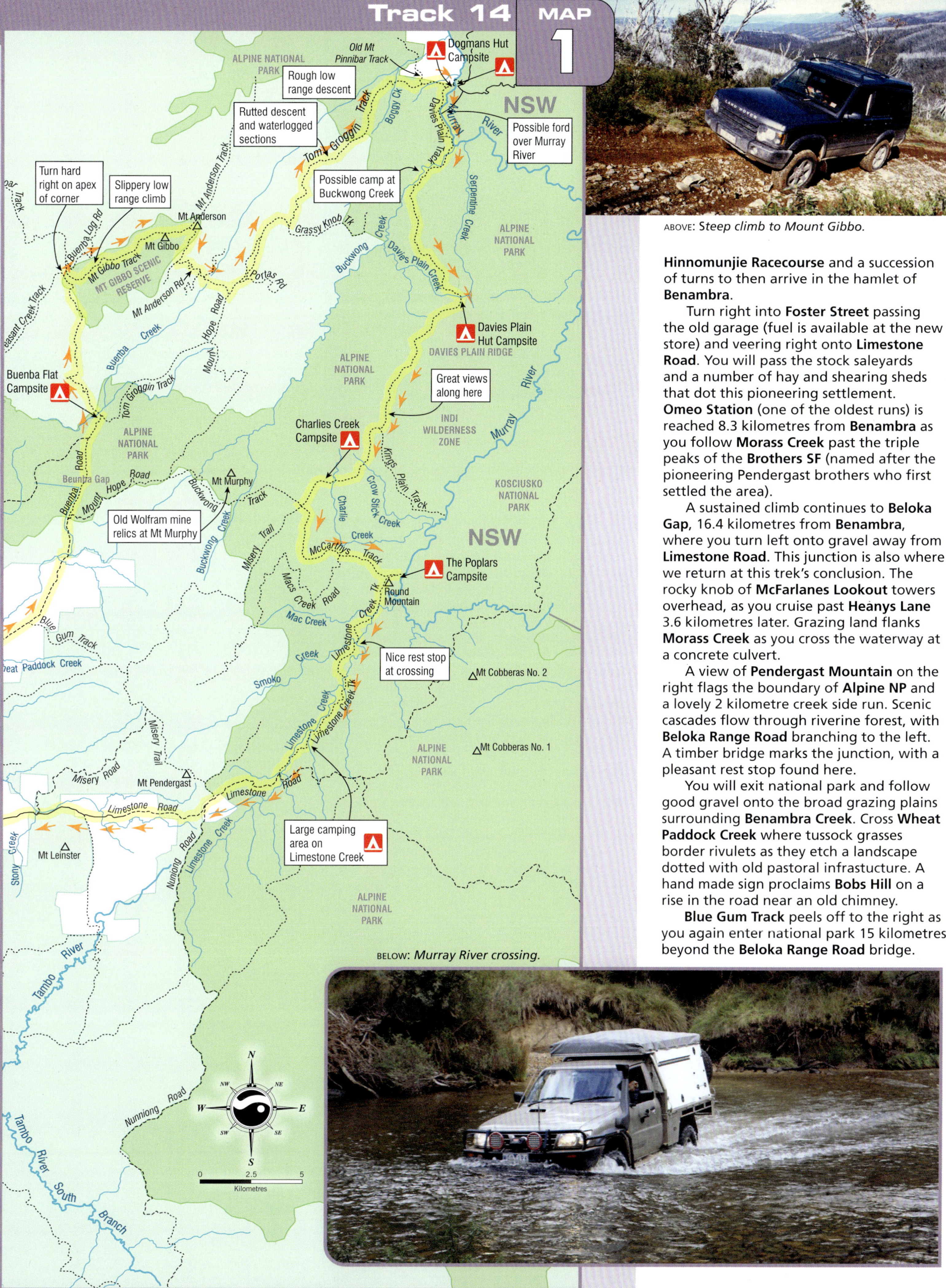

ABOVE: *Steep climb to Mount Gibbo.*

Hinnomunjie Racecourse and a succession of turns to then arrive in the hamlet of **Benambra**.

Turn right into **Foster Street** passing the old garage (fuel is available at the new store) and veering right onto **Limestone Road**. You will pass the stock saleyards and a number of hay and shearing sheds that dot this pioneering settlement. **Omeo Station** (one of the oldest runs) is reached 8.3 kilometres from **Benambra** as you follow **Morass Creek** past the triple peaks of the **Brothers SF** (named after the pioneering Pendergast brothers who first settled the area).

A sustained climb continues to **Beloka Gap**, 16.4 kilometres from **Benambra**, where you turn left onto gravel away from **Limestone Road**. This junction is also where we return at this trek's conclusion. The rocky knob of **McFarlanes Lookout** towers overhead, as you cruise past **Heanys Lane** 3.6 kilometres later. Grazing land flanks **Morass Creek** as you cross the waterway at a concrete culvert.

A view of **Pendergast Mountain** on the right flags the boundary of **Alpine NP** and a lovely 2 kilometre creek side run. Scenic cascades flow through riverine forest, with **Beloka Range Road** branching to the left. A timber bridge marks the junction, with a pleasant rest stop found here.

You will exit national park and follow good gravel onto the broad grazing plains surrounding **Benambra Creek**. Cross **Wheat Paddock Creek** where tussock grasses border rivulets as they etch a landscape dotted with old pastoral infrastucture. A hand made sign proclaims **Bobs Hill** on a rise in the road near an old chimney.

Blue Gum Track peels off to the right as you again enter national park 15 kilometres beyond the **Beloka Range Road** bridge.

BELOW: *Murray River crossing.*

ABOVE: *Heading south from Dogman Hut.*

Veer left onto **Buenba Road** at the **Mount Hope Road** junction (the latter offers access to old wolfram mine ruins at **Mount Murphy**), to take the low road on a much narrower pathway. Less surface rock makes this a dry weather only section, as you reach **Buenba Gap** (no views).

Trace the descent from here through broken views to **Buenba Gap Track** on the left 1.7 kilometres later. Keep straight at the junction to cross a bridge, climbing to **Tom Groggin Track** on the right a couple of kilometres later. Keep left at the junction to find **Buenba Flat Camping Area** just prior to a creek. Its large open area has fireplaces, but no other facilities.

Exit the camp via the small creek to reach the more significant **Buenba Creek** shortly after. Cross a bridge here at a very scenic location to begin a sustained climb along **Buenba Road**. You will enter the **Mount Gibbo Scenic Reserve** 6.6 kilometres later to be greeted with broken views through range country now recovering from a large blaze. Keep straight away from **Pheasant Creek Track** on the left 3 kilometres later, to reach a tee intersection 1 kilometre beyond that.

Wild Boar Track heads left here (access to **Mount Sassafras**) and **Buenba Log Road** to the right (access to **Wheelers Creek Hut**), but we turn hard right on the apex of the corner to begin the climb along **Mount Gibbo Track**. You will head through a seasonally closed gate to follow a track that was once quite difficult. Much of the loose rock and tricky shelves have been dug out or bypassed, although the earthen surface is still very slippery if wet.

It is a low range slog through snow gums, with broken views at periodic intervals. You will reach the summit of **Mount Gibbo** some 8 kilometres later, where a cairn indicates its 1750 metre peak. Superb views extend from here into NSW, with **Mount Townsend** and the **Rams Head Ranges** seen in the background.

Leave the summit via a sudden drop off with rocky steps to neighbouring **Mount Anderson**. You will reach a tee intersection on the lofty peak with the left turn heading further into the sky at **Mount Pinnibar**. We will turn right however on an easier track through roof high shrubs and beneath burnt trees. Dusty daisy bushes and native flax lilies colour the descent through the scenic reserve. Alpine grevillea and fishbone ferns are found in the sheltered zones as you return to state forest 2.2 kilometres later.

Drive through a seasonally closed gate and turn left onto **Mount Anderson Road** at a junction. Follow this winding road past logging coupes and beyond **Mount Anderson Saddle Track** on the right 2.6 kilometres later. You will pass **Fiasco Trail** and other logging tracks, reaching a tee intersection on **Mount Hope Road**. Turn left here, then keep straight to pass **Porters Road** on the right 2.6 kilometres later, remaining on **Mount Hope Road** (there is a parallel track in this section – we will follow the eastern link, signposted **'Mount Hope Road'**, but referred to as **Tom Groggin Track** on some maps).

The earthen surface is smothered in leaf litter and has waterlogged sections, but does see regular traffic. Swing left at **Grassy Knob Track** to remain on the priority road, following a rutted descent through substantial eucalypts and magnificent forest. The trail narrows as it nudges massive trees to reach national park, 8 kilometres beyond **Grassy Knob Track**.

A rougher descent offers views of the plains around **Tom Groggin Station**, before you drop into low range for the final stretch past **Mount Pinnibar Track** on the left 5 kilometres later. Cross the bridge over **Boggy Creek** as you follow the boundary of **Tom Groggin Station** and reach the old **Pinnibar** track at a locked gate.

Keep right as you follow the **Alpine Walking Track** over seriously big erosion control mounds and drainage scrapes. The undulations allow for great views over the **Murray Valley** as you reach **Davies Plain Track** on the right, 3 kilometres from the bridge. We will turn right here to exit, but for now continue straight to **Dogman Hut** 500 metres further on for camping possibilities on the **Murray River**. Basic facilities are provided, with a clearing for tents and walking access to the river.

Return to **Davies Plain Track** to turn south over a creek crossing 1.6 kilometres later (pleasant stop here) and past a left turn 500 metres later. (Left turn follows rough descent to the **Murray River** and potential waterway crossing between December and May. Water levels can be deep and fast flowing – this is not a place to take risks. But a camping area adjacent to the sealed **Alpine Way** in NSW can be reached by taking a clockwise arc across the river in suitable conditions.)

Continue south to reach national park and head through a seasonally closed gate to a creek crossing. Pass a track on the left (river access) and occasional river views on a descent to a lumpy and deeper crossing at **Buckwong Creek**. Grassy sites and fireplace define the camping here near a water gauging station, with **Davies Plain Track** closed at a gate here from May 1st to December 1st anually.

A couple of creek crossings mark the drive out into the **Indi Wilderness** with eroded obstacles and sharp climbs to deal with. A more sustained climb follows a rutted and possibly slippery path past native pines and bluebells. You will need to pick your line carefully on some of the rougher sections as the consistently steep terrain holds you in the lowest gears.

As you approach the **Davies High Plain** you reach an enchanting forest of alpine ash and a thick cluster of understorey, dotted with wildflower colour. A trickling rivulet and old fenceline flag a grassy treeless area fringed with character snowgums and granite boulders. This is the start of the **Davies High Plains** and is a great place to

RIGHT: *A water crossing at Buckwong Creek flags the beginning of a climb on Davies Plain Track.*

pull up to absorb the remote atmosphere.

You will ford **Davies Plain Creek** 14 kilometres from the seasonally closed gate with a couple of possible smaller camps on either side of the crossing. Sheltered country and lichen cloaked forest frames **Davies Plains Hut** and a more open camping area adjacent to **Charlies Creek**. This is an iconic high country location, and well worth staying the night, even though this hut is a newer building – the original 1892 structure was burnt to the ground in the inferno of 1939.

Continue past a set of yards on **Davies Plain Ridge** for broken views from its 1741 metre peak. The undulating ridge drive passes small natural plains ringed by multi trunked snowgums – some reduced to almost bonsai dimensions from the bleak winters and incessant freezing winds.

Great views can be made from a saddle 8.3 kilometres beyond the hut, with outlooks both east and west. Shortly after you will pass **Kings Plain Track** on the left (access to **Murray River** in dry weather) and cross **Crow Stick Creek**. A seasonally closed gate is reached 4.9 kilometres later, where you reach **Charlies Creek** for a very nice camp with toilets and fireplace. This is a popular camp for horse riders, with a large open area, fenced off to protect the more fragile vegetation.

Three kilometres later you will reach a four way intersection with **Buckwong Track** on the right and **Misery Trail** directly ahead. We will turn left onto **McCarthys Track** at the junction, to follow a descent punctuated with erosion mounds and great views. An abrupt drop off 4.2 kilometres later will peg you back to the lower gears as you pass **Mac Creek Road** on the right, to reach **Limestone Creek Track** 9.4 kilometres from the four way junction.

We will turn right here, but we are just over a kilometre away from the **Murray River** at **The Poplars** and it is worth a look via the access track directly ahead. The descent passes a helipad on **Round Mountain** (great views of the **Cobberas Mountains**), before reaching a camping strip along the river frontage. Basic facilities are provided here, with ready river access and fishing possibilities.

Return to **Limestone Creek Track** and head south west on a surface peppered with rock, to cross **Cottonwood Creek** and take in open views of the **Cobberas Mountains**. If weather conditions are favourable the boulder capped summit of **Mount Cobberas No.2** will dominate the skyline. At 1838 metres, it is the highest point in the eastern section of Victoria's **Great Dividing Range**. The subsequent crossing of **Mac Creek** flags a lengthy scramble to an unmarked junction, where you keep left to descend to **Limestone Creek** for some excellent views.

You will cross **Smoko Creek** with its inky waters reflecting the tea tree understorey at a lovely rest stop, before a gravelly scramble takes you on to **Limestone Creek**. Take your time fording this waterway to enjoy the vision of trees leaning over the water's edge and some sculpted rocky shelves. Olive green snowgums shelter tussock grasses that define the contours of this silky waterway.

The route along **Limestone Creek** was blazed in the 1830s by cattlemen droving stock from the Monaro Tablelands in NSW to the lush Gippsland pastures. Cattle still roam the area in small allotments of private land. Limestone caves and sinkholes pocket the creek banks along here, in a bizarre chain of grottoes and hidden overhangs thought to have been created up to 400 million years ago.

A crossing of **Stony Creek** lives up to its name, as you head further up **Limestone Creek** to even more colourful snowgums and lichen cloaked forest. You will pass another seasonally closed gate into a camping area with basic facilities and potential sites spread over 300 metres. A block of private land is situated on the right 1 kilometre later, as you make the final climb to **Limestone Road** at a tee intersection.

Turn right here onto substantial winding gravel to again cross **Limestone Creek** at the site of a collapsed hut. A few sheets of iron are all that is left to mark its passing, but the grassy site is a rather pleasant stop. Continue west past **Misery Trail** on the right and **Nuniong Road** on the left (access to **Nuniong Plains** and **Moscow Villa Hut**). You will pass **Mount Leinster** and the other end of **Misery Trail**, before reaching the **Beloka Road** back at **Beloka Gap**. Retrace your steps from here to **Omeo**.

ABOVE: *Snowgum and grassland, Davies Plain.*

Davies Plain Hut.

TRACK 15 BILLY GOAT BLUFF

HIGH COUNTRY

Much of Billy Goat Bluff Track is within national park.

*The frightening reputation of **Bllly Goat Bluff Track** may be well deserved, but it is not the most difficult climb or descent to be tackled in **Victoria's High Country**. Other tracks such as **Sarah Spur Track** and **Herne Spur Track** should be approached with even greater caution, and indeed avoided at the first hint of moisture. That said, the climb up **Billy Goat Bluff Track** is tricky and probably impassable to vehicles without traction control or locking rear differentials. Its descent is equally demanding, but more manageable for most experienced drivers.*

*This trek sets the scene with a low range climb to **The Pinnacles**, before all of your hard won altitude is wiped off on a 10 kilometre roller coaster ride to the **Wonnangatta River.** Camping options are found along the magic waterways en route, with great views available from the higher peaks.*

Begin by heading south from **Dargo** following the sealed road past the old **Exhibition Battery** and caravan park at **Waterford**. Cross the **Wonnangatta River** bridge to follow the bubbling waterway to **Meyers Flat Camping Area** – a popular stop just off the **Dargo Road**.

Continue on to swing more south westerly at **Castleburn Creek Road** on the left. Follow the blacktop for a further 3.1 kilometres to reach one of two entrances to **Trails Track** on the right. They are difficult turns to see from the main road, and the southern one especially requires a hard right turn when travelling from this direction, so look out for other road users as you turn.

View from The Pinnacles

BASIC CHECK LIST . . .

- ☑ **Steep Climbs**
- ☑ **Water Crossings**
- ☑ **Good Clearance Needed**
- ☑ **Avoid Wet Weather**

TRACK SNAPSHOT

TOUR ROUTE
Dargo and return via The Pinnacles and Billy Goat Bluff.

DURATION AND DISTANCE
This 90 kilometre run is a good day trip out of Dargo.

TRACK DETAILS
Consistently steep country and a loose descent down Billy Goat Bluff Track demands a high clearance vehicle with low range gears.

WHEN TO GO
Although open all year round, this trek should only be undertaken in dry weather for both safety and environmental reasons. The view from The Pinnacles is best in clear weather. Avoid days of extreme fire danger.

CAMPING
Camping on the Wonnangatta River at Meyers Flat and Black Snake Creek. Bush camping at Kingswell Bridge.

FUEL AND SUPPLIES
Dargo and Waterford have fuel and basic supplies.

MAPS
Rooftop: Dargo – Wonnangatta

OTHER INFORMATION
Nearby Mount Kent is an interesting side trip from Billy Goat Bluff, and is worth the extra drive if you have a few hours up your sleeve.

You will cross **Castleburn Creek** immediately as you look for low range to deal with a subsequent loose climb and notable switchback. Gravity pushes you back into your seat as you reach the boundary of national park, 4.2 kilometres from the turn. Dense undergrowth tickles the paintwork as you reach a tee intersection on **Scrubby Creek Track**, 5 kilometres into national park, where you turn left.

A sudden descent keeps you in low range for the drop off to **Castleburn Creek** and its lovely forest of creamy trunked trees and bracken. The trickling waters and tree fern glen invites visitors to stop for a while, with a small clearing found just off the track.

Just beyond this oasis you turn right onto **Junction Spur Track**, crossing one branch of the creek where massive orange coloured rocks jut up from the poisoned blackberry. Much debris has collected here, with tree trunks washed into the gully from previous flood events. A sharp eroded exit and another small clearing mark the return to another uphill slog.

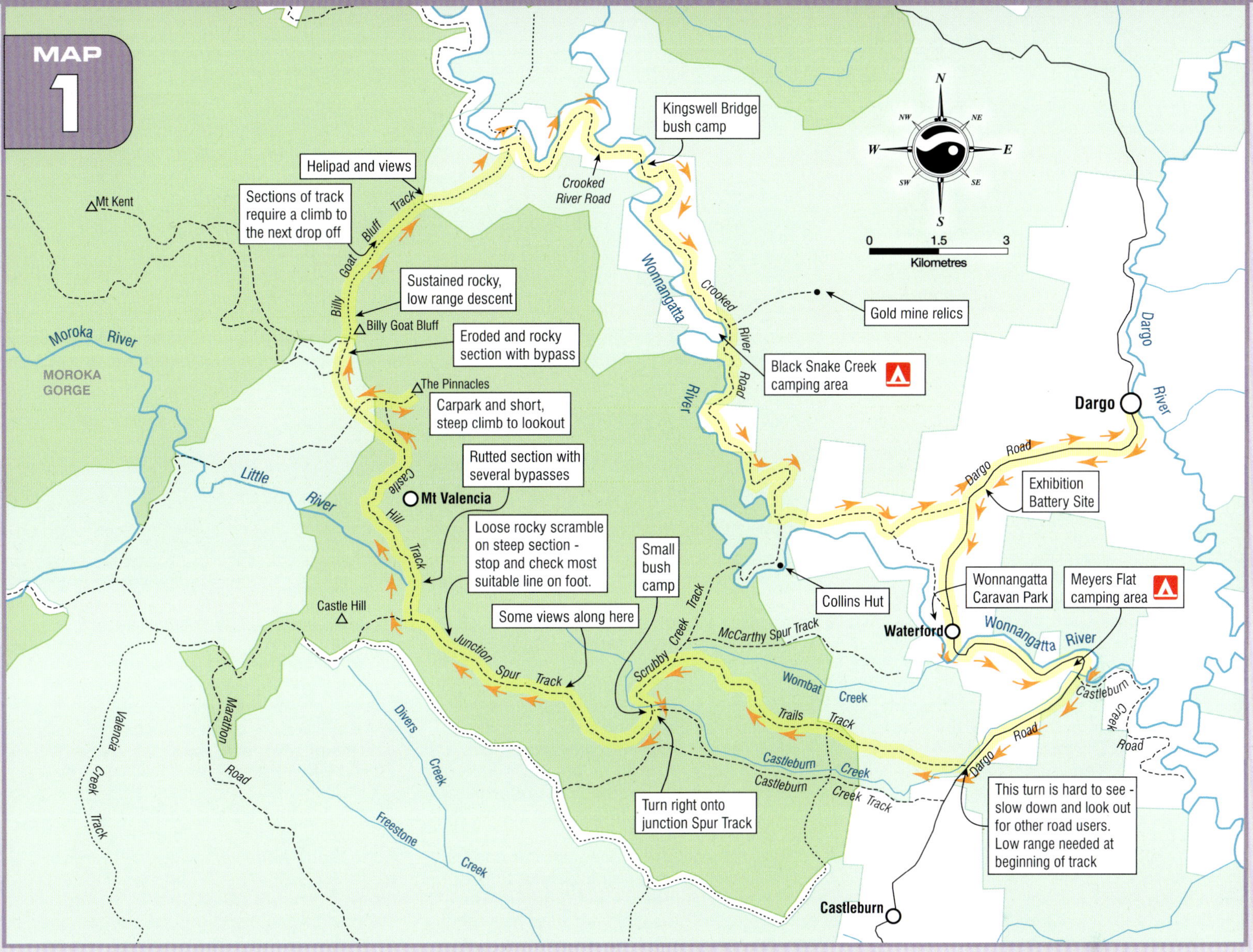
MAP
1
Helipad and views
Sections of track require a climb to the next drop off
Mt Kent
Kingswell Bridge bush camp
Crooked River Road
N
NW
NE
W
E
SW
SE
S
0
1.5
3
Kilometres
Sustained rocky, low range descent
Billy Goat Bluff Track
Billy Goat Bluff
Eroded and rocky section with bypass
Moroka River
MOROKA GORGE
The Pinnacles
Carpark and short, steep climb to lookout
Wonnangatta River
Crooked River Road
Gold mine relics
Black Snake Creek camping area
Dargo
Dargo River
Rutted section with several bypasses
Little River
Castle Hill Track
Mt Valencia
Dargo Road
Exhibition Battery Site
Loose rocky scramble on steep section - stop and check most suitable line on foot.
Small bush camp
Collins Hut
Wonnangatta Caravan Park
Meyers Flat camping area
Castle Hill
Some views along here
Scrubby Creek Track
McCarthy Spur Track
Waterford
Wonnangatta River
Junction Spur Track
Wombat Creek
Trails Track
Castleburn Creek Road
Valencia Creek Track
Marathon Road
Divers Creek
Castleburn Creek
Castleburn Creek Track
Dargo Road
Freestone Creek
Turn right onto junction Spur Track
This turn is hard to see - slow down and look out for other road users. Low range needed at beginning of track
Castleburn

Another clearing, 3 kilometres beyond the creek, offers broken views as some native pines colour the landscape. An especially testing section of track is reached 3.6 kilometres later, with loose rock preceding a scramble to a gnarly stretch of rock sheets and multiple paths.

Stop to assess the obstacle if you are not confident, to plan the most suitable line through it. Previous wheel marks will offer some guidance, while a spotter to direct your progress could help avoid becoming cross axled or even hung up. Use all of your traction aids and drop a little tyre pressure if all else fails. Don't rush the process, and avoid using momentum as your saviour – it rarely helps with a lengthy obstacle, and can contribute to a vehicle bouncing sideways with possible roll-over consequences.

Just beyond this obstacle you will turn right onto **Castle Hill Track** for a more sedate drive through lovely alpine ash, with wildflowers colouring the forest floor. Misty cloud is possible at this higher altitude, with regular rain part of the deal.

A rutted section of track is reached about 3 kilometres from **Junction Spur Track**, which will require choosing the best route around a corner. Take a look ahead before charging in to see where the ruts are likely to take you. Several bypasses offer other options.

Mount Valencia marks a small clearing and snowgum forest near its 1380 metre peak, with a track fork 1.3 kilometres beyond the clearing. Keep left here to enjoy a better road surface, before arriving at a tee intersection on the **Pinnacles Road**, 1.9 kilometres later.

Turn right onto the 2WD road, reaching **Billy Goat Bluff Track** on the left, 100 metres later. We will return here for our exit, but for now continue straight to **The Pinnacles** carpark 1.6 kilometres further on.

It is a steep 15 minute walk to the lookout and fire watcher's tower from the carpark, with unobstructed views from the 1445 metre

SJB-636
Rock shelves are a hazard on this trek.

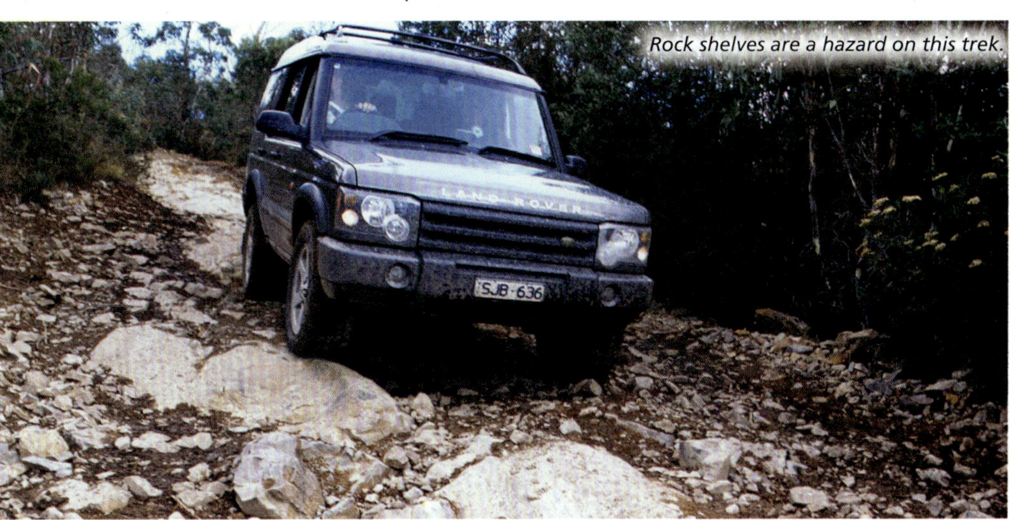

outlook. Fog and low cloud can be partners to this location, but if clear the views seem endless.

Return to **Billy Goat Bluff Track** and turn right to reach the first of two tracks heading west to **Mount Kent**. (The drive to **Mount Kent** is a beauty, following an escarpment track over a network of rivulets to sheltered slopes dripping with mothershield fern. Some slippery sections and possible fallen trees slow progress for a final climb to a helipad at the summit. Walkers can rock hop the last few metres to commanding lookouts taking in the **Wonnangatta River** and the impressive bulk of **Dawson Ridge**.)

However this trek continues straight along **Billy Goat Bluff Track**, as you drop into low range to deal with deep holes and a rocky lurching section complete with bypass track. You pass the second turn off to **Mount Kent** 2.2 kilometres from the **Pinnacles Road** to begin a lengthy sustained descent.

Use your UHF to communicate with others tackling this track, as there are numerous bottlenecks on the route, where an untimely meeting could present difficulties for vehicles to pass. This is especially so at the rocky section around the bluff itself.

Most of the descent is best done in low first using the engine as your primary braking mechanism. You may need to feather the foot brake as well to deal with particularly steep sections, but avoid locking the wheels, as this will affect steering control.

Regular track maintenance is undertaken along **Billy Goat Bluff Track**, but constant use, especially by vehicles scrambling their way up, has cut holes and dislodged rocks, making the track surface rather variable. At its worst, sheets of rock become exposed, ready to catch lower slung vehicles.

Choose your line carefully over these obstacles and build the track up if necessary to fill in any deep holes. Look at the worn path chosen by previous vehicles as a guide to how your vehicle may fare on the descent. Gouges and tyre scuffs can tell an eye opening story.

Look out for oncoming vehicles on Billy Goat Bluff Track.

Once committed to the descent there is really no turning back, so travel slowly looking out for oncoming vehicles, and a possible ramp if your vehicle starts to run away. It is better to stop on any flat sections to reset your speed, rather than undertaking the next drop off with more momentum than is comfortable to peg back.

While the drivers may have their hands full, the passengers can enjoy some of the best views to be had of the **Wonnangatta Valley**. There is a helipad just over half way down that offers limited parking and the chance to stretch your legs. Beyond here, the worst of the descent is over, with vehicles reaching the **Wonnangatta Road** at a clearing.

Turn right here for a welcome drive on relatively flat single lane gravel, with lovely river views at nearly every turn. You will reach a bush camp at **Kingswell Bridge** to cross the **Wonnangatta** and follow the **Crooked River Road** south to **Black Snake Creek**.

Camping with basic facilities is popular here, while walkers can reach the old **Kong Meng Mine** via a track and carpark to the left just after the bridge. Winding gravel continues to follow the river to **Short Cut Road**, reaching the **Dargo Road** at the **Exhibition Battery**. Trace the final 6 kilometres back into **Dargo**.

Great views are part of this drive.

TRACK 16 MOROKA RANGE

HIGH COUNTRY

Looking west from The Sentinels

TRACK SNAPSHOT

TOUR ROUTE
Arbuckle Junction to The Pinnacles via Neilson Crag, Mount Wellington and Moroka Hut.

DURATION AND DISTANCE
The tour as described is a 90 kilometre run, but you will need to factor in the return drive, be it back to Arbuckle Junction or via other options. Allow two days for the complete trek if you visit both Neilson Crag and Mount Wellington.

TRACK DETAILS
Arbuckle Junction to The Pinnacles via Moroka Road is suitable for all vehicles, but low range and high clearance is needed for the side trips.

WHEN TO GO
A seasonal road closure on Mount Wellington Track limits access to the warmer months, but avoid any wet weather regardless. Days of catastrophic fire danger will see areas of national park closed to visitors.

CAMPING
Defined camps at Millers Hut and Horseyard Flat, with some other bush options.

FUEL AND SUPPLIES
Nothing along this route. Licola is the closest centre.

MAPS
Rooftop: Dargo – Wonnangatta.

OTHER INFORMATION
The three bushwalks mentioned here are very demanding for various reasons; Neilson Crag is heavily overgrown, Tali Karng is located in steep country and Moroka Gorge uses sections of rough country.

*Although originally cut in the 1950s as a logging road to access valuable stands of alpine ash, the **Moroka Road** offers much more to the visitors of today. The lofty peaks of **Mount Wellington** and **Neilson Crag** are accessible to bush enthusiasts, while cross country skiers and hikers can reach some superb alpine country. The main **Moroka Road** is well surfaced and suitable for AWDs from **Arbuckle Junction** to as far as **The Pinnacles** fire tower.*

This trek utilises the main road as the primary tour route, but expands on the drive with some tempting low range excursions into the rough country. Like other parts of The Alps, rain and snow are potential partners at any time of the year here, so be prepared for all weather conditions. Bushwalks are often part of visitor activities to this region and some options are quite demanding – do not undertake any hike that is not within your group's capability.

Begin the tour at **Arbuckle Junction**, located some 47 kilometres north of Licola (see seperate tour **'Howqua High Plains'**).Head east from the junction following winding gravel past a surveyors camp on the left. You will reach **Doolans Plain Road** also on the left, 4.1 kilometres beyond **Arbuckle Junction**. Turn left to follow a rough road through tall snowgums. Remain on the main track passing a forestry trail on the left and **Moroka Range Track** on the right (track ends at a locked gate on the boundary of national park).

Leaf litter and boggy patches pave the way further north over **Doolans Plain** to an unsignposted turn on the left 3.7 kilometres from **Moroka Road**. Keep right here (left option leads to flat open area near the head of **Surveyor Creek** that would make a reasonable bush camp within **Carey River SF**).

Scrubby tea tree with lomanda and dianella define a section of overgrown track with views through the bush toward **Mount Kent**. Fallen trees and loose rocks holds you back in the lower gears for a slow drive to a carpark 7.8 kilometres from **Moroka Road**, under the shadow of **Neilson Crag**.

This rocky ridge looks over both **Carey Creek** and the **Moroka River**, while giving hikers a vantage point from which to appreciate the distant but impressive, **Snowy Bluff**. Visitors must make an informal and overgrown 800 metre walk from the carpark to reach the viewpoint, but the effort is well worthwhile. Those individuals brimming with energy can roam the immediate area to gain alternative views of this spectacular bushland, although only well prepared and experienced climbers can continue on to the distinctive peak of **'The Watchtower'**.

Return to the **Moroka Road** and swing east for about a kilometre to a roadside viewpoint overlooking **Snowy Bluff** and **Dawson Ridge**. Although a devastating bushfire claimed 35,000ha of this country in 1998, regrowth is gradually greening the bush again. **McMillans Walking Track** continues at this point, following **Playboy Creek** to the **Wonnangatta River**.

McFarlane Road peels off to the right 4.8 kilometres later, before you enter **Alpine NP** and a parking area at McFarlane Saddle. Bush

BASIC CHECK LIST . . .

- ☑ Trailers with Care
- ☑ Steep Climbs
- ☑ Water Crossings
- ☑ Good Clearance Needed
- ☑ Road Tyres
- ☑ Avoid Wet Weather

Moroka River at Horseyard Flat

MOROKA RANGE

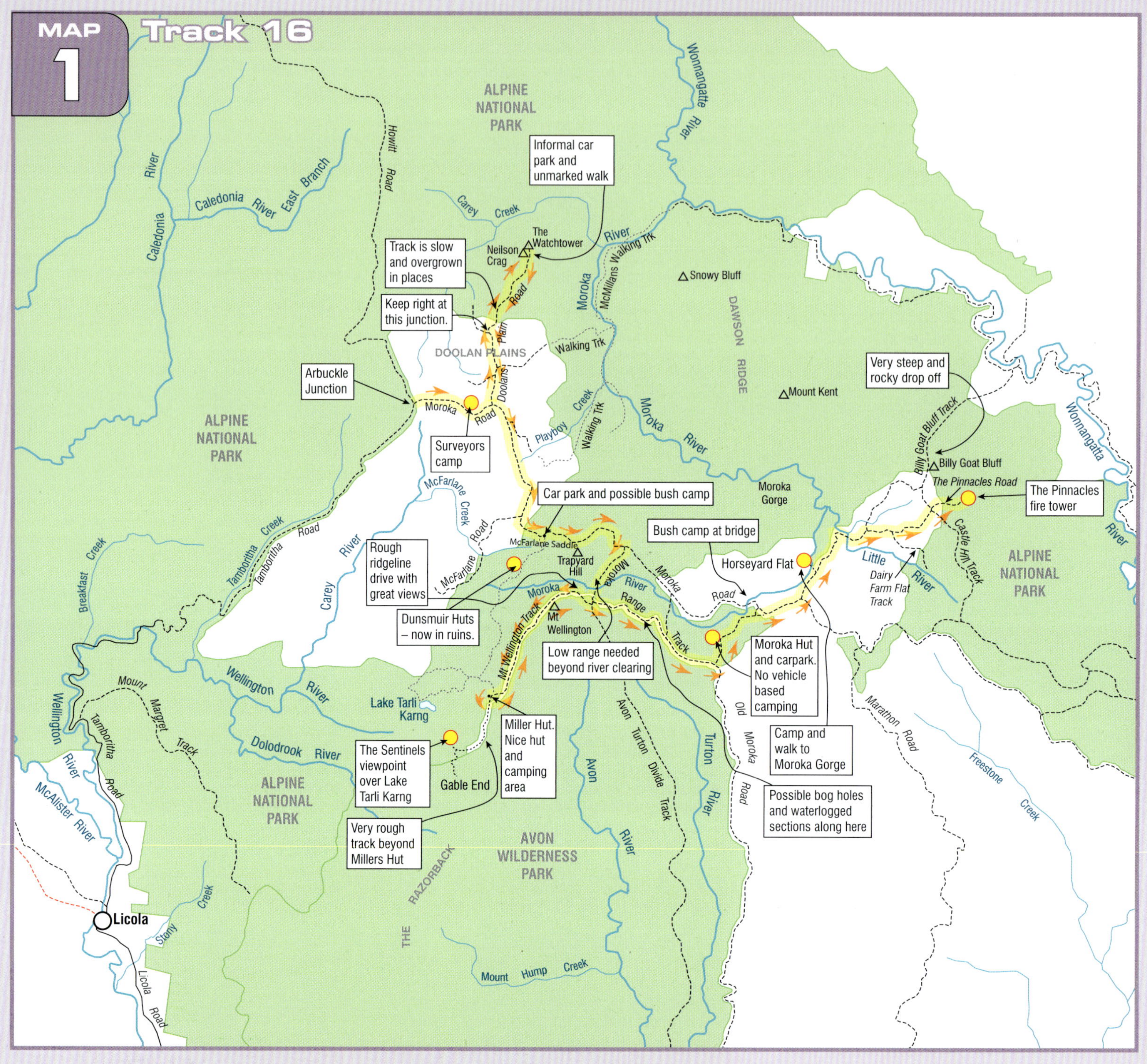

camping is possible here, and a nine hour return walk to **Lake Tarli Karng** originates at this point. In summer the alpine plains are alive with wildflowers making the alternative hike to **Dunsmuir Huts** (now in ruins) a colourful experience.

Continue east past **Trapyard Hill** to **Moroka Range Track** some 5.5 kilometres later, and turn right onto an earthen track. You will slither under alpine ash and slender snowgums to a clearing just prior to the **Moroka River.** Slip into low range beyond this potential bush camp and ford the river to begin a climb to a junction 1 kilometre later.

Turn right at this point onto **Mount Wellington Track** to pass through a seasonally closed gate for a scrambling journey beside the **Avon Wilderness**. Switchbacks and rock keep a lid on your speed as you follow an undulating ridge drive with views to both sides.

A cairn marks the 1634 metre summit of **Mount Wellington** just off the track, where snow daisies and brachycomes colour the grassland. There are great views to be had in all directions (in clear weather), especially toward **The Razorback** and extensive **Wellington Plains**. The crumpled landscape to the east makes up part of the **Moroka Range**, while somewhere in the shadows the **Avon River** is beginning its mighty journey.

Follow a gradual descent through a particularly colourful stand of snowgum; streaked vivid green and orange in the colder months in contrast with the silver trunked alpine wattle. You will reach an unmarked track on the left after about 4 kilometres (possible camp 300 metres in, with broken views, but good shelter).

Keep right to reach **Millers Hut** 800 metres later, with a big camp clearing adjacent. Buttercups flower around the timber framed slab hut, now sheeted in iron, and this location is the closest you

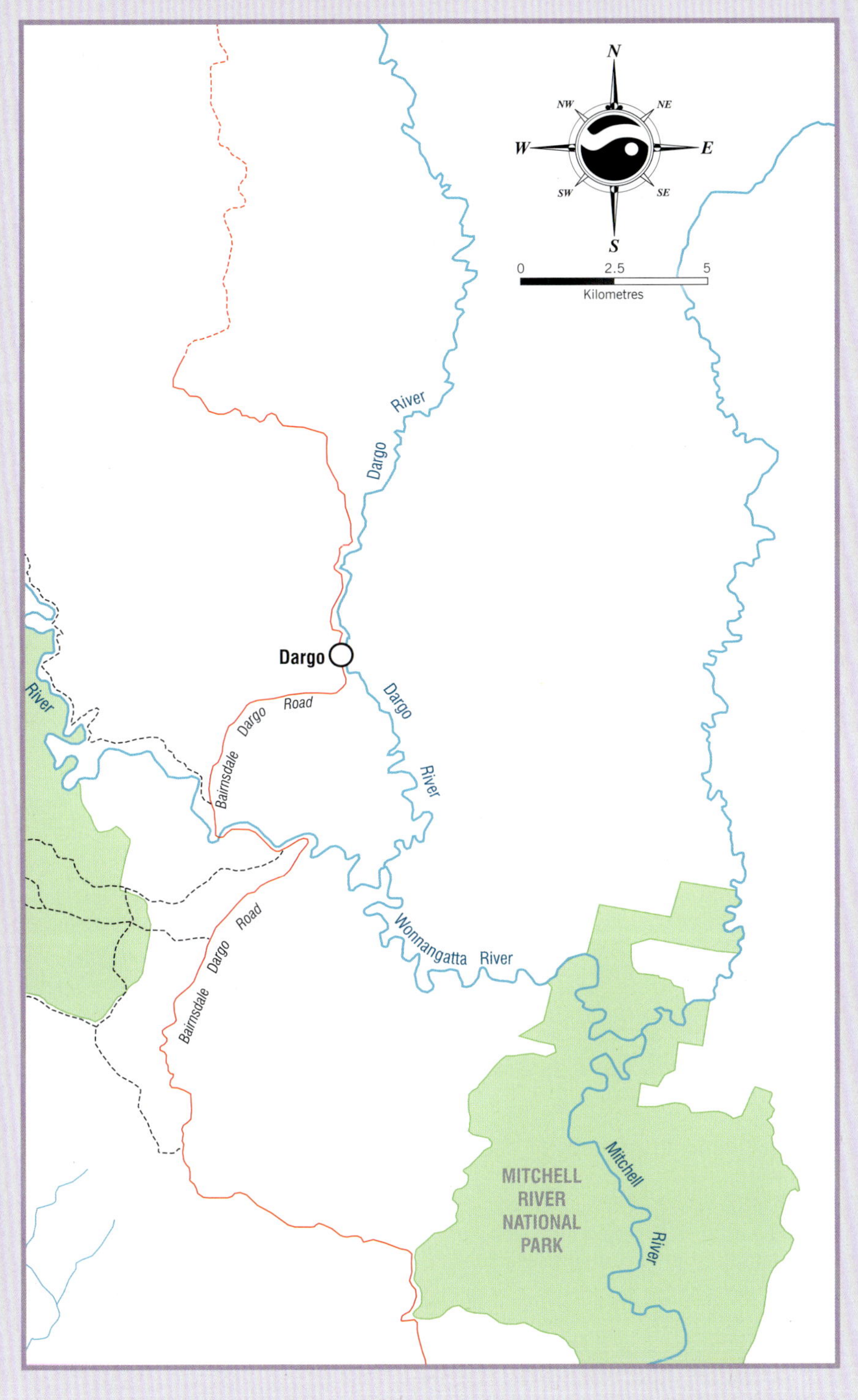

BELOW: *Millers Hut*

can drive to **Lake Tali Karng**. The walking access via **Gillios Track** is relatively short but still very steep and demanding – requiring three hours for the hike in, and perhaps four hours for the return. However **Tali Karng** is a destination that is hard to resist – some enormous trees on the western shore, a hidden waterfall and remote trout fishing are just a few of the highlights.

Lake Tarli Karng covers an area of only 15 ha, but is believed to be up to 50 metres deep. It may have been formed as recently as 500AD, when a massive landslide funnelled rocks and soil into this remote valley, damming the waters of **Nightingale** and **Nigothoruk Creeks**. Subsoil characteristics have prevented the formation of a conventional spillway – instead the waters seep undergound to emerge as the infant **Wellington River**, perhaps one kilometre to the west.

Vehicle access beyond the hut is limited by the boulder strewn track surface that leads to **The Sentinels** and beyond to **Gable End**. It is a very scenic journey however, and a worthy tour extension if you have the time, with pockets of open heathland supporting stands of mountain needlewood and bottlebrush. Other significant species survive harsh extremes of weather on the plateau, where annual precipitation totals more than 1400 mm, and snow drifts can remain until November. Excellent views from **The Sentinels** take in just a section of **Tali Karng**, while those who continue on foot to **Gable End** will enjoy a broad view along **The Razorback** to the southern foothills. The track is little used, slow and overgrown in places. It may be easy to get lost.

Return to **Moroka Range Track** and turn right for a potentially slippery run to the **Old Moroka Road**. Erosion mounds and waterlogged sections can be tricky if it is too wet, so turn back prior to a significant descent if this is the case (you can return to the main **Moroka Road** to continue eastward). Otherwise take the descent past an unsignposted link track on the left, and keep left at the **Old Moroka Road junction**.

Follow the track signposted **'Moroka Hut'** for 1.2 kilometres, then turn left again following the track for 600 metres to a carpark near **Moroka Hut**. There is no vehicle based camping at this site, nor at the hut, which is a 250 metre walk away. The hut is hidden within lovely snowgum woodland, bordered by post and rail fence, and an intricate network of trickling water. Its chock log construction has stood the test of time, having been built by local cattlemen in 1946. Only a few other huts of this type still stand in the alps today.

Return to **Moroka Range Track** and continue east for 3 kilometres, reaching the **Moroka Road** at a forked exit option. Bush camping is a possibility on the left fork near the bridge. Continue eastward for 2.2 kilometres to pass **Marathon Road** on the right (rough, steep and potentially slippery route to **Briagolong**) and the turn off to **Horseyard Flat** 1.8 kilometres later.

Camping is popular here, with basic facilities and grassy, shady sites adjacent to the **Moroka River.** Black sallee woodland frames the site of old horseyards built by John Hubbard, a local horse breeder from the pioneering days. The original yards now no longer stand, but some remains can be found when walking around the area. A demanding 12 kilometre walk originates at the flat, visiting **Moroka Gorge** and several of its falls. The hike involves some rock hopping and negotiating uneven terrain, and will take a day to complete, although it should not be attempted with high river levels.

The gorge was originally revealed to Europeans in the 1860s when explorer **Alfred Howitt** was opening up the goldfields and their access routes. His party including artist **Eugene von Guerard**, traced the gorge's location largely by sound as they headed in the direction of roaring water, such was the inability to see in this dense part of the alps. Some difficulty in retracing his steps meant that few others walked into this remote region of Victoria for almost a century.

Vehicles heading further east cross the **Little River Bridge** to reach a rocky section of track, keeping right at the first of the **Billy Goat Bluff** access tracks. Continue past **Dairy Farm Flat Track** and **Castle Hill Track** to reach the second access track to **Billy Goat Bluff** on the left and **The Pinnacles Road** on the right.

Keep right for a sustained climb to a carpark at The Pinnacles fire tower. From here a steep 350 metre walk brings you to a vantage point taking in much of the **Wonnangatta Valley**.

Mount Wellington Track

Options for the return drive from here include retracing your steps to **Arbuckle Junction**, following **Marathon Road** to **Briagolong**, or jumping into the deep end by following **Billy Goat Bluff Track** into **Dargo**. The latter two options will require some rough country experience, especially the **Billy Goat Bluff** choice which is very steep and demanding (see separate tour: **Billy Goat Bluff**).

Looking over the Carey Valley from Neilson Crag

TRACK 17 JAMIESON TO LICOLA

HIGH COUNTRY

TRACK SNAPSHOT

TOUR ROUTE

Jamieson to Licola via Mount Skene.

DURATION AND DISTANCE

This 100 kilometre run is easily done as a day trip.

TRACK DETAILS

Routine unsealed roads, with the possibility of slippery sections making it suitable for all types of 4WD vehicles.

WHEN TO GO

Closed over winter due to regular snowfalls. This tour is best undertaken between November and June. Avoid days of extreme fire danger.

CAMPING

Good camping at Grannys Flat on the Jamieson River, and bush options at Connors Plain or the Barkly River Bridge.

FUEL AND SUPPLIES

Jamieson and Licola can provide fuel and basic supplies.

MAPS

Rooftop: Jamieson – Licola.

OTHER INFORMATION

A great introductory trip to the Victorian High Country with brilliant views from the peak of Mount Skene and some superb alpine flora.

BASIC CHECK LIST . . .

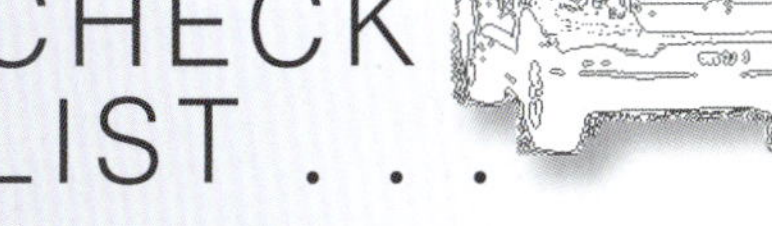

- ☑ **Soft Roaders**
- ☑ **Trailers with Care**
- ☑ **Road Tyres**
- ☑ **Avoid Wet Weather**

The road surface is usually quite good

BELOW: *The Goulburn Inlet near Jamieson*

*The scenic run from **Jamieson** to **Licola** is one of the iconic High Country drives, cresting the **Great Divide** for some outstanding views. In ideal conditions the journey can be made by conventional vehicles, but those in a 4WD will enjoy a greater sense of security. The lofty section across **Mount Skene** is especially vulnerable to the changeable weather, and can become very slippery at any time of the year.*

*Snow views are likely early in the touring season, with distant alpine peaks retaining a dusting of white, sometimes into November and beyond. Campers will find good choices along the **Jamieson River**, on **Connors Plain** and beside the **Barkly River**.*

We start the tour at **Jamieson**, a now quiet holiday escape some 190 kilometres north east of Melbourne. Once a booming gold rush town with 14 hotels and two breweries, **Jamieson's** claim to fame these days is its close proximity to **Lake Eildon**, Victoria's largest man made lake - and venue for the trout chasing brigade who frequent here in considerable numbers. The original red brick church and school hide under a canopy of deciduous trees, while a commercial caravan park enjoys prime river frontage.

Leave **Jamieson** via the **Heyfield Road** crossing the **Jamieson River** at **Brewery Bridge**. Turn left onto gravel toward signposted **'Licola'** noting a warning that the road ahead is unsuitable for semi-trailers, caravans and buses. You pass the historic **Jamieson Cemetery** and begin a rural drive past small vineyards and tourist accommodation.

Private land and weekenders make up much of the valley where deciduous trees provide autumn colour. Follow a winding path into **Jamieson State Forest**, to reach **Grannys Flat Camp** 8 kilometres from **Jamieson**. An access track leads to river side camps with grassy sites and basic facilities. Creamy manna gums and exotic trees line the sheltered valley along a lengthy stretch of water, with **Gallows Track** providing a very steep low range 4WD link back to the **Heyfield Road**.

JAMIESON TO LICOLA

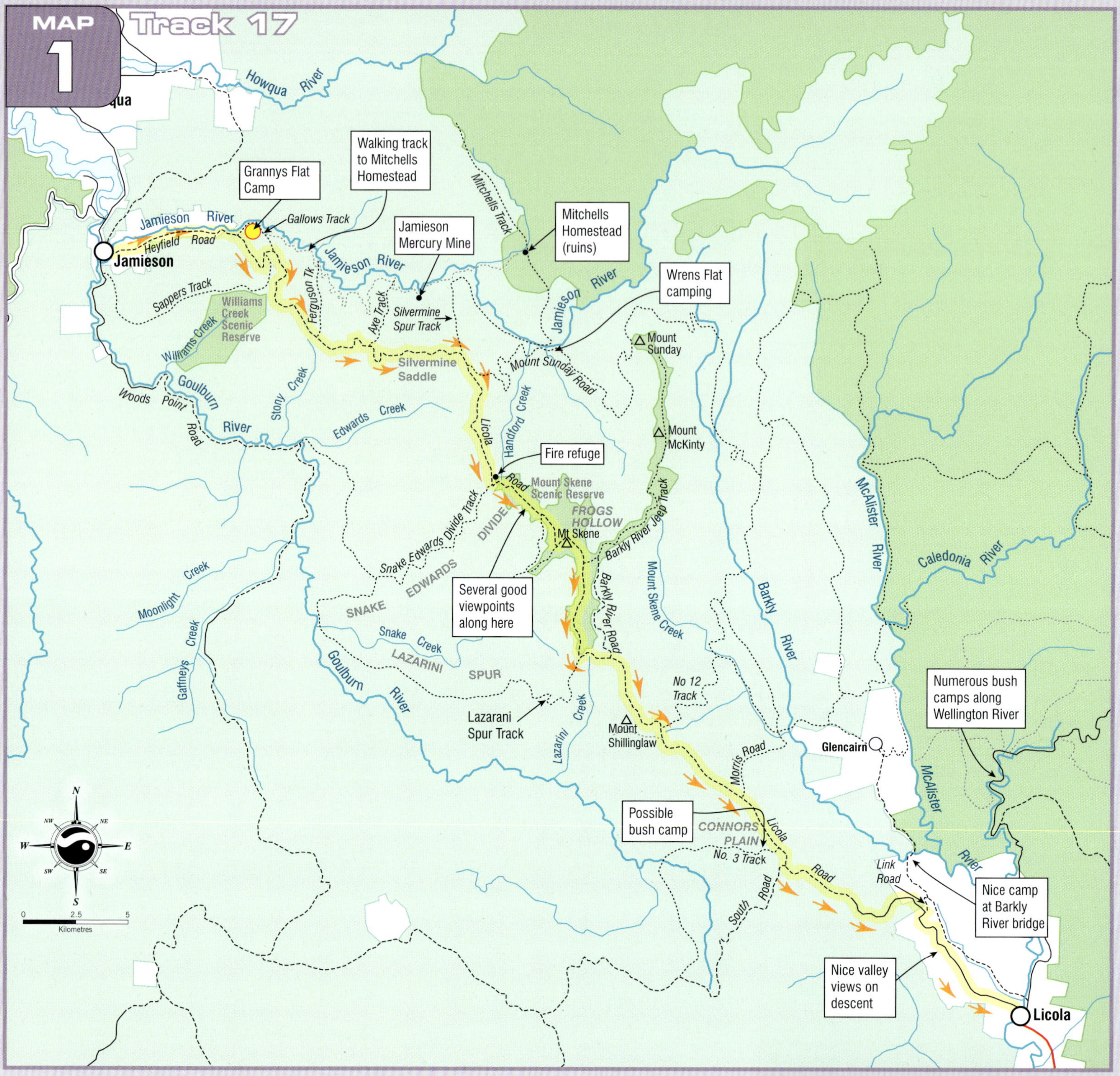

MAP 1 Track 17

Grannys Flat Camp

Walking track to Mitchells Homestead

Jamieson Mercury Mine

Mitchells Homestead (ruins)

Wrens Flat camping

Fire refuge

Several good viewpoints along here

Numerous bush camps along Wellington River

Possible bush camp

Nice camp at Barkly River bridge

Nice valley views on descent

Dedicated hikers can make a 24 kilometre two day hike to **Mitchells Homestead** (now in ruins) from the flat, following the most tortuous section of the **Jamieson River**. An old mercury mine, now largely lost to the bush following its destruction in 1919, marks the historic trail first cut in the early 1900s. Back then local farmer **George Hoskin** used the path to drive cattle single file from **Mitchells** to the **Jamieson** markets.

You begin the climb beyond **Grannys Flat** following a serpentine route through verdant forest with native pine and tree fern gullies to the **Sappers Track (Jamieson Lookout)** turn off. Continue from here past **Gallows Track** on the left on a largely smooth run roughed up with corrugated corners. **Ferguson Track** and **Axe Track** fan off to the left (4WD access to river) before you reach **Silvermine Saddle** and some fire affected country.

The uphill lug continues with good views to the south west through burnt trees, exposing crumpled mountain folds and a succession of ridges. Road markers coloured in orange indicate the transition to snow country and the **Mount Sunday Road** turn

Snowgum forest at Mount Skene

Exotic trees on Connors Plain

off, about 33 kilometres from **Jamieson**.

This junction also marks the seasonal road closure point over winter for the Licola Road, with the next 38 kilometres subject to regular snow falls. If open, continue ahead for some great views over **Snake Edwards Divide** visible on the right. You will pass a fire refuge on the left, 8 kilometres beyond the **Mount Sunday Road**, just prior to **Snake Edwards Divide Track**.

A tree fern gully on **Hanford Creek** flags the boundary of the **Mount Skene Scenic Reserve**, where tall eucalypts crowd out the sky. We follow the boundary of this reserve on a noticeable climb into more exposed country, with windswept snowgums.

Veer left to a scenic look out 2 kilometres into the reserve for broken views through the trees. Lichen streaked table and seats mark the stop at the northern end of the reserve. Follow a ridgeline descent through fire damaged forest with occasional views along the **Dividing Range**.

A switchback and more table and seats mark the next lookout some 4 kilometres later, although the outlook is rather restricted. Continue past alpine meadows where delicate ground covers enjoy a reprieve from the winter snow. The largest meadow marks the road's highest point at 1558 metres, with the summit of **Mount Skene** just a 200 metre walk from here. One kilometre further on by road brings you to another scenic lookout, with views looking over **Frogs Hollow** and **Mount McKinty**.

The **Licola Road** continues past the **Barkly River Jeep Track**, on a gradual descent to **Lazarini Spur Track** 5.5 kilometres later. Keep left at the junction, heading east into more sheltered bush, with a transition to alpine ash and verdant gullies of tree fern. Gravel road topping makes for easier travel as you pass the **Barkly River Road**, signposted '**Middle Range Road**'.

You will continue past a walking track on the right (foot access to **Mount Shillinglaw**) then **No.21 Track** on the left. Seven kilometres later you leave the **Mansfield Shire** and head into the **Wellington Shire**, with **Morris Road** peeling off on the left.

You will reach the fenced off area of **Connors Plain** about 2.8 kilometres later, where **No.3 Track** heads east. Exotic cypress, cedar and spruce trees perhaps a century old grow near here, where redundant pipe and concrete relics hark back to an earlier time. Perhaps once used for stock management purposes, there is now a fireplace and potential bush camp on the large grassy area.

Some 1.6 kilometres later you reach a major junction, with **South Road** peeling to the right, and the **Licola Road** continuing straight ahead. Keep straight on a steady descent to reach sealed road 5.5 kilometres beyond **South Road**. Broken views appear periodically as you reach **Link Road** on the left (access to nice camp at the **Barkly River bridge**). The outlook opens up beyond this junction with clear views extending into the **Macalister Valley**. You will reach **Licola** 9 kilometres beyond **Link Road** to find a general store, fuel and a rather clunky timber bridge spanning the **Macalister River**.

Cloud rolls into the upper Jamieson Valley at Mount Skene.

TRACK 18

Howitt High Plains

HIGH COUNTRY

Guys Hut

BASIC CHECK LIST . . .

- ☑ Soft Roaders
- ☑ Trailers with Care
- ☑ Road Tyres
- ☑ Avoid Wet Weather

TRACK SNAPSHOT

TOUR ROUTE
Licola to the Howitt High Plains via the Wellington River and Bryce Plain.

DURATION AND DISTANCE
Allow a day for the 80 kilometre drive, bearing in mind the return journey.

TRACK DETAILS
Routine driving along gravel and other unsealed surfaces; suitable for all vehicles and trailers.

WHEN TO GO
This route beyond Arbuckle Junction is closed over winter, typically from early June until the end of October, but can be closed at other times as well. Avoid days of extreme fire danger.

CAMPING
Riverside camps along Tamboritha Road and bush camping detailed on map and in text.

FUEL AND SUPPLIES
Licola has fuel and a range of basic supplies.

MAPS
Rooftop: Dargo – Wonnangatta

OTHER INFORMATION
Kellys Lane is an optional bypass around Arbuckle Junction and is a beaut drive in drier conditions. Two classic high country huts feature on the drive, but beware of potentially boggy ground.

*The drive from **Licola** to the **Howitt High Plains** is an inspiring journey from the **High Country** foothills to the lofty meadows of **Mount Howitt.** The winding and sustained climb catches spectacular views on a run established by pioneering graziers. Rustic huts and other hand built infrastructure provides glimpses into this historical route as you pass by a series of alpine plains.*

*Although subject to ice and snow (potentially at any time of the year) the drive is generally suitable for AWDs, although it will be closed just beyond **Arbuckle Junction** over winter. Camping opportunities are numerous along the **Wellington River**, and rather more exposed the higher you climb. Marked bushwalks vary from easy to very demanding, with some great views on **Bryces Plain**.*

Leave **Licola** via the **Tamboritha Road** following the blacktop on the eastern side of the **Macalister River.** Open farmland and grazing cattle back onto the broad water as you negotiate a series of single lane bridges and pass by the first of many bush camps. Look out for fallen rock on the road from numerous cuttings as you reach **Mount Margaret Walking Track**, 4.5 kilometres from **Licola.**

A gradual climb offers lofty views over the **Wellington River**, and the 400 million year old siltstones forming its ancient valley, as you enter national park with information board and table and seats marking the boundary. Continue northward to round a major hairpin bend, with **Mount Margaret Track** branching to the right just beyond the bend. You will cross the river to reach more water side camping areas extending over the next 5 kilometres or so.

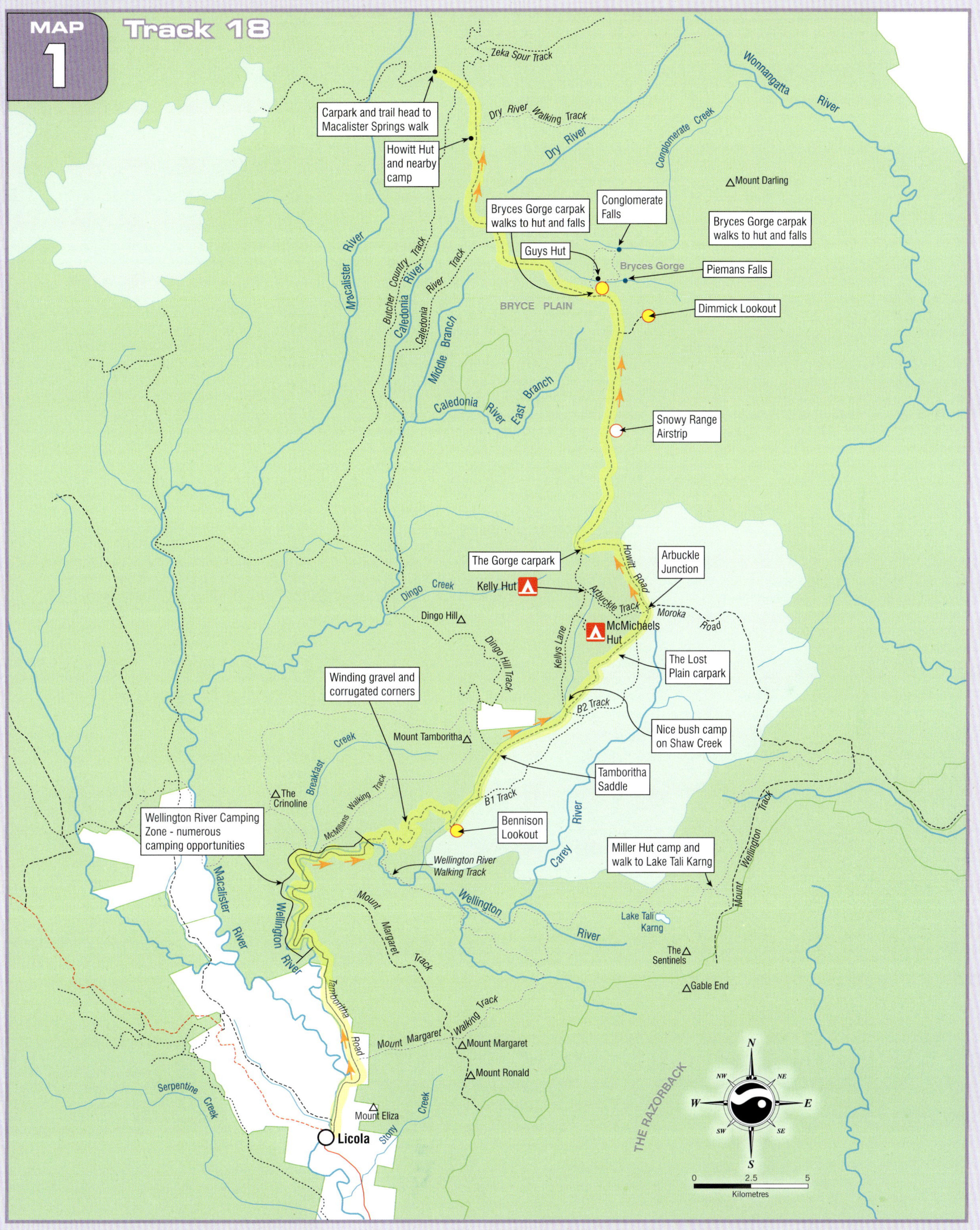

MAP 1
Track 18
Carpark and trail head to Macalister Springs walk
Howitt Hut and nearby camp
Bryces Gorge carpak walks to hut and falls
Conglomerate Falls
Bryces Gorge carpak walks to hut and falls
Guys Hut
Piemans Falls
Dimmick Lookout
Snowy Range Airstrip
The Gorge carpark
Kelly Hut
Arbuckle Junction
McMichaels Hut
The Lost Plain carpark
Winding gravel and corrugated corners
Nice bush camp on Shaw Creek
Tamboritha Saddle
Bennison Lookout
Wellington River Camping Zone - numerous camping opportunities
Miller Hut camp and walk to Lake Tali Karng
Zeka Spur Track
Dry River Walking Track
Dry River
Wonnangatta River
Conglomerate Creek
Mount Darling
Bryces Gorge
BRYCE PLAIN
Macalister River
Butcher Country Track
Caledonia River
Caledonia River Track
Middle Branch
Caledonia River East Branch
Howitt Road
Dingo Creek
Dingo Hill
Dingo Hill Track
Arbuckle Track
Moroka Road
Kellys Lane
B2 Track
Mount Tamboritha
Breakfast Creek
The Crinoline
McMillans Walking Track
B1 Track
Carey River
Wellington River Walking Track
Wellington River
Macalister River
Mount Margaret Track
Lake Tali Karng
The Sentinels
Mount Wellington Track
Gable End
Tamboritha Road
Mount Margaret Walking Track
Mount Margaret
Mount Ronald
Serpentine Creek
Mount Eliza
Stony Creek
Licola
THE RAZORBACK
N
NE
E
SE
S
SW
W
NW
0
2.5
5
Kilometres

HOWITT HIGH PLAINS

Some 5 kilometres beyond **Mount Margaret Track** you will find **The Crinoline Walking Track** and **Breakfast Creek Camp** on the left. **McMillans Walking Track** fans east and west from the camp, offering a lengthy trail to dedicated walkers.

The sealed road continues for about another 4 kilometres to **Campsite 17** and a parking area marking the **Wellington River Walking Track**. This track is a challenging route to **Lake Tali Karng**, suitable only in good weather, and requiring an overnight stop at the lake.

Gravel paves the way now as you climb on a winding run over corrugated corners and occasional outlooks. Signposted **'Bennison Lookout'** is reached 9.2 kilometres into the gravel run with broad views over the **Carey River SF, The Razorback, Gable End** and **The Sentinels**.

Continue north past **B1 Track** on the right to see **Mount Tamboritha** on the northern horizon. **Dingo Hill Track** fans off to the left 2.4 kilometres later, with a stockramp and old fencelines marking the junction at **Tamboritha Saddle**. An informal camp can be made here, but there are other options up the road.

Keep heading north east past several huts and a block of private land, for 3.5 kilometres to **B2 Track** on the right, then **Kellys Lane** access 50 metres further on the left. (There is a lovely camp 400 metres along this side track with basic facilities, a cascading water course, and surrounding snowgums streaked in olive green colours. The access track continues past **McMichaels Hut** and **Kelly Hut** – both photogenic structures near pleasant waterways. Access by 4WD is limited by an extended seasonal road closure from May 1st until November 30th, due to the frequently waterlogged terrain around here.)

So remain on **Tamboritha Road** to reach a carpark at **Lost Plain** (a popular cross country ski venue), then **Arbuckle Junction**, some 47 kilometres from **Licola**. **Moroka Road** branches to the east here (see separate tour **'Moroka Range'**), but we will continue north along **Howitt Road**.

Follow the snowgrass landscape to **The Gorge** carpark 5 kilometres later (northern access to **Kellys Lane**), then continue through a seasonally closed gate (closed in winter and during heavy snow events) to follow **Shaws Creek**. Jagged mountain scenery ushers the journey to **Snowy Range Airstrip** 6.3 kilometres later; Australia's highest airstrip. The turn off to **Dimmick Lookout** is reached 4.1 kilometres later, with a 2 kilometre access track leading east to a picnic spot overlooking **Conglomerate Creek Valley** and **Mount Darling**.

Two kilometres later **Bryce Gorge** carpark is reached on the right. An 8 kilometre walking track visits both **Pieman** and **Conglomerate Falls** on a relatively flat hike via historic **Guys Hut**. The latter structure was built in 1939 using chock log style construction methods, while the falls plunge over a basalt cap to an eroded sandstone bed. Sheer gorge walls are a spectacular feature, but potentially dangerous, so supervise children on the walk.

Beyond **Bryce Gorge** you will travel over **Bryce Plain** with its appealing snowgum woodland and remnant fences, before a more noticeable climb begins. You will trace a lofty path to the **Caledonia River Track** on the left (demanding 4WD track to **Caledonia River**), and reach **Howitt Hut** 5.8 kilometres after that.

Old fenceline surrounds this significant cattleman's hut built around 1900. It has survived recent fires and is a great spot to enjoy a break. Nearby camping is available with basic facilities on a lovely patch of elevated grassland 8 kilometres long and about 1 kilometre wide. **Dry River Walking Track** begins 800 metres further north – a strenuous hike into the **Wonnangatta Valley**.

Kelly Hut

A few kilometres beyond that will bring you to the **Howitt High Plains** proper, where a carpark marks a trail head. A pleasant walk to **Macalister Springs** and **Vallejo Gantner Hut** follows a lengthy but reasonably easy trail to the 1970s refuge hut, while those with a day to spare could continue to **Mount Howitt** for unparalleled mountain views. Walkers should be prepared for any weather conditions on the hike, and let others know of their intentions.

There are four options for vehicle travel beyond this point. The easiest option by far is to return the way you came. Other choices are to exit via **Butcher Country Track** (demanding low range descent to the **Macalister River**) or follow **Zeka Spur** to **Wonnangatta Station** (see separate tour **'Wonnangatta Valley'**). Those who continue along **Howitt Road** will reach **King Billy Track** for a scenic and rugged journey over bowling ball sized rocks to **Mount Lovick** and the **Howqua Hills Historic Area**.

Lake Tali Karng is an overnight walk from the Tamboritha Road

TRACK 19

DARGO TO OMEO

HIGH COUNTRY

BASIC CHECK LIST . . .

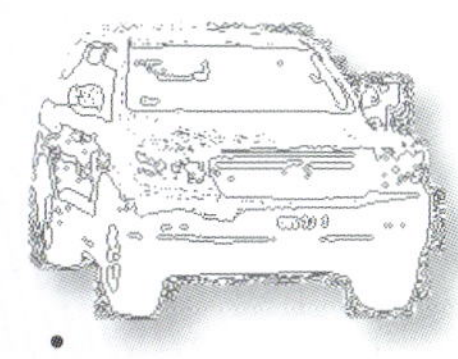

- ☑ Soft Roaders
- ☑ Trailers with Care
- ☑ Road Tyres
- ☑ Avoid Wet Weather

Livingstone Valley view near Omeo

TRACK SNAPSHOT

TOUR ROUTE
Dargo to Omeo via Mount Birregun and Dogs Grave.

DURATION AND DISTANCE
This 90 kilometre drive is easily done as a day trip, but why not camp for a night somewhere along the way?

TRACK DETAILS
Routine bush driving suitable for all vehicles. Side trips are likely to be more rugged, requiring low range and good clearances.

WHEN TO GO
This route is open all year round, but avoid wet weather and days of extreme fire danger.

CAMPING
Lovely camps on the Dargo River with another option at Dogs Grave. Dispersed bush camping possible.

FUEL AND SUPPLIES
Dargo and Omeo can cater for most needs.

MAPS
Rooftop: Bairnsdale – Dargo – Omeo

OTHER INFORMATION
Signs of early gold mining activity are found at both ends of this tour – allow some time to look around and get a feel for those who suffered great hardship in their quest for wealth.

__Dargo__ and __Omeo__ are both strong contenders for the unofficial title of 'Capital of the Victorian High Country'. Each town is steeped in early European history when gold prospectors and graziers first developed the area. Their characters are founded on the main focus of each region – __Dargo__ is built on bush architecture reflective of its rough and tumble mining history, while __Omeo__, also moulded on gold rush foundations, features more open grazing country and several grand colonial buildings.

This tour follows an easy run over the range country separating the two rivals. There is superb bush camping along the way, some iconic views, and even a quirky bush destination in '__Dogs Grave__'.

Leave **Dargo** via the **High Plains Road**, heading north past walnut and chestnut orchards. The sealed road narrows as you follow the river along a potential log truck route (scan channel 40 for any movements). River views open up on the winding climb, where you turn right onto the **Upper Dargo Road** 5.8 kilometres from town at **The Farm** junction.

Bellbirds ring in the valley on the undulating gravel run past numerous campsites on the **Dargo River. Two Mile Flat** marks the first of the riverside camps, which are very popular over summer, but not all have facilities. The string of potential camps end at the **Upper Dargo Road** junction, some 8.2 kilometres from **The Farm** junction.

There is an especially nice rest area here at the bridge under the shade of enormous walnut trees – **Dargo's** signature crop. Keep right at the junction to follow **Jones Road** on a wider sustained climb via substantial cuttings and all weather road surface. The topping deteriorates after the **Gidley Track** junction 7 kilometres later, as broken views open up over the **Wentworth Valley**.

Turn left onto **Birregun Road** 1.8 kilometres later, as **Rudolph Gap Road** breaks away to the east. You will climb further into the alps along a route dotted with yellow paper daisies to **Murdering Spur Track** on the right (seasonally closed gate and access to the **Wentworth River**). Keep straight at the junction to be rewarded with lovely views of the **Dargo Valley** and high plains to the north.

You will reach **Stock Route Track** on the left at a bend (very steep drop off to the **Dargo River** crossing at **Mathesons Flat** and nearby **Harrisons Cut**). Continue the climb from here to **Mount Birregun Spur Track** 5.8 kilometres later. Just under 1 kilometre beyond that you will reach a helipad on **Mount Birregun** with views to **Hotham Heights**.

Continue past **Danes Spur Track** then **Messmate Spur Track** to **Triggy Track** (signposted Twiggy Track) 6.5 kilometres beyond the helipad. Keep right here and travel 1.4 kilometres further to turn right at signposted **'Dogs Grave'**. A short access track leads to an elaborate headstone dedicated to a loyal dog. Toilets and basic facilities mark a pleasant camp here on **Phipps Creek**.

Return to the **Birregan Road** and turn right to reach **Dinner Plain Track** on the left 3 kilometres later (scenic 4WD run over grassy plains to **Dinner Plain Resort**). We will keep right here though to pass rarely used **Carneek Track** and the adjacent helipad (only limited views).

You will skirt the **Spring Creek Reference Area**, breaking to the south east at **Mount Phipps Track** on the left. Continue past **Groves Gap Road** 900 metres later to proceed through alpine ash bushland and past some logging roads. **Old Hut Track** on the right flags **Seymours Hut** and a descent past tree fern gullies.

Zig Zag Track heralds a grid and private grazing land as you reach the **Livingstone Creek** bridge. Turn left after the bridge onto **Upper Livingstone Road**, reaching sealed road 6 kilometres later. Turn left here onto **Cassilis Road**, passing under the shadow of

DARGO TO OMEO

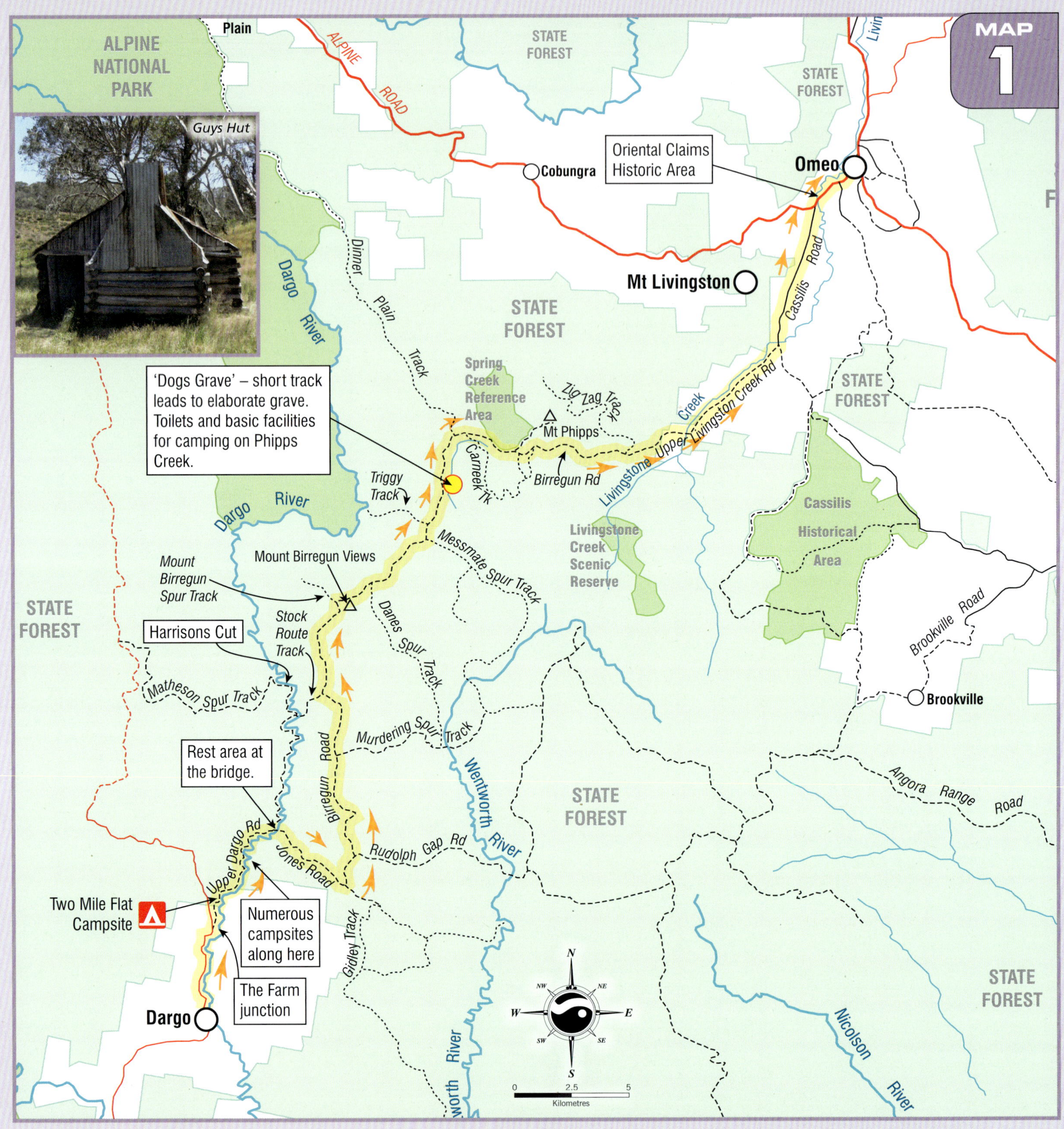

Mount Livingstone. You will reach the **Great Alpine Road** at a tee intersection, turning right to pass the **Oriental Claims Historical Area**, and its strange facade of sculpted river bank that dates from the 1856 gold rush.

For more than 50 years this area was washed of gold in what developed into a massive operation. A complex network of water races, powering high pressure hoses, gouged tonnes of clay and rock from the **Livingstone Creek** cliffs and into the waiting sieves and cradles of the miners. The furrows left – some up to 20 metres high – have eroded further in successive winters, leaving a grotesquely damaged landscape reminiscent of the wild west.

Weekend prospectors still find good colour along **Livingstone Creek**, while specimens of petrified wood are lying amongst the piles of discarded rock. Interested visitors can explore the area on foot along an extensive network of trails, before driving the final few kilometres into **Omeo**.

TRACK 20 Buckland Valley

HIGH COUNTRY

Buckland River crossing near The Junction

TRACK SNAPSHOT

TOUR ROUTE
Porepunkah to Mount Murray via the Buckland Valley.

DURATION AND DISTANCE
This 60 kilometre tour can easily be done in a day (but allow for the return leg, either retracing your steps, or via a different route). Many travellers will enjoy bush camping on the Buckland for a day or three.

TRACK DETAILS
Routine travel to Mount Murray North Track, where some rough country will probably spell the end of the tour for AWDs. Easy enough for full size 4WDs in the dry, and trailers OK.

WHEN TO GO
The Buckland Valley is open all year round, but a seasonal road closure applies to travel up onto Mount Murray. Sections of national park will be closed on days of catastrophic fire danger.

CAMPING
Many options for bush camping along the Buckland River, with a rather more exposed option just below the peak of Mount Murray.

FUEL AND SUPPLIES
Supplies from Porepunkah and Bright.

MAPS
Rooftop: Bright – Mansfield.

OTHER INFORMATION
Supervise children near old gold mining areas – unguarded pits and collapsing drives are sometimes hidden in the bush.

*Once the site of a frenzied gold rush, the **Buckland Valley** now offers relaxed camping in a bush setting on an unchecked and scenic river. Access as far as **Beveridges Station** is easy and suitable for all vehicles and travellers, although those who press on to **Mount Murray** will need high clearance and low range gears.*

*Visitors interested in our European history will appreciate the relics and stories left behind in the gold rush wake, while fishers and less active folk can dabble along the waterway. Those who continue to **Mount Murray** will not leave disappointed – in clear weather, the views appear endless.*

Leave **Porepunkah** on the **Buckland Valley Road** heading south through rural country. Grazing stock, grapes and apple orchards are just some of the commercial activities of the valley, but garlic, olives and various nuts are also harvested. Yellow flowering dogwood trees pop out from a patchwork background of pine plantation and avenue of maples.

You cross **Devils Creek** 6.5 kilometres out of town to pass rustic farm houses and some tourist accommodation. **Devils Elbow Hill** and a notable dairy farm preceed a view of **Howells Falls** on the right, about 9.8 kilometres from **Porepunkah**. There is no access to the falls or indeed to any of the sheer rock faces of adjacent **Mount Buffalo NP** at this point, so continue south to enter **Buckland Valley SF**.

The granite boulders and tors of **Buffalo** disappear from view as you cross the **Buckland River** at a bridge and picnic area, where **Goldie Spur Track** peels off to the right. Keep left to pass old tobacco drying sheds, where gravel replaces the sealed road. Stock ramps continue the rural theme, with walnuts, false wattles and blackberry hugging the river flats.

You reach the old township site of **Buckland** at a private residence, but the historic cemetery adjacent is open to the public. Graves dating from the goldrush, and a memorial to the infamous Chinese Riots make sombre but interesting reading. Although the valley proved somewhat productive in gold won, it did so at a price. Colonial fever swept across the valley, bringing death to large numbers of residents in the first few years of the gold rush.

In latter years the **Buckland Riots** brought the area further notoriety as European miners began harassing the Chinese prospectors. The ratio of three Orientals to every European was a cause for concern, particularly as the Chinese seemed to be more efficient at extracting the precious metal. The rioting extended along the **Buckland**, with widespread violence and property damage. Police were summoned to deal with the unrest, with **Robert O'Hara Burke** leading the outfit; an individual who later achieved greater recognition as one half of the ill-fated **Burke and Wills expedition** into northern Australia.

A series of camping flats mark the next few kilometres of river travel with **Ah Youngs Campground** reached 2 kilometres beyond the cemetery, where basic facilities and shade are found. A deep dredge hole and plenty of disturbed ground is part of the terrain here (and elsewhere along the **Buckland River**), so be sure to supervise children.

BASIC CHECK LIST . . .

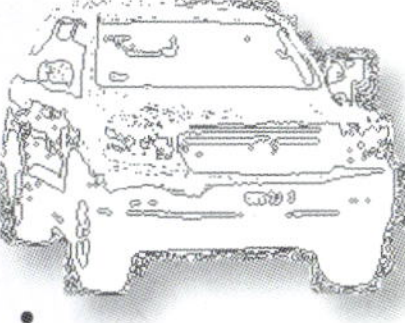

- ☑ Trailers with Care
- ☑ Good Clearance Needed
- ☑ Road Tyres
- ☑ Avoid Wet Weather

Buckland Valley bushland

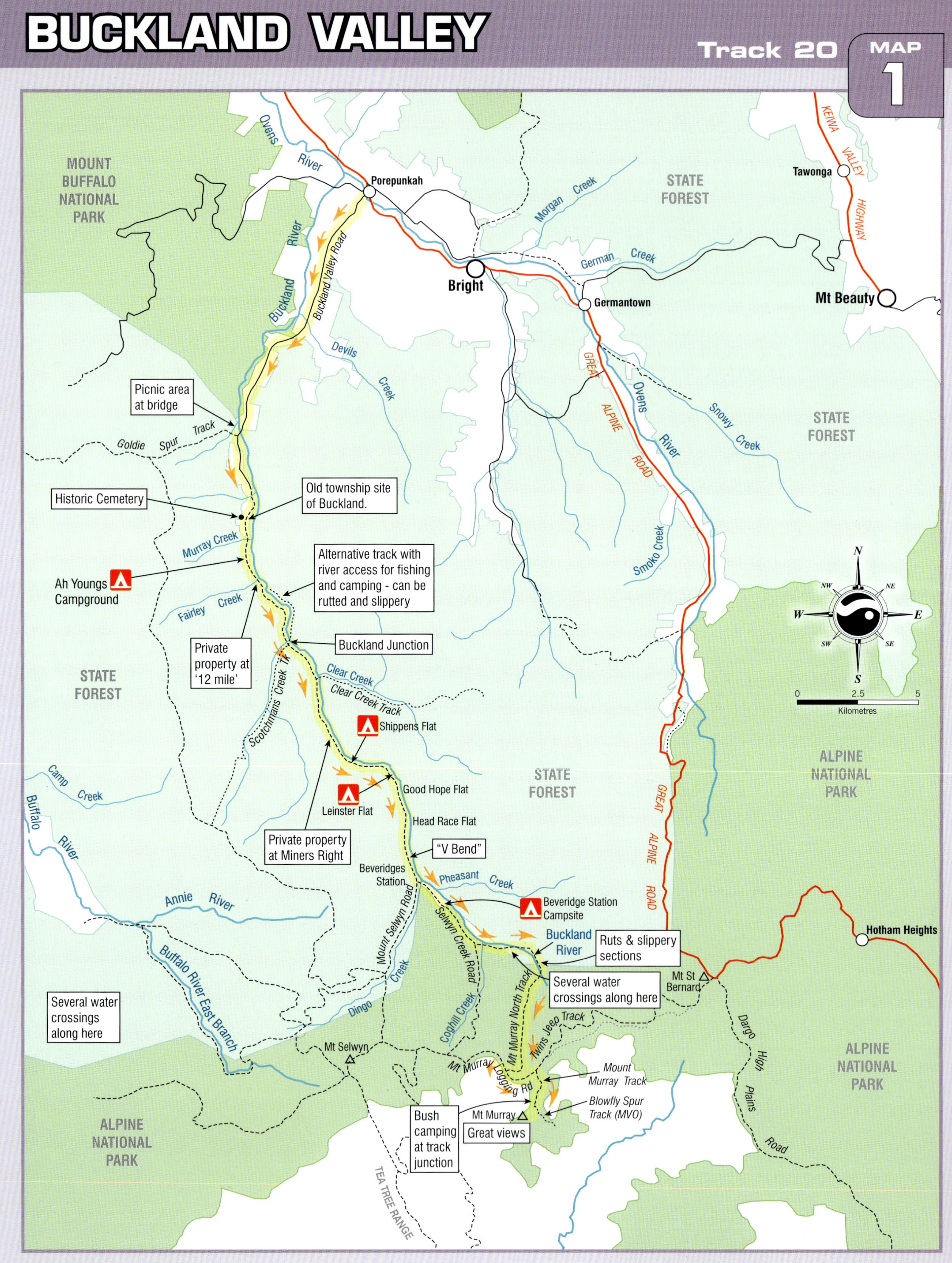

MOUNT BUFFALO NATIONAL PARK
Ovens River
Porepunkah
Bright
Germantown
Tawonga
Mt Beauty
KIEWA VALLEY HIGHWAY
STATE FOREST
Morgan Creek
German Creek
Buckland River
Buckland Valley Road
Devils Creek
GREAT ALPINE ROAD
Ovens River
Snowy Creek
Picnic area at bridge
Goldie Spur Track
Historic Cemetery
Old township site of Buckland.
Murray Creek
Alternative track with river access for fishing and camping - can be rutted and slippery
Ah Youngs Campground
Fairley Creek
Smoko Creek
Private property at '12 mile'
Buckland Junction
STATE FOREST
Clear Creek
Clear Creek Track
Scotchmans Creek Tk
Shippens Flat
Good Hope Flat
Leinster Flat
Head Race Flat
Camp Creek
Buffalo River
Private property at Miners Right
"V Bend"
Beveridges Station
Pheasant Creek
Beveridge Station Campsite
Annie River
Mount Selwyn Road
Selwyn Creek Road
Buckland River
Ruts & slippery sections
Buffalo River East Branch
Mt Murray North Track
Several water crossings along here
Mt St Bernard
Hotham Heights
ALPINE NATIONAL PARK
Several water crossings along here
Dingo Creek
Coghill Creek
Twins Jeep Track
Mt Selwyn
Mt Murray Logging Rd
Mount Murray Track
Blowfly Spur Track (MVO)
Mt Murray
Great views
Bush camping at track junction
Dargo High Plains Road
TEA TREE RANGE
ALPINE NATIONAL PARK
N
S
E
W
NW
NE
SW
SE
0
2.5
5
Kilometres

View from Mount Murray

You will reach a lovely spread at '**12 Mile**' (private property with grassed area and ornamental trees) where **Fairley Creek** enters the **Buckland**. It is just beyond this point that a parallel track follows the river for 3 kilometres on its east bank. Those who ford the river at the crossing pass more camping opportunities with many side tracks fishboning to secluded clearings. Rutted sections and some bogholes feature on this slow drive, where old fence posts, naturalised corn poppies and stone footings lay witness to a previous era.

This area known as **Buckland Junction** was once a mining settlement bustling with frantic activity. Many residents arrived with dreams of striking it rich, but some settled to undertake the mundane yet probably more lucrative pursuit of other commercial ventures. The **Junction Hotel** operated for many years, while a store and post office fulfilled other necessary functions for the township.

The main road and parallel track merge at **Junction Bridge**, where **Scotchmans Creek Track** branches to the right. Keep left here to follow the main river branch to **Clear Creek Track** on the left 2 kilometres later (a small clearing marks the **Buckland** crossing at this junction).

Water crossing on Mount Murray North Track

Avoid smaller tracks fanning off to the river and keep heading south to the old township of **Miners Right**, 3 kilometres later. A character house and disused timber trams mark this quirky patch of private property, where exotic trees shade a lovely garden.

Just over 1 kilometre later you will reach **Shippens Flat** on the left, with **Leinster Flat** found 1 kilometre beyond that. Both sites offer self contained bush camping with fireplaces and plenty of shade. **Leinster Flat** is particularly attractive with bubbling cascades and the remains of a water race. **Good Hope Flat** and **Head Race Flat** maintain the frontier theme as you reach **Mount Selwyn Road** on the right, some 800 metres beyond **'V Bend'** – yet another bush camp on the **Buckland**.

Keep left at this junction to follow **Selwyn Creek Road** into national park at a bridge spanning **Dingo Creek**. You will pass the private holding of **Beveridges Station** (no camping at this site) to find an elevated view over the old homestead and its galvanised iron clad hut on the river flat. Chestnut trees grow near the old homestead, while an enormous walnut tree may date back to the pioneering days, when a 30 head stamper rang out across the valley.

Bush camping is available near **Beveridges** with the turn off found 2.5 kilometres from the **Selwyn Creek Road** junction. Those who turn left here will find dispersed camping opportunities along the river, on a broad site with plenty of grassy clearings and shade if needed.

Follow **Sandy Creek Track** further south to **Mount Murray North Track** just over 1 kilometre later. Keep left here past a clearing to cross **Coghill Creek** and continue through a seasonally closed gate. This is a much narrower track that follows a tortuous path along the **Buckland's** upper reaches. Fern filled pockets and bluebells dot the drive over successive water crossings; some testing for lower slung vehicles.

An especially nice piece of forest is found 3 kilometres into the drive where the river winds around some impressive tall timber, and brachycomes flower on embankments that see plenty of sunlight. Ruts and slippery sections mark pockets of disturbed ground, turned over in the mining rampage of 150 years ago.

Erosion control mounds flag the increasing altitude, and swathes of burnt trees, as you follow the **Buckland's** west branch to a seasonally closed gate and tee intersection on the **Mount Murray Logging Road** (signposted **Twins Jeep Track**).

Turn left at the junction to follow a section of Alpine Walking Track over a saddle to another seasonally closed gate, 1 kilometre later. Great views extending to **Mount Buffalo** mark the drive as you trace snowgum forest along the **Dividing Range**'s spine.

Turn right 1.3 kilometres beyond the gate onto **Mount Murray Track**, with the dominant rounded peak defining the view ahead. **Blowfly Spur Track** (MVO) peels off to the left 2.1 kilometres later as you reach an open grassy area, with bush camping within the relatively sheltered saddle.

A locked gate allows final access to the 1650 metre peak of **Mount Murray** to walkers only. The 300 metre walk is steep but worthwhile, rewarding visitors with a 360 degree view over the windswept snowgums. Many of the **High Country**'s most impressive peaks can be seen from here on a clear day.

Retrace your steps from here to **Porepunkah**, or as an alternative, follow the **Twins Jeep Track** on a lofty ridge run east to **Mount St Bernard** and the **Great Alpine Road**. Other options include heading west to **Mount Selwyn** and following **Tea Tree Range** over **Mount Sarah** to **Talbotville**. Both of these options require a full size 4WD and bush driving experience.

TRACK 21

GRANT GOLDFIELDS

HIGH COUNTRY

A sustained grade keeps you in low range on the Bulltown Spur

BASIC CHECK LIST . . .

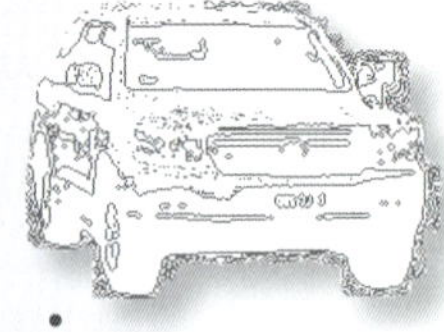

- ☑ Steep Climbs
- ☑ Water Crossings
- ☑ Good Clearance Needed
- ☑ Avoid Wet Weather

TRACK SNAPSHOT

TOUR ROUTE
Dargo and return via the Wonnangatta River, Crooked River Track and Grant Historic Area.

DURATION AND DISTANCE
The 100 kilometre trek is an ideal day trip from Dargo.

TRACK DETAILS
Routine bush driving in the main, with a rugged loop along the Crooked River Track and Bulltown Spur. These tracks require high clearance and low range, but can be avoided by taking McMillan Road out of Talbotville.

WHEN TO GO
This tour can be undertaken all year round, but should not be attempted in wet weather or if river levels are well up. Avoid the area on days of extreme fire danger.

CAMPING
Designated camping at Black Snake Creek, Talbotville and Grant. Bush camping at Kingswell Bridge.

FUEL AND SUPPLIES
Dargo has fuel and supplies.

MAPS
Rooftop: Dargo – Wonnangatta

OTHER INFORMATION
A trailer could be towed along most of this route if you avoid the Crooked River Track and Bulltown Spur Track, by remaining on McMillans Road.

*These days it is hard to imagine the frenzied activity that once shook the goldfields of **Grant**. Many hundreds of miners dug, crushed and sieved their way through largely inhospitable country, with patchy reward for most. Much of the action ceased before the 1890s and the region was all but deserted by the turn of the century.*

*This trek follows in the footsteps of those hopeful individuals with an easy run along the **Wonnangatta River**, then a slower lug through the goldfields. Numerous rough river crossings punctuating the **Crooked River**, and the low range lug up the **Bulltown Spur** limit travel to full size 4WDs. There is excellent bush camping on the **Wongungarra River** and at the old township sites of **Talbotville** and **Grant**.*

Head south from **Dargo** following the blacktop past the **Lower Dargo Road**. Veer right onto gravel at **Short Cut Road** some 6 kilometres from town, to begin a descent to the **Wonnangatta River**. Sweeping views open up through the bush before you turn right onto the **Crooked River Road**.

Follow undulating gravel to **Scrubby Creek Track** 4 kilometres later, where you keep right at a bend (left turn drops down to **Collins Hut**; one of the more elaborate high country huts, with fibro walls and even glass windows). Orchards and exotic trees colour the valley with pockets of private land and cottages enjoying the peaceful outlook.

A camping area at **Black Snake Creek** flags a minor track on the right, some 8.8 kilometres beyond **Scrubby Creek Track**. Travellers can follow this rough track to a carpark, for a challenging walk to the old **Kong Meng Mine** and its remnant components. Campers will find grassy river front sites with basic facilities, at an open area just prior to the **Black Snake Creek** bridge.

Deciduous trees line the Wonnangatta River

GRANT GOLDFIELDS

MAP 1

Numerous river crossings on this track
Very steep low range climb
Site of Hogtown
Site of Stonewall
Site of Talbotville and camp
Numerous mining relics around here
Camping area at the site of Grant – the cemetery is worth a visit.
Helipad
Old dredge buckets
GREAT HISTORIC AREA
Grant Junction
Several camps along here
Potentially deep river crossing
Sustained descent - use low gears and avoid over heating your breaks
Turn right just before Kingswell Bridge
Winding drive through private land with great valley views
Kong Meng Mine
Black Creek Snake Campsite
Dargo
Wonnangatta Caravan Park
Collins Hut

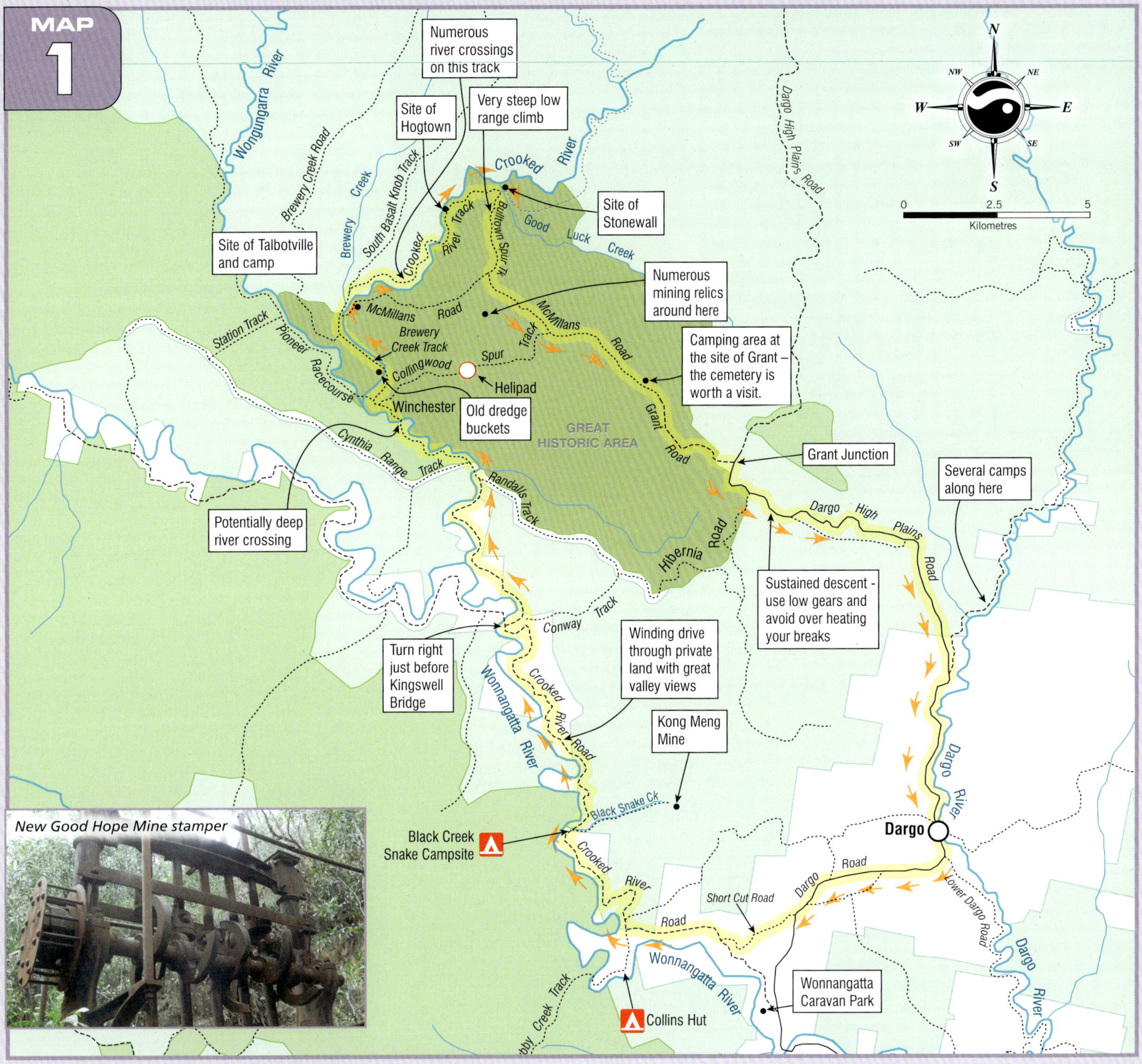

New Good Hope Mine stamper

Beyond the bridge you will pass a pedestrian suspension bridge and a cluster of adjacent sheds and cottages. The scenic valley drive continues to **Kingswell Bridge** for more bush camping options. We turn right just prior to the bridge, following the **Crooked River Track** toward **Talbotville**.

This narrower track is topped with less stone now, as numerous cottages mark the transition to 4WD territory. You will pass **Conway Track** on the right (very steep access into the **Grant Historic Mining Area**), about 1 kilometre from the bridge. Sheep grazing and fencelines define more sections of private land, before the track breaks away from the **Wonnangatta** to follow the pretty **Wongungarra River**.

A couple of lumpy water crossings flag the boundary of the **Grant Historic Area** as you reach **Cynthia Range Track** on the left and **Randalls Track** on the right (both are sustained low range climbs from here). Continue straight on the **Crooked River Track** to pass an open area of cattle grazing and cross the river 3.3 kilometres later near the old town of **Winchester**. You will follow an arc along a row of rocks indicating a deeper part of the river.

Old gold dredge, Wongungarra River

Drive for another kilometre to pass **Collingwood Spur Track** on the right (steep lug to helipad for views), then **Pioneer Racecourse** on the left. Keep right at this junction to leave the river and follow **Brewery Creek Track** to an old gold dredge abandoned on the creek bank.

A pleasant cleared area ushers your journey through to **Brewery Creek Road**, 3.2 kilometres from **Collingwood Spur Track**. Turn right here to cross the creek and arrive at an open area at the site of **Talbotville**.

Talbotville was once a small commercial hub for local mining activity, with dwellings and support services maintaining the goldfield. In latter years, as the gold became depleted, the population drifted away, leaving just market gardens to carry **Talbotville**'s flag. However the remote location and freezing winters soon saw the end of even these endeavours, reducing the community to all but a memory.

Camping is popular here with easy access via **McMillans Road** and basic facilities. There is some shade and plenty of grassy sites along the creek frontage. Mine ruins dot the area, so keep a close watch on children here – many shafts are left open and unguarded.

Leave **Talbotville** via the **Crooked River Track**, keeping left away from **McMillans Road**. The water crossings begin soon enough, with two fordings in quick succession, before passing **Basalt Knob South Track** on the left. Large bog holes mark the next creek crossing 100 metres later, and become a routine obstacle with many more punctuating the slow drive to **Stonewall**.

A number of mine shafts are seen trackside (most with fences) as you negotiate the string of obstacles dealt out by the **Crooked River Track**. Tree fern and wattle colour the understorey, as you reach the old alluvial mining centre of **Hogtown**, some 6 kilometres beyond **Talbotville**. A few clearings are passed en route, with some making a nice rest stop. Visitors will find widespread disturbed ground around here, with some building footings and the occasional relic from the short lived boom days.

An especially gnarly creek crossing marks the site of **Stonewall,** as the track swings south to become the **Bulltown Spur Track**. The sustained low range run up will have you in low first or second for the relentless climb over erosion mounds and around hairpin bends. Some scrambling sections of loose rock can be tricky, but always drive keeping an eye out for oncoming traffic – as those on the ascent usually need to make way for those heading down.

You will reach **McMillans Road** after 3.3 kilometres of looking to the sky, where you turn left for easy travel past **Collingwood Spur Track**. The corrugated gravel passes several side tracks before arriving at a camping area at **Grant**. Today, little remains of this once bustling township which boasted of hotels, banks, and a variety of stores, but the cemetery is worth a visit. Engraved headstones recount some of the hardships of the goldfields, while eerie unnamed graves dot the surrounding bushland. The **Jolly Sailor Mine** lies nearby and can be reached via a walking track.

Follow **Grant Road** now for five kilometres to **Grant Junction** on the **Dargo High Plains Road**. Ruins from the old **Bandicoot Arms Hotel** mark the tee intersection, where you swing right onto sealed road. The **Freda Family Tree Reserve** protects a section of alpine ash and tree fern bush here, although much has been lost to recent bushfires.

Pass **Hibernia Road** on the right to continue a steep and sustained descent around a series of switchbacks. Avoid the temptation to ride your brakes on the descent, as it is a punishing ordeal for any vehicle – especially one with an automatic transmission. Hold a lower gear and let your engine do most of the work.

Follow the descent for views of the **Dargo Valley** and the **Upper Dargo Road** on your left, about 11.3 kilometres from **Grant Junction** (there are numerous camping possibilities at a series of river flats along here). Continue along the walnut tree lined run into **Dargo**, just 6 kilometres away.

Mining relics at the Good Hope Mine

Grant cemetery

TRACK 22

SHEEPYARD FLAT

HIGH COUNTRY

Crossing the Jamieson River at Upper Jamieson Hut.

The ***Howqua Hills Historic Area*** *once rang out with the sound of frenzied activity as mining companies turned over gold bearing ore along a lengthy stretch of the* ***Howqua River****. The action petered out in the late 1800s, and the valley was returned to graziers, who soon established local stock runs.*

These days horse riders and general bush enthusiasts frequent the area in considerable numbers, with the excellent camping flats and easy river access being hard to resist. This trek begins in nearby ***Merrijig*** *and follows the* ***Howqua Hills Track*** *westward, before tracing a low range circuit to the* ***Jamieson River****. The subsequent drive takes in more scenic camping opportunities, then returns to the* ***Howqua*** *via the* ***Upper Jamieson Hut.***

Begin by leaving **Merrijig**, taking the **Howqua Track** south on winding gravel road past **Mount Timbertop** and its walking track. Keep left on the narrow corrugated trail to pass a couple of side tracks and reach **Sheepyard Flat** over the **Howqua River Bridge**. Turn right here to follow **Howqua Hills Track** along the bubbling waterway past a sizable camping area with basic facilities.

You will reach the turn off to **Frys Hut** soon after (1930s cattleman's timber dwelling adjacent to a large camp, again with basic facilities). Keep left here to climb past a walking trail head that peels off to **Castle Hill** and the **Upper Jamieson Hut** (both demanding walks, especially the lengthy latter option). Continue through a seasonally closed gate past a couple of side tracks to drop down to **Tobacco Flat** for more camping possibilities. Cross **Lickhole Creek** to drive by some private property with great elevated river views.

You will pass the **Howqua Feeder Walk** some 4.9 kilometres beyond **Frys Hut** for a steep climb over sizable erosion control mounds and broken views into crumpled range country. Alpine ash give way to snow gums at the higher points of the track, as you step from one saddle to the next. Native pines flag a seasonally closed gate and a potentially slippery clay track surface to a tee intersection on **Steiners Road** 200 metres later.

Turn left here for more skyline views as sheets of slate pave the drive. Swing hard right onto **Mitchells Track** 4.1 kilometres beyond **Steiners** to reach an old slate mine 300 metres later on the crest of a hill. Uninterrupted views through the tailings pile extend over the **Jamieson** and **Howqua Valleys** from here, although trees are gradually reclaiming the site. The track deteriorates now as you proceed through a seasonally closed gate to deal with a sustained drop off and only a few erosion control mounds, as you enter national park.

Pick your line carefully, perhaps feathering the brake as you negotiate some of the especially steep sections where views extend over the historic site of **Mitchells Homestead**. A wattle grove and summer flowering snow daisies herald the crossing of **Mitchell Creek,** where you veer left at a junction to the old homestead site 300 metres later. Little remains of this 1860's outpost which once was a vital resupply point for local gold miners looking for beef, pork and vegetables. The property was sold near the end of the rush and the 1000 odd acres maintained as a market garden until 1936, when the remote land holding was finally abandoned.

Destroyed by a camp fire some years ago, the hut ruins have yielded to the elements over subsequent years, while the old pines and an enormous apple tree were razed in a 2006 bushfire. Various other exotics including sycamores and hazelnuts have been removed, reducing the hard won endeavour to just a memory. The camping is rather pleasant here however, with some creek side sites on the grassy flats. Energetic and experienced hikers can follow a bridle trail along the boulder strewn creek to the **Jamieson River** (and all of the way to **Grannys Flat** near the township of **Jamieson** if you have a couple of days and a complete backpack up your sleeve).

Continue south from **Mitchells** on a potentially slippery clay based track over erosion control mounds and some rutted boggy sections. You will leave the national park at **Potato Patch** before proceeding through a seasonally closed gate to reach a single lane concrete bridge over the **Jamieson**, some 8 kilometres beyond **Mitchells**.

TRACK SNAPSHOT

TOUR ROUTE

Merrijig to Sheepyard Flat and loop drive via Howqua Hills and the Jamieson River.

DURATION AND DISTANCE

The 120 kilometre circuit from Merrijig and back to Sheepyard Flat is a great day trip, but can be extended with an overnight camp at one of several appealing locations.

TRACK DETAILS

Medium standard bush drive with low range climbs and descents, water crossings and boggy sections.

WHEN TO GO

Seasonal Road Closures limit the trek to between November and June. Summer and Easter holiday periods are very busy around Sheepyard, so try to time your visit outside of these periods.

CAMPING

Nice camps with basic facilities around Sheepyard Flat and along the Howqua River. Wrens Flat and the Upper Jamieson Hut are other options, with more bush camping possibilities marked on the map.

FUEL AND SUPPLIES

You will need to stock up at Mansfield before setting out on this tour.

MAPS

Rooftops: Mansfield – Mount Howitt.

OTHER INFORMATION

Frys Hut is a magnificent example of Australian bush architecture, and is well worth visiting. The original hut located here was constructed for the gold mine manager, then was occupied by local stockman Jim Fry. His nephew, Fred, took over the residence in later years and rebuilt the structure around 1940.

BASIC CHECK LIST . . .

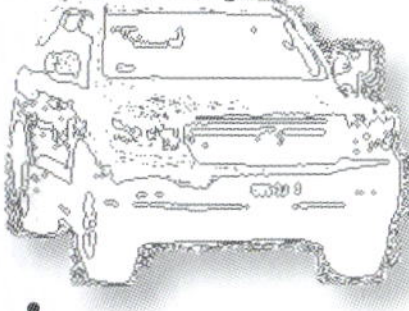

- ☑ Trailers with Care
- ☑ Steep Climbs
- ☑ Water Crossings
- ☑ Good Clearance Needed
- ☑ Avoid Wet Weather

SHEEPYARD FLAT

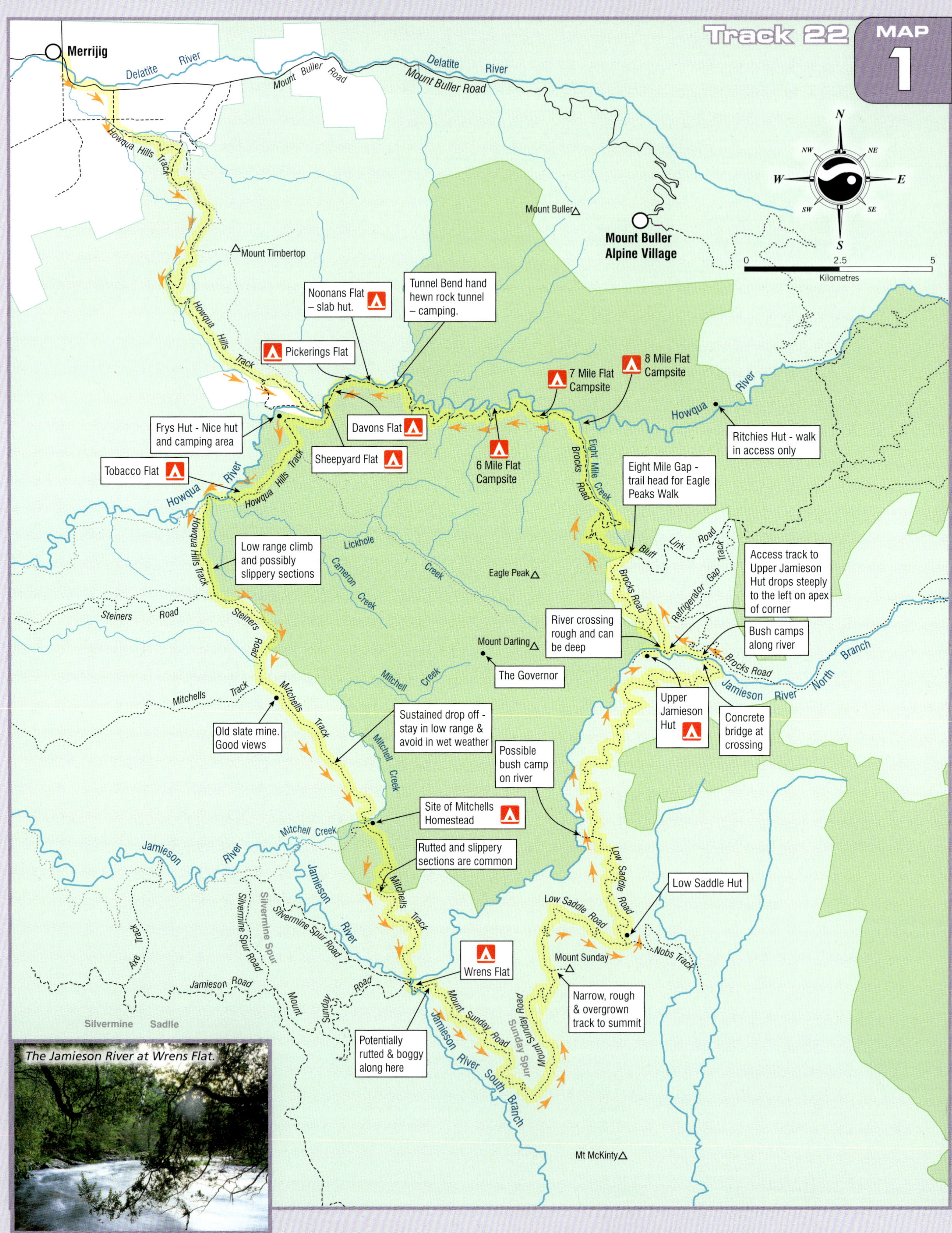

Cross the waterway to an unmarked junction 300 metres later. We will turn left here to continue the trek on **Mount Sunday Road**, but those who turn right will descend to another bridge at **Wrens Flat**, where the north and south branches of the **Jamieson** merge. Camping is popular here, with tables, seats and fireplaces provided and some more informal campsites found off **Silvermine Spur Track** – a sometimes testing trail that follows the river downstream.

From **Wrens Flat** head east through potentially boggy terrain to follow **Mount Sunday Road** on a winding run past tree fern clad slopes and some substantial cuttings. Excellent views extend down the valley as you negotiate a series of switchbacks coloured with bluebells and large flower clematis. Some blackberry has also taken a toehold here, but specimens of weeping native pine about one metre in height are a hidden highlight of the location.

Mount Sunday Road swings suddenly northward about 7.5 kilometres from **Wrens Flat** at a large tree stump shrine, adorned with chainsaw bars. Views of **Mount McKinty** appear between the alpine ash on your right, as you descend through some superb fern glades, especially in the sheltered areas.

Low Saddle Road marks a junction some 5.6 kilometres beyond the northward turn, where you continue north in a seamless transition. (The right turn at this intersection remains **Mount Sunday Road**, but it deteriorates quickly to a narrow and overgrown track. Those who press on will fight a rocky and uneven trail featuring a nasty rock shelf. The trig point at **Mount Sunday** offers broken views through burnt snowgum – an outlook that is probably equalled by other vantage points further north on **Low Saddle Road**).

So follow the undulations of **Low Saddle Road** for 5.4 kilometres to **Nobs Track** on the right at the site of a tiny hut. Camping is possible here at **The Low Saddle**, but there are no views and the hut is far from grand; however it could be a lifesaver in extreme weather.

Keep left at **Nobs Track** to reach an unmarked track on the left 4.3 kilometres later (clearing and camp, but access restricted by fallen tree on our most recent visit). You will reach another turn off on the left 600 metres later which is worth following for another 600 metres to a clearing and camp. From here a short walk takes you to a lovely section of the **Jamieson River**.

Follow **Low Saddle Road** on a pleasant run north on a well surfaced track. The impressive bulk of **Mount Darling** and **The Governor** tower over the western skyline as you descend to a concrete bridge spanning the **Jamieson River's North Branch**. A small and average camp marks the crossing, where you reach **Brocks Road** at a tee. Turn left here (right turn follows state forest to the **Jamieson River** headwaters at the **King Billy Mountains**) to pass a much larger camp with table, seats and fireplace.

Follow the river downstream past another bush camp to a sharp right bend. The access track to the **Upper Jamieson Hut** falls away to the left here on the apex of a bend, and is well worth making a detour to visit. You will proceed through a seasonally closed gate and follow a steep low range drop off to a fording of the **Jamieson River** 300 metres later.

A small clearing (possible camp) marks the rather lumpy crossing, and a much larger camping area 600 metres further on near the hut. The hut itself is a popular destination with a fireplace that draws well, and an appealing layout that includes elaborate bunk beds, although camping in high country huts should be left as a last resort.

Return to **Brocks Road** and turn hard left over a creek spanned by a bridge with views of **The Bluff** dominating the driver's side windows. The serpentine road makes its way skyward to **Eight Mile Gap**, 6.3 kilometres later, where **Bluff Link Road** fans off to the east (see tour **Merrijig** to **Porepunkah** for details). You will re-enter Alpine NP now at a parking area (walk to Eagle Peak from here – a steep 3 kilometre slog taking at least two hours).

Keep left to follow **Brocks Road** on a downhill run laced with numerous switchbacks. Spectacular views open up around the countless corners, with **Mount Buller** being the most significant landmark. You will follow **Eight Mile Creek** to the **Eight Mile Flat** turn off, some 7.3 kilometres beyond **Eight Mile Gap**. The flat at **Eight Mile** flags the first of many camping opportunities on the **Howqua River**, and is the perfect staging point for a hike along the **Howqua Feeder Walking Track** to **Ritchies Hut** and beyond. Although the old hut at **Eight Mile** has long since gone, the tall manna gum and peppermint trees provide nice shelter.

Continue west on **Brocks Road** to pass **Seven Mile Flat** and **Six Mile Flat** on a perpetually winding route overlooking picturesque river bends and rapids. The valley drive follows a series of flats, reputedly used as a stock route in the 1840s. You will reach historic **Tunnel Bend** 9 kilometres beyond **Eight Mile** to find camping and an amazing hand hewn rock tunnel cut 100 metres through solid rock in 1884. The remarkable project was undertaken to gain access to gold bearing deposits in the river bed and to divert part of the **Howqua**'s flow to a water race.

Works on the water race entailed further back breaking labour as a 4 kilometre long channel was cut by hand to power a water wheel some 18 metres in diameter. Gold ore was crushed by the water wheel powered plant, before the precious metal was extracted in a local smelter.

The slab hut at **Noonans Flat** is always popular with campers, although I prefer a quieter stretch of river if it can be found – a tough ask around here in peak season. **Pickerings, Davons** and **Sheepyard Flats** mark a return to this trek's beginning at **Howqua Hills**. You can return to **Mansfield**, consider the slightly more demanding trek from here to **Porepunkah** via **Lake Cobbler**, or just chill out on the **Howqua**. When the weather is pleasant and time is your friend, there can be few more satisfying places to be.

Mount Sunday Road is often rutted and boggy.

Upper Jamieson Hut.

Chapter 3

WESTERN VICTORIA

◀ *Sunset over Lake Crosbie.*

TRACK 23

SUNSET COUNTRY

WESTERN VICTORIA

The soft sand will require a tyre pressure reduction.

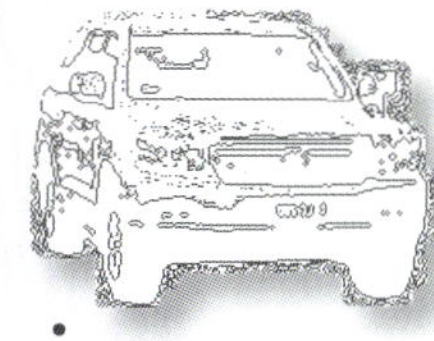

BASIC CHECK LIST . . .

- ☑ Trailers with Care
- ☑ Good Clearance Needed
- ☑ Road Tyres
- ☑ Avoid Wet Weather

TRACK SNAPSHOT

TOUR ROUTE
Underbool to Nowingi via the Pink Lakes and Murray-Sunset NP.

DURATION AND DISTANCE
Allow two days for the 180 kilometre trek route.

TRACK DETAILS
Sandy tracks with some minor dunes and rough sections best tackled by a full sized 4WD, but a capable AWD could follow this trek in the company of other full sized vehicles. Lower tyre pressures required, and don't drive on the salt lakes.

WHEN TO GO
Autumn and Spring are the best times to explore north west Victoria, however be prepared for cold nights. Summer is very hot making travel uncomfortable and the sand very soft.

CAMPING
Camping with basic facilities at the Pink Lakes, Mount Crozier, Mopoke Hut and Rocket Lake. Bush camping at Large Tank and Cattleyards.

FUEL AND SUPPLIES
Mildura and Ouyen are the larger centres, but fuel and basic supplies are available at Underbool and Hattah.

MAPS
Meridian Productions: Victoria's Deserts

OTHER INFORMATION
Always carry plenty of drinking water in this region and preferably travel in company as there is little passing traffic.

***Murray-Sunset** is Victoria's second largest national park protecting lovely mallee eucalypts, sand ridges and colourful salt lakes. Its 633 000 hectares are criss crossed with access tracks – some dating back 150 years when pioneering graziers first pushed stock into the relatively remote north west corner of this state.*

*Visitors of today will see historic pastoral sites, in addition to the area's natural attractions of spring wildflowers and mallee fauna, such as kangaroos, reptiles and a large bird population. This tour looks at the eastern flank of **Murray-Sunset**, picking up the impressive **Pink Lakes**, old grazing infrastructure and many bush camping opportunities.*

Leave **Underbool** via the **Mallee Highway** heading west toward the locality of **Linga**. Turn right after 10 kilometres to leave the blacktop, cross the rail line and follow **Pink Lakes Road** past several intersecting roads. You will enter the **Pink Lakes** area and reach the southern tip of **Lake Hardy** 11 kilometres later, where you swing left to reach **Pioneer Drive** on the right. Make a note of this location as we will return here to continue the trek.

Veer right onto **Pioneer Drive** at the site of an old tennis court to follow the western shore of **Lake Hardy** to a parking and day use area at its northern tip. Elevated views of the lake usually depict it in a pinkish tinge – the result of salt tolerant algae excreting beta-carotene. Other salt lakes in the area exhibit the same colouring, with the thick salty crust harvested for commercial purposes a century ago.

Pass the former state school site on the left and turn right 500 metres later to follow a north east heading past cropping country to the old township ruins on the east shore of **Lake Kenyon**. Little of the once isolated community remains except for some rusting relics and an information board.

Continue past **Mount Crozier Track** on the right 1 kilometre later to drive through mallee and some more open country dotted with sheoaks. Proceed past **Salt Bush Flat Track** on the right to reach a camping area at **Lake Becking** 1 kilometre later. Basic facilities are found here, with the lake hidden behind a prominent dune. Walkers can follow a short trail to the lake shore and take a look

A gypsum hopper dominates the Raak Plain

at 1920s rail equipment from the salt mining days.

Travel east on **Pioneer Drive** beyond **Lake Becking** for 1.1 kilometres to reach a large pile of harvested salt (estimated to weigh 2 300 tonnes) and open air machinery museum. Information boards shed light on the early days when large scale salt collection was undertaken within the **Pink Lakes** area. Abandoned scrapers, elevators and other relics lie around the site, where at one time up to 240 camels carted the raw product to market.

Continue the drive past a nature walk and lookout over **Lake Kenyon**, to a camping area at **Lake Crosbie**. A turn off on the right leads to the **Pink Lakes Camp** 300 metres later where basic facilities are provided, but with limited shade for tents. Informal walks can be made onto the lake, however be aware that native and feral bees are a regular visitor around any water sources, including water tanks, food and even human perspiration.

Head south from camp and return to the first intersection that you arrived at near the old tennis courts, where you turn right. Follow the road past an unnamed salt lake on the left to the junction of **Grub Track**, some 3.2 kilometres later. Keep left at the turn onto a sandy road, and pull over somewhere to drop some air from your tyres, as there is some deep sand to come.

You will pass **Lake Roulton** and an unsignposted access track on the left 1.8 kilometres later. Ten kilometres from the beginning of **Grub Track** you will reach a cross roads with **Honeymoon Hut Track** branching to the right and **Clay Lake Track** branching to the left. These are both lake bypass tracks that link to their respective main tracks via the shoreline of **Grub Lake**.

Keep straight at the junction to begin a lengthy drive over the saltbush flats of **Grub Lake** following a new track alignment. A large dune on the west side guides you toward the southern shoreline of **Clay Lake**, some 3 kilometres into the lake drive, to reach its access walking track 1 kilometre later.

Sand furrows through the spinifex continue past **Underbool Tank Track** on the left (access to dam 400 metres away) and a link track on the right (short cut to **Underbool Track**) about 2 kilometres later. Keep straight to reach **Cattleyards Camp** on the left, with the old yards marking the turn off. Only table and fireplace are provided here, on the edge of the **Sunset Wilderness Area**.

Head west to leave the yards and turn right onto

The pinkish colouring of Lake Hardy is evident from the lookout.

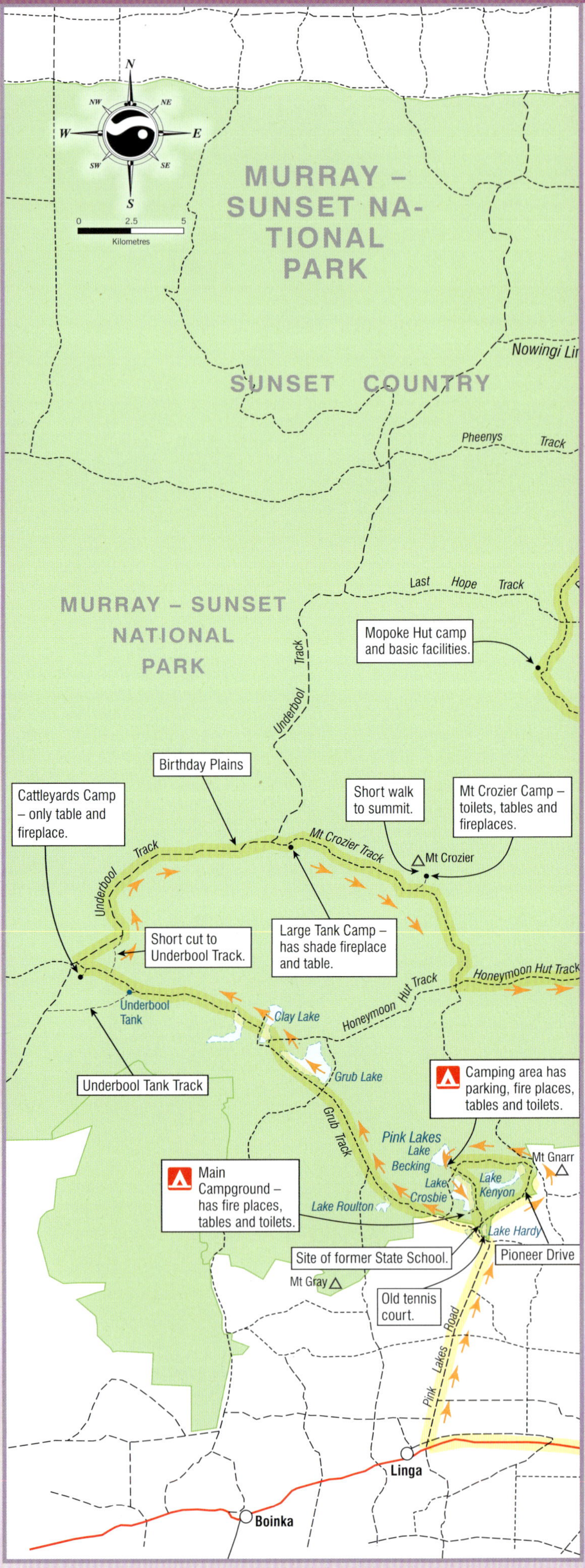

MURRAY – SUNSET NATIONAL PARK
SUNSET COUNTRY
Mopoke Hut camp and basic facilities.
Birthday Plains
Cattleyards Camp – only table and fireplace.
Short walk to summit.
Mt Crozier Camp – toilets, tables and fireplaces.
Short cut to Underbool Track.
Large Tank Camp – has shade fireplace and table.
Underbool Tank Track
Camping area has parking, fire places, tables and toilets.
Main Campground – has fire places, tables and toilets.
Site of former State School.
Pioneer Drive
Old tennis court.
Linga
Boinka

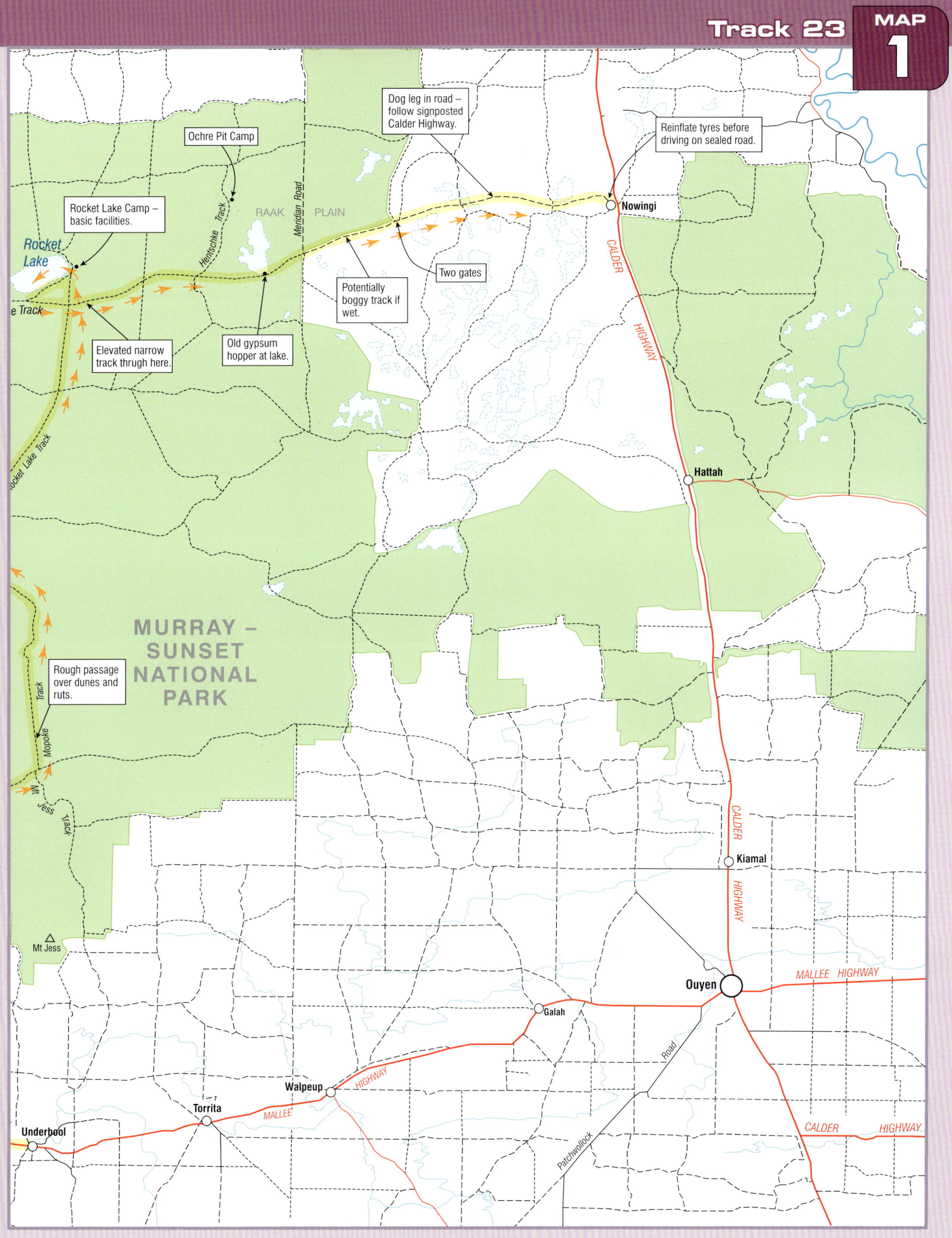
Dog leg in road – follow signposted Calder Highway.
Reinflate tyres before driving on sealed road.
Ochre Pit Camp
Rocket Lake Camp – basic facilities.
Rocket Lake
Nowingi
RAAK PLAIN
Meridian Road
Hentschke Track
Two gates
Potentially boggy track if wet.
e Track
Elevated narrow track thrugh here.
Old gypsum hopper at lake.
CALDER HIGHWAY
ocket Lake Track
Hattah
MURRAY – SUNSET NATIONAL PARK
Rough passage over dunes and ruts.
Mt Mopoke Track
Jess Track
Kiamal
Mt Jess
Ouyen
MALLEE HIGHWAY
Galah
Road
Walpeup
HIGHWAY
Torrita
MALLEE
Underbool
Patchwollock
CALDER HIGHWAY

Mopoke Hut once housed local drovers.

Underbool Track 300 metres later. Some surface gravel provides easier travel as you pass the **Grub Track Link** about 3 kilometres from the yards. You will cross **Birthday Plains** (a 50 000 acre block mooted for grazing and wheat growing) and reach the **Mount Crozier Track** junction 15.7 kilometres beyond the yards. Keep straight at the turn off (**Underbool Track** peels off to the left), and arrive at **Large Tank Camp** 1 kilometre later. Fireplace and table are provided with some shade within the nice clump of mallee.

Follow **Mount Crozier Track** over increasingly larger dunes to a turn off on the left 10 kilometres from **Large Tank Camp**.

Mopoke Track will keep the driver alert.

Turn left here to arrive at **Mount Crozier Camp** 600 metres later. Toilets, tables and fireplaces are found across this popular camp with bollards restricting some vehicle access. A short walk to the summit of **Mount Crozier** begins here, allowing visitors reasonable views across the desert from a point only 111 metres above sea level.

Continue along **Mount Crozier Track** heading more southerly to the **Honeymoon Hut Track** intersection, 6.3 kilometres later. Turn left and follow an easy run via the dune swales to pass **Mount Jess Track** on the right after 9.8 kilometres. You will turn left 200 metres later onto **Mopoke Track** at a broad clearing.

Begin the entertaining drive northward with a large dune to crest, then a roller coaster ride, as you lurch over wheel ruts and deal with powdery corners. Keen eyed travellers will notice many animal tracks in the sandy track verge, with emus, kangaroos and feral goats being the larger species, and lizards also very well represented.

Turn left onto **Mopoke Track** after 18.6 kilometres, to arrive at the renovated hut 700 metres later. The original hut was built in 1962 to house local stock drovers, and features a welcome section of flywire to help keep the interior bearable during the hot summers. The fireplace has been decommissioned, and the original notched post and rail yards remain standing (but only just). Camping is permitted nearby with basic facilities and a local walking trail.

Return to the main **Mopoke Track** and turn left to **No Hope Track** 3.4 kilometres later. Keep straight as the track becomes **Rocket Lake Track**, crossing **Pheenys Track** at an offset intersection. You will reach **Nowingi Line Track** about 6.5 kilometres further on, keeping straight to arrive at **Rocket Lake Camp** 2.5 kilometres after that.

Again basic facilities are provided here, with the large expanse of **Rocket Lake** just walking distance away. The lake basin is rimmed by sand dunes of a consistent height and carpeted with low growing salt bush. Vehicles are not permitted to drive across the lake (its surface can be very soft), but a shoreline perimeter track heads south west from camp, enabling travellers to appreciate the sheer scale of this desert feature.

The link track reaches **Nowingi Line** 8.4 kilometres later where you turn left and head east to cross **Rocket Lake Track**. Follow the rather elevated track on a good surface which is narrow for some distance, and not an ideal spot to find oncoming traffic. Fortunately the flat country offers excellent views to the distance as you pass **Henschke Track** on the left (access to **Ochre Pit Camp** 7 kilometres away), 9.4 kilometres from **Rocket Lake Track**.

Keep heading straight to reach the southern end of a large salt lake, with a prominent mineral hopper standing trackside. Gypsum flakes lie scattered in the area, although commercial harvesting is no longer active at this site. An old rail line runs from here toward the **Sunraysia Highway**, although it is now almost completely gone, except for the odd sleeper to mark its passing.

You now begin to cross the infamous **Raak Plains** – a lowland of potentially muddy substrate that has claimed many vehicles over the years. Proceed only if the road is dry and no "Track Closed" signs have been erected. An old fenceline and gate flags **Meridian Road** on the left as you head eastward past some tanks and more fenceline on the right.

Leave **Murray-Sunset NP** with **Boundary Track** on the left and two gates in succession. A set of old stockyards some 11.1 kilometres beyond **Meridian Road** flag a dogleg in the road 800 metres later (follow signposted "**Calder Highway**"). A burnt out truck tanker sits on a nearby salt lake as you cross a grid to reach another set of yards on the right.

Three kilometres later you swing right to cross the **Mildura** rail line and meet the **Calder Highway** just after, at the locality of **Nowingi**. Remember to reinflate your tyres before turning onto the sealed road, with **Mildura** about 50 kilometres to the north and **Ouyen** some 45 kilometres to the south.

Salt pile and old machinery at the open air museum.

TRACK 24 THE BIG DESERT

WESTERN VICTORIA

Driving along Firebreak Track.

BASIC CHECK LIST . . .

- ☑ Steep Climbs
- ☑ Good Clearance Needed
- ☑ Road Tyres
- ☑ Avoid Wet Weather

TRACK SNAPSHOT

TOUR ROUTE
Murrayville and return via the Big Desert State Forest.

DURATION AND DISTANCE
The 160 kilometre run could be done in a day, but an overnight camp would be a better option.

TRACK DETAILS
Big sand dunes demand full size 4WDs and the possible use of low range gearing. Difficult country for trailers.

WHEN TO GO
Autumn and Spring are best. Summer is very hot during the day and Winter nights can be freezing. Avoid wet weather as the Murrayville Road has clay sections which become very slippery.

CAMPING
Bush camping at Coburns Pines, The Red Gums and White Springs. Camping with basic facilities at Big Billy Bore on the Murrayville Track.

FUEL AND SUPPLIES
Murrayville can supply most requirements.

MAPS
Meridian Productions: Victoria's Deserts

OTHER INFORMATION
Carry water and preferably tyre repair gear – deflated tyres are easily punctured on a rock or burnt tree root.

*Christening a small block of Victoria's Mallee "**The Big Desert**" seems hard to justify, when a single desert elsewhere in Australia covers more ground than this entire state. Indeed the **Great Victoria Desert** of **South** and **Western Australia** spans two time zones, and dwarfs north west **Victoria** by an embarrassing margin. However what the **Big Desert** lacks in size is more than compensated for by ease of access and diversity of attraction – it may be small but you will find it to be a great Victorian desert.*

*Boxed in to the north and south by the **Mallee** and **Western Highways**, the **Big Desert** reaches the **South Australia** border, and extends eastward into the **Wimmera**. Its western block is declared a Wilderness Area, with limited vehicular access, while the eastern block is protected by **Wyperfeld National Park**. This trek follows a loop trail from **Murrayville**, criss crossing the **Big Desert State Forest** via some testing dune country. There are great viewpoints and superb mallee bush camps, with a little bit of recent European history thrown in.*

Leave **Murrayville** via the single lane sealed **Nhill Road** passing the old state school site. You will pass **South Road** on the left and **Ngallo Road** shortly after on your right. Drive through cropping country to reach gravel at the **South Five Chain Road** intersection.

Continue straight to arrive at the boundary of **Big Desert State Forest**, some 10.9 kilometres from **Murrayville**, and turn right immediately onto **Firebreak Trail**. Drop some air from your tyres near here to deal with a lot of dry, loose sand dunes to come. (20 psi – 138kPa - is a good starting point, but warmer weather may require a further reduction).

Head west to pass the **Old Murrayville Road** on your left 200 metres later, to crest the first of many sand dunes. Small native pines form a corridor as you drive past good views of the northern farmland, and reach **Cactus Bore Track** 4.3 kilometres into the state forest.

Keep straight at the junction to pass an unsignposted turn off on the left and reach a track dogleg 4.5 kilometres from **Cactus Bore Track**. Continue west to a tee intersection on **Ngallo South Road**, where you turn left and reach a three way junction with **Firebreak Trail** peeling off to the right, and **Coburns Track** branching to the left. (The centre

The Murrayville Road is easily rain affected.

option follows a lumpy overgrown path for 2.2 kilometres to **Coburns Pines** – a large camp near the mature pines that survived an unsuccessful attempt to grow various softwood plantation species in this desert environment).

Follow **Coburns Track** south east through broom bush and scrub country to arrive at **The Redgums** 5.6 kilometres later. This is a superb and unexpected camp, with a shallow depression holding enough water to establish a beautiful stand of red gums. A table and seat are the only facilities, but it is a nice place to pitch a tent or stop for lunch – just not directly beneath a red gum though, as these trees are known to drop branches without warning.

Six kilometres further on you will reach a substantial sand dune and fork in the track. The track directly ahead follows a ridge to **Thomson Peaks Lookout** – an abrupt 200 metre low range climb with unparalleled views over the **Big Desert Wilderness**. The left track bypasses this major dune meeting the ridge top track 1.2 kilometres later at a subsequent intersection.

Those not willing to undertake a vehicle climb should walk up if possible so as not to miss out on seeing the vast sea of khaki at your feet from the summit. **Jaffle Iron Rocks** jut up from the desertscape with **Mount Rodney** dominating the dunes. Continue along the sand ridge by vehicle to pass another access track on the left, before reaching the exit track (also on the left) one kilometre later. At this junction another steep and lurching climb awaits those who continue directly ahead, but it is very difficult with limited parking and room to turn around, so consider doing this section at least, on foot.

Make your way down the dune and turn right onto the byppass track to reach **Cactus Bore Track** 5 kilometres later at a tee intersection. Swing right here to pass an unsignposted track on the left 300 metres later (a lumpy and overgrown alternative route to **Cactus Bore**), so keep straight to reach the c1929 bore via a turn off 400 metres beyond that.

Cactus Bore features some pipe work at this once vital water point, together with a thick garden of towering American Aloe plants. Head east from the bore through low growing scrub with the **Big Desert Wilderness Area** on your right. Veer right at the **Old Murrayville Road** junction to remain on **Cactus Bore Track**, meeting a tee intersection on the main **Murrayville Road** near **Sim Perrys Bore**.

Turn left at the tee, then right onto **White Springs Track** 1.6 kilometres later. You will drive through native pines to reach another tee intersection 7 kilometres later, where you turn left onto the **Cowangie – Nhill Track**. You will reach another tee 1 kilometre later, with **St Johns Bore Track** heading left and **White**

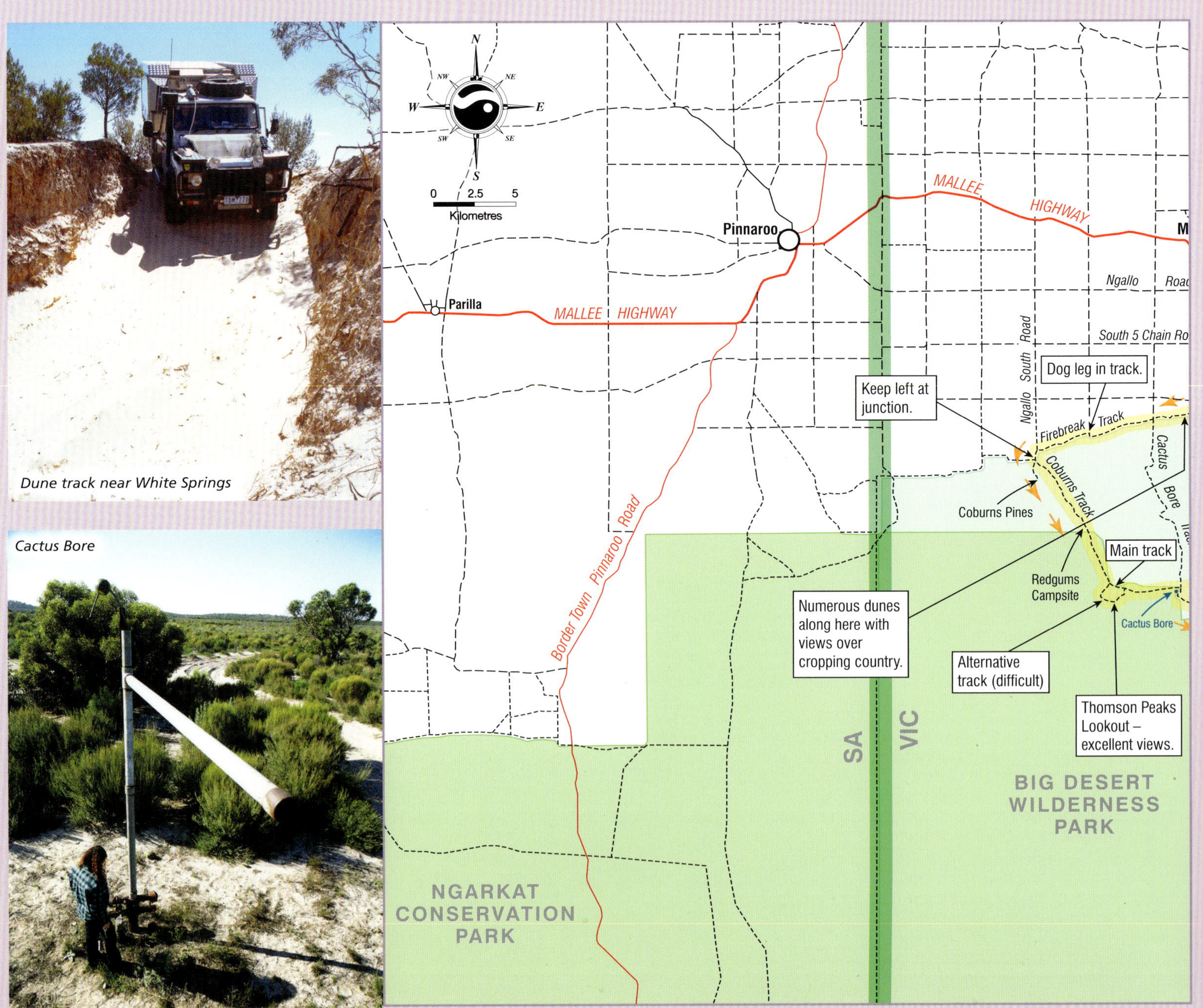

Dune track near White Springs

Cactus Bore

Springs Track branching to the right.

We will continue right at this junction, but for now turn left to pass the **Cowangie – Nhill Track** on the right 500 metres later, and reach **Johns Bore** 200 metres after that. Little remains of the old bore – just some pipework, old trough and a tiny weathered plaque – but it is worth reflecting upon the remarkable work done by the pioneering pastoralists.

Return to the **Johns Bore Track** junction and head south east through nice mallee and dune country. A rocky section slows progress as you reach **Lone Pine** 3.3 kilometres from the last junction. An unusual expanse of grassland (for this desert country) and a solitary native pine provide interest as you cross a patch of gypsum and reach **Big Dune Track** on the right (the massive dune that you admire to the south will be visited in due course!)

Keep straight to cross a yellow carpet of wildflowers and native grasses defining an area known as the **"Sand Bucket"**. The track then weaves through mallee thicket to **Brushcutters Track** on the right, some 10.5 kilometres beyond **Big Dune Track**.

We will turn right here, but the location of **White Springs** is reached just a couple of hundred metres to the left. A claypan and boggy patch flag the springs, where succulents colour a possible bush campsite. A steep dune climb and overgrown ridge drive loop mark the nearby lookout, although it is best to walk this particular section.

Return to **Brushcutter Track** and head south past **Campbell Track** to a grassy area at **Brushcutters Flat** 10 kilometres later. Turn right onto **Delisio Track** here to begin the sand ridge drive. You will pass the other end of **Campbell Track** to deal with increasingly bigger dunes – some present double headed obstacles, with the track over swinging back on itself, before cresting the second ridge. Stay alert and drop some more air if your vehicle is struggling.

You will reach **Clarence Ranges Track** on the left 11 kilometres from **Brushcutters Flat**, where you will keep right to continue the trek. However a left turn brings you to **Big Dune** and **Big K Lookout** – with several vehicle tracks gouged into this desert giant. Again walking access is best with several locations suitable for parking.

Follow the dune system further west, past the **Cowangie – Nhill track** intersection to arrive on the **Murrayville Road** 2 kilometres later. If you are still looking for sand dune excitement you can cross the main road to find a dune lookout on the west side as well. Back on the **Murrayville Road** it is 8 kilometres south to **Big Billy Bore** for camping (basic facilities and large camp area), or return to **Murrayville**, 27 kilometres to the north.

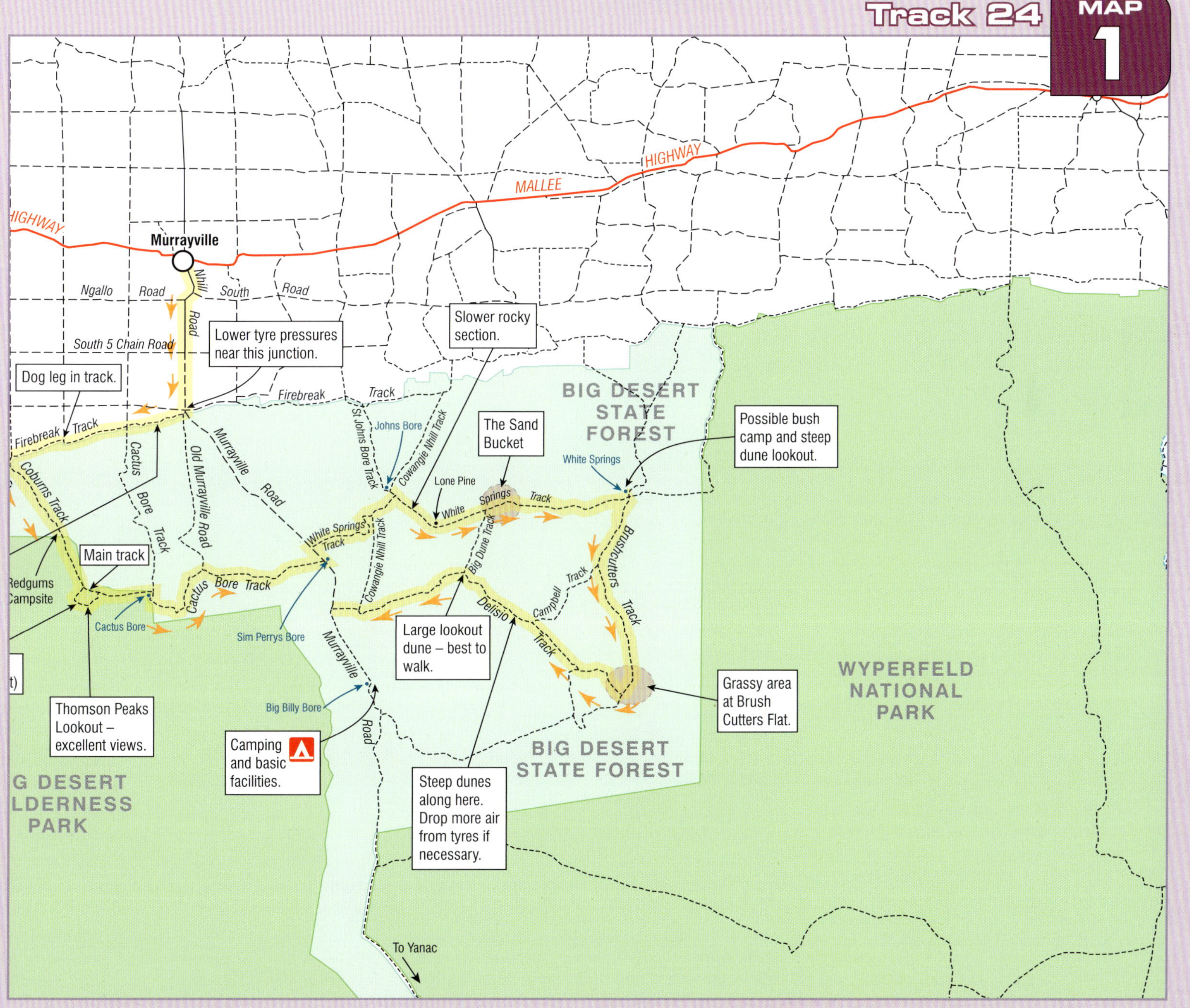

TRACK 25

EAST WYPERFELD

WESTERN VICTORIA

Lower your tyre pressures for the soft sand on Purra Track.

*The eastern reaches of **Wyperfeld National Park** are scalloped with dry lakes, clay pans and potential floodplains. Sprawling creek tentacles link many of these shallow depressions, although it is a very infrequent event to see water actually flowing within the system. Local rains provide some assistance in filling the waterways, but it has been the **Wimmera River** that did most of the heavy lifting, as occasional floodwaters flowed north from **Lake Hindmarsh** into **Lake Albacutya** spilling over into the desert via **Outlet Creek**.*

*Visitors to the area will see where intermittent flooding has established red gum and black box forests, adjacent to the dry waterways, and perhaps identify some of the other 450 species of plants which have adapted to the unique conditions. Unfortunately back to back droughts and weirs on the **Wimmera River** have taken their toll on water output, with a consequent impact on these forests in particular. The local bird population has suffered as well, but with 200 odd species still calling the area home, you are likely to at least see some desert wildlife on the tour.*

The trek route follows the major drainage lines north through the park to some lookouts and more lengthy bushwalking opportunites. The 4WD track system is largely sandy and occasionally demanding, but a pleasant drive for those who appreciate the desert environment. Bush camps are dotted along the route for those looking to extend their stay.

We begin at **Rainbow**, heading north on the **Hopetoun Road**, but keeping left 8 kilometres later at signposted "**Lake Albacutya**". Follow the narrower bitumen left away from **Wembulin Track** at the locality of **Albacutya** to reach **Outlet Creek** 6 kilometres later, at a bridge commissioned in 1919.

Veer right at a picnic area just after the bridge and follow the dry shoreline of Lake **Albacutya** to a camping area at **Western Beach** several kilometres from **Outlet Creek**. Cold showers and flushing toilets are a rare luxury at a free bush camp, with shady

BASIC CHECK LIST . . .

- ☑ **Good Clearance Needed**
- ☑ **Road Tyres**
- ☑ **Avoid Wet Weather**
- ☑ **Navigational Skills**

TRACK SNAPSHOT

TOUR ROUTE
Rainbow to Underbool via Lake Albacutya and Wyperfeld NP.

DURATION AND DISTANCE
Travellers following this 190 kilometre trek will need at least two days to really absorb the mallee atmosphere.

TRACK DETAILS
A combination of some sealed and gravel roads is routine, but soft sand is a feature of Purra Track and North South Track. AWDs will probably struggle in the deep sand furrows and trailers are not permitted on some sections of this trek.

WHEN TO GO
Avoid Summer with its extreme heat, and the wetter months when travel may be restricted.

CAMPING
Basic facilities at Western Beach, OTIT Camp, Casuarina Camp and Snowdrift Camp. Popular camp at Wonga Hut, but fees apply here.

FUEL AND SUPPLIES
Rainbow and Underbool can cater for most basic needs.

MAPS
Meridian Productions: Victoria's Deserts

OTHER INFORMATION
This is a great trip for nature enthusiasts – numerous walks and lookouts, with desert flora and fauna at every turn.

Red gums are common along the floodplains.

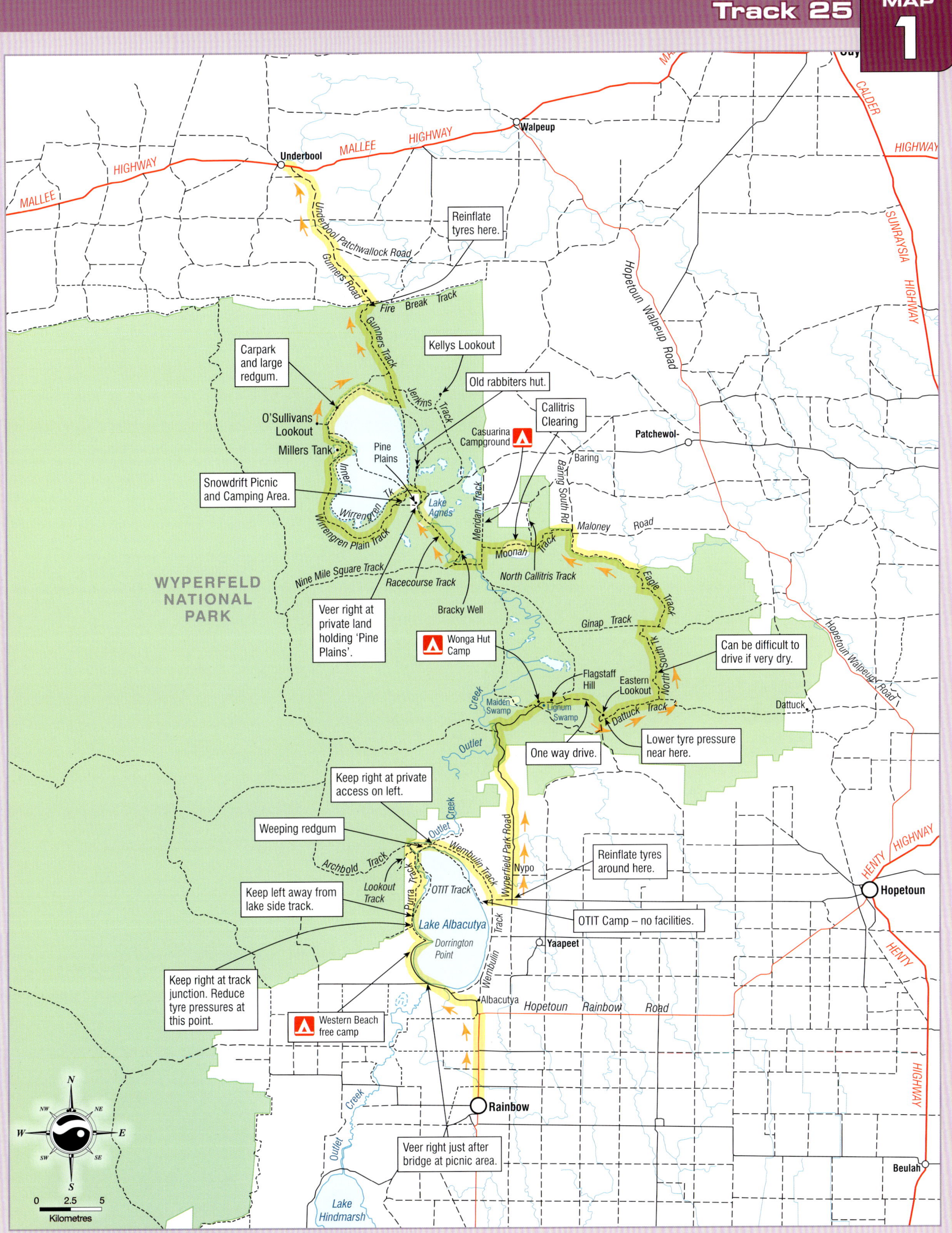

Underbool
Walpeup
MALLEE HIGHWAY
CALDER HIGHWAY
SUNRAYSIA HIGHWAY
HENTY HIGHWAY
Reinflate tyres here.
Underbool Patchwallock Road
Gunners Road
Fire Break Track
Gunners Track
Kellys Lookout
Carpark and large redgum.
Old rabbiters hut.
Jenkins Track
Callitris Clearing
Casuarina Campground
O'Sullivans Lookout
Millers Tank
Pine Plains
Patchewollock
Baring
Hopetoun Walpeup Road
Snowdrift Picnic and Camping Area.
Inner Wirrengren Tk
Wirrengren Plain Track
Lake Agnes
Meridan Track
Baring South Rd
Maloney Road
Moonah Track
North Callitris Track
Eagle Track
WYPERFELD NATIONAL PARK
Nine Mile Square Track
Racecourse Track
Bracky Well
Veer right at private land holding 'Pine Plains'.
Wonga Hut Camp
Ginap Track
North South Tk
Can be difficult to drive if very dry.
Flagstaff Hill
Eastern Lookout
Maiden Swamp
Lignum Swamp
Dattuck Track
Dattuck
Outlet Creek
One way drive.
Lower tyre pressure near here.
Keep right at private access on left.
Weeping redgum
Archbold Track
Wembulin Track
Wyperfeld Park Road
Nypo
Reinflate tyres around here.
Keep left away from lake side track.
Lookout Track
Purra Track
OTIT Track
OTIT Camp – no facilities.
Hopetoun
Lake Albacutya
Dorrington Point
Yaapeet
Keep right at track junction. Reduce tyre pressures at this point.
Western Beach free camp
Albacutya
Hopetoun Rainbow Road
Rainbow
Veer right just after bridge at picnic area.
Beulah
Lake Hindmarsh
0 2.5 5
Kilometres
N S E W NE NW SE SW

sites nearby and a boat ramp for the most optimistic of folk. An informal track system crosses the dry lake bed in an east – west line and a north – south line, but can only be driven on following a lengthy spell of dry weather.

We will head north following the main shoreline route passing a wool shed and **Dorrington Point** on the right. You will reach a junction on the left 3.3 kilometres from camp, where you keep straight on **Purra Track** (left turn follows boundary of national park to **Pella Track**). Drop some air from your tyres somewhere around here in preparation for the lengthy stretches of soft sand to come (try 20 psi – 138kPa - as a starting point, and perhaps lower if it is especially powdery in the warmer months).

Follow the sandy furrows past native pines to reach a fork some 4.2 kilometres from **Western Beach Camp**. Keep right here (left fork crests large dune), and follow the orange diamond markers tracing the route.

Open dune country ushers the way past a track on the right (access to lake and the **Inner Purra Track**) some 9.6 kilometres from camp. Continue straight to a cross road 1.6 kilometres later, where you turn left (track on right crosses **Outlet Creek** to **Freeway Track** and the lake drive, with the straight ahead option being a dry weather bypass on **Purra Track**).

Follow the main **Purra Track** past a lookout track to reach **Archbolds Track** on the left (MVO). Keep right at this junction to cross **Outlet Creek** and follow a path between the dry creek and northern shoreline of **Lake Albacutya**. You will drive a short distance to reach a small parking area where walkers can take a closer look at a rare weeping red gum, 50 metres away. Further on, keep right at the junction of **Wembulin Track** to follow the improving road surface eastward.

Cropping country dominates the left view as you trace **Lake Albacutya**'s north east shoreline past unsignposted **Jordan Valley Track** (access to several bush camping areas) to **O.T.I.T. Track** some 6 kilometres from the Wembulin Track junction (**OTIT Track** was named after the local wood cutting brothers; Owen and Ian Thomas). Turn right here to cross the beach track 800 metres later, and reach **O.T.I.T. Camp** 600 metres beyond that. Red gums fringe a nice camp here, with toilet, fireplaces and table provided, however the last section of access can be boggy so take care.

Back track from camp to **Wembulin Track** and keep heading east to leave the national park remembering that you should inflate your tyres for the higher speed section of road ahead. Farming infrastructure dots the country here with some buildings well elevated to deal with the rare flooding events.

You will reach a tee intersection on **Wyperfeld Park Road**, where you turn left and cruise the bitumen past the gypsum mine and old state school chimney at **Nypo**. Several side roads intersect, before you reach the boundary of **Wyperfeld NP** and an information board (camping permits for **Wonga Hut Camp** available here).

Keep following the sealed road past a few side tracks (mostly bike paths) to the main camping area at **Wonga Hut**, some 9 kilometres into the park. A broad camping area here offers basic facilities together with displays of pioneering farm equipment and land management methods. Numerous walks and bike paths fan out from the camp, with others accessible from nearby car parks.

Continue east through the park to hit gravel at the prominent dune of **Flagstaff Hill**, then a one way circuit drive beyond that. Keep left at the junction to pass **Lignum Swamp** and the **Eastern Lookout Walk**, with **Dattuck Track** branching left 8.5 kilometres from camp.

Turn left here and find a place to lower your tyre pressures again as you pass a sign indicating **"No Trailers or Caravans"**. Head east through lovely eucalypt mallee, turning left onto **North South Track** 6.1 kilometres later. It is an especially powdery climb as you head north, with lumpy corners and multiple wheel furrows. Watch out for oncoming traffic and drop some more air from your tyres if progress proves too difficult.

You will reach another tee intersection on **Ginap Track** where you turn right and drive for 1.3 kilometres, then swing left onto **Eagle Track** at a locked gate. Weave your way north past **Maroong Rise**, turning left 7.3 kilometres later to remain on **Eagle Track**, signposted **"Pine Plains"**. Follow the boundary fence of national park with cropping country and an old shearing shed on the right. Better road paves the way to the **Moloney Road** junction, where you keep straight on the **Baring South Road**, turning left onto **Moonah Track** 400 metres later.

You will pass **North Callitris Track** on the right and enter **Callitris Clearing** where an open area of wildflowers colour a yellow

Rusting relics at Millers Bore.

Wildflowers and mallee on North South Track.

carpet under the native pines. The clearing ends 2 kilometres beyond the junction, with **Moonah Track** finishing at a tee intersection on **Meridan Track**. (If you turn right here and drive 2.4 kilometres, you will reach **Casuarina Campground** with basic facilities and three hour loop walk).

We will however turn left at this junction to follow a narrower track through native pine, before reaching a locked gate 1.6 kilometres later. Turn right here onto **Nine Mile Square Track**, crossing **Outlet Creek** (usually dry) 700 metres later. Turn right onto **Racecourse Track** 1.7 kilometres beyond the creek making an uneven descent into the creek system. An historic dog leg fence (utilizing tree trunks laid horizontally in a zig zag fashion without the need for supporting posts) marks the crossing.

Follow **Racecourse Road** past **Bracky Well** and several intersecting side tracks (all MVO). A patchwork of open and treed country is home to plenty of kangaroos with parrots and cockatoos in good numbers. You will reach the southern shoreline of **Lake Agnes** and cross its dry bed, veering right at a management track near **Pine Plains Lodge** (private land holding and prearranged accommodation).

Follow the fenceline past an old log stockyard to a cross roads on **Outlet Creek Track**. We will turn left to continue the trek, but those interested can keep heading straight along **Racecourse Track** to an old rabbiter's hut 1.4 kilometres later. The now roofless iron hut ruins mark a time in this country's past when rabbiters, timber cutters and pioneer graziers managed to live a simple life with few luxuries

Return to **Outlet Creek Track** and head west for 1.4 kilometres to the **Gunners Track** intersection. Keep left at the junction on **Wirrengren Plain Track** to cross **Outlet Creek**, keeping left again away from the **Inner Wirrengren Plain Track** turn off 600 metres later.

Follow the track past a junction on your left to **Pine Plains Lodge** (no access), reaching **The Snowdrift Picnic and Camping Area** 700 metres later. Toilets, fireplaces, shelter shed and tables are provided under the shade of local casuarinas, with a large sand dune adjacent. Kids and energetic adults will enjoy climbing the gleaming white dune for sand play or just to get a view.

Wyperfeld's sand dune system was formed about 15 000 years ago following the receding of an inland sea. The residual sand was picked up by the prevailing westerly winds, gradually transforming ripples into ridges. The process continues to this day with dunes like the **Snowdrifts** slowly engulfing parts of the mallee.

Continue beyond the **Snowdrifts** to pass **Red Hill Track** on a trail marked with orange arrows. You will reach the **Inner Wirrengren Plain Track** on your right (access to historical soak) where you keep left to reach the northern end of Inner Wirrengren Plain Track 5.9 kilometres later.

Keep left here to reach a turn off to **Millers Tank** 3 kilomeres later (alternative route via dam and nearby disused bore pump facility). Remain on **Wirrengren Plain Track** to pass **Millers Track** on the right 1.1 kilometres later (dry weather access across lake to **Pine Plains Lodge**), with a concrete water tank and troughing flagging the turn off to **O'Sullivans Lookout** about 1.3 kilometres from the tank.

Turn left at the junction to arrive at a parking area 800 metres later. A one hour return walk punishes hikers with a steep dune face climb, that leads to 360 degree views from the crest. The open expanse of **Wirrengren Plain** stretches for kilometres, and can be readily appreciated from this lofty peak.

Return to the main track and turn left to reach a carpark 3.4 kilometres later. A huge red gum with its canopy touching the ground lives nearby, making it a worthwhile stop. Continue past a management track on the left to reach a tee intersection on **Gunners Track**, where you turn left to begin the drive out.

You will pass **Jenkins Track** on the right (short drive, then walk to **Kellys Lookout**), then a management track on the left to reach **Firebreak Track** marking the boundary of **Wyperfeld NP**. Keep left here to follow the improving surface of **Gunner Road** past a dry well, where you can stop to put some air back into your vehicle's tyres.

Improving road passes an old stockyard and cropping country to the **Patchewollock Road**, some 6.4 kilometres beyond **Firebreak Track**. Turn left here to follow a corridor of scrub over **Stockroute Road** and into **Underbool** on the **Mallee Highway**.

Major Mitchell cockatoos are just one of the 200 bird species across Wyperfeld.

TRACK 26 SOUTH WYPERFELD

WESTERN VICTORIA

Lake Hindmarsh can be dry, but it's a lovely destination when full.

BASIC CHECK LIST . . .

- ☑ Trailers with Care
- ☑ Steep Climbs
- ☑ Good Clearance Needed
- ☑ Road Tyres
- ☑ Avoid Wet Weather

TRACK SNAPSHOT

TOUR ROUTE
Rainbow to Nhill via Lake Hindmarsh and the South Wyperfeld Wilderness Area.

DURATION AND DISTANCE
The 170 kilometre run can be done as a day trip, but with excellent bush camping why not take a couple of days?

TRACK DETAILS
Mostly routine desert driving, but with some dunes to negotiate on Milmed Rock Track. Just a little tough for AWDs and trailers will need a capable vehicle pulling them.

WHEN TO GO
Avoid wet weather when the clay pans and Murrayville road turn into skating rinks. Summer is probably too hot for comfort.

CAMPING
Great bush camping at The Wattles, Williamson Beach, The Springs and Moonlight Tank. Basic facilities at Round Swamp and Broken Bucket Camp.

FUEL AND SUPPLIES
Rainbow and Nhill can provide for most needs.

MAPS
Meridian Productions: Victoria's Deserts.

OTHER INFORMATION
History buffs will enjoy an interesting drive via numerous pioneering pastoral endeavours. Old bores, windmills and the Murrayville Track stock route are all well worth seeing.

Victoria's ***Wimmera*** *reaches north to an arbitrary line separating it from the* ***Big Desert*** *of the state's north west. The southern flank of* ***Wyperfeld NP*** *protects a corridor of this transition to mallee, where the sand dunes have grown bigger, the cropping land has become more marginal, and the populated centres are even sparser.*

This is great country to explore by 4WD with sand ridges to test your driving skills, and access to a string of waterholes and springs for pleasant bush camping. Our trek clips the northern tip of ***Lake Hindmarsh****, before making an authentic desert run across* ***Wyperfeld****, returning via the historic* ***Murrayville Track*** *stockroute.*

Leave **Rainbow** by travelling south on the main street (**King Street**) to **Lake Street** on the right. Turn west then veer left on the **Rainbow – Nhill Road**, following its sealed surface on a dogleg route through cropping country. Several roads and tracks intersect with the main road, but stick to the blacktop to reach a turn off to **The Wattles**, just prior to the bridge spanning **Outlet Creek**.

A dirt track heads south along **Outlet Creek** (usually dry) to a bush camp on the northern tip of **Lake Hindmarsh**. There are no facilities at **The Wattles**, but the site offers a pleasant sandy beach and good views over the lake; which may or may not be endowed with any water depending on the season. **Hindmarsh** marks the beginning of the end for the **Wimmera River** however, which flows in a northerly direction into its shallow basin, spilling over into nearby **Lake Albacutya** and beyond only in very wet years.

Sunset at Hermie Strauss's Garden.

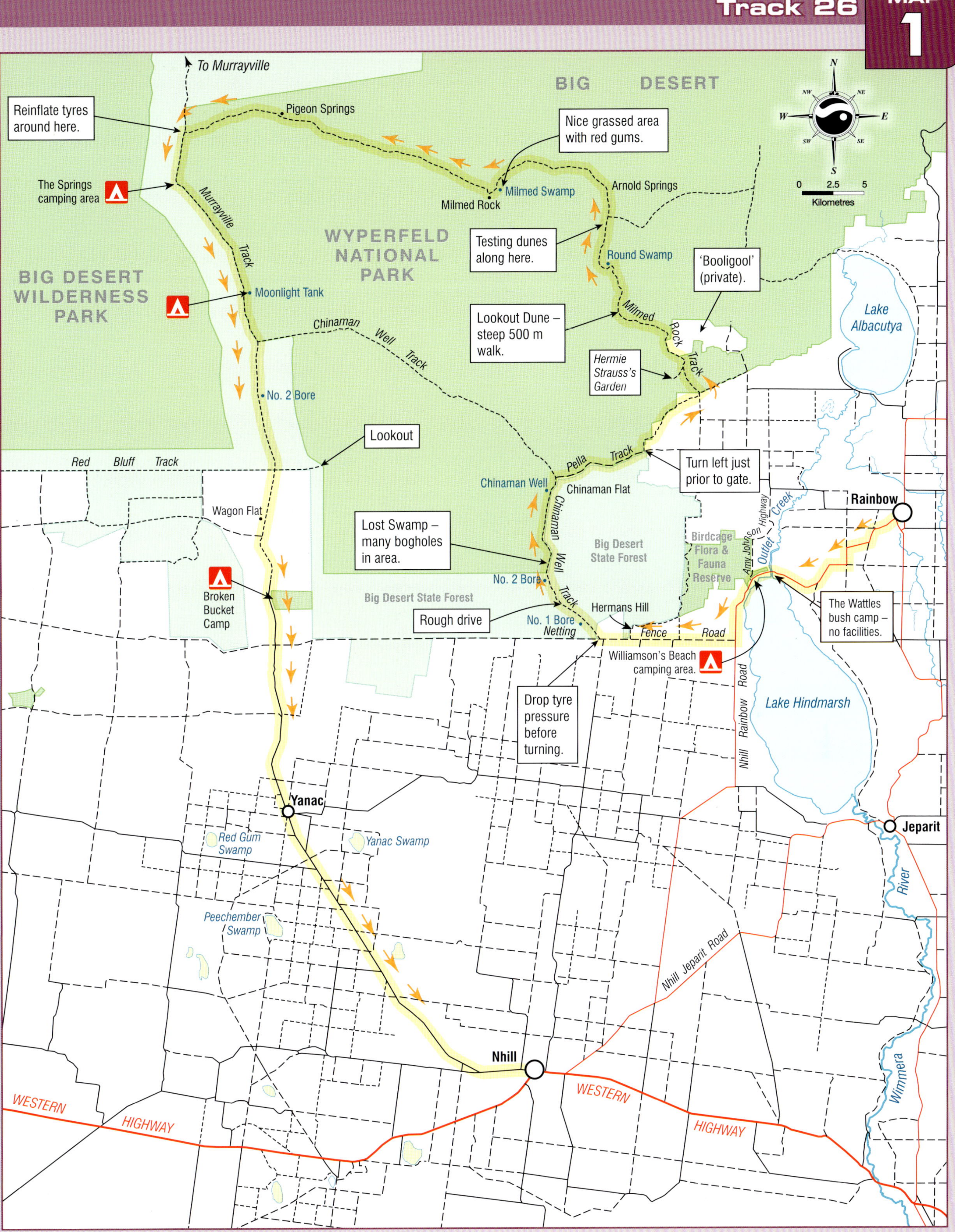

To Murrayville
BIG DESERT
Reinflate tyres around here.
Pigeon Springs
Nice grassed area with red gums.
Milmed Swamp
Milmed Rock
Arnold Springs
The Springs camping area
Murrayville Track
WYPERFELD NATIONAL PARK
Testing dunes along here.
Round Swamp
'Booligool' (private).
BIG DESERT WILDERNESS PARK
Moonlight Tank
Lake Albacutya
Chinaman Well Track
Lookout Dune – steep 500 m walk.
Milmed Rock Track
Hermie Strauss's Garden
No. 2 Bore
Lookout
Red Bluff Track
Pella Track
Turn left just prior to gate.
Chinaman Well
Chinaman Flat
Rainbow
Wagon Flat
Lost Swamp – many bogholes in area.
Big Desert State Forest
Birdcage Flora & Fauna Reserve
Amy Johnson Highway
Outlet Creek
No. 2 Bore
Broken Bucket Camp
Big Desert State Forest
Hermans Hill
The Wattles bush camp – no facilities.
Rough drive
No. 1 Bore
Netting Fence Road
Williamson's Beach camping area.
Drop tyre pressure before turning.
Nhill Rainbow Road
Lake Hindmarsh
Yanac
Jeparit
Red Gum Swamp
Yanac Swamp
River
Peechember Swamp
Nhill Jeparit Road
Wimmera
Nhill
WESTERN HIGHWAY
WESTERN HIGHWAY
0 2.5 5 Kilometres
N S E W NE NW SE SW

SOUTH WYPERFELD

Old bore equipment on Chinaman Well Track

Follow the single lane bitumen west from the bridge over **Outlet Creek** to trace a corridor of yellow gum bushland within the **Birdcage Flora and Fauna Reserve**, where wildflowers and rare butterflies may be seen. A camping area at **Williamsons Beach** marks an intersection and the north heading track of **Amy Johnson Highway**, before you again reach cropping country and **Netting Fence Road** heading west.

Turn right at this junction and follow the gravel past a couple of sidetracks for 9.9 kilometres to signposted "**Hermans Hill**" (short drive then 300 metre walk to trig point with subsequent views over the **Big Desert State Forest** and broad acres of cropping country). Drop the pressures in your tyres somewhere around here in preparation for the soft sand to come. Try something like 20 psi (138kPa) to start with, but you may have to go lower if it is especially dry and the sand more powdery.

Clumps of mallee eucalypt close in as you reach a junction 2.6 kilometres beyond the Hermans Hill turn off. Turn right here onto the soft sand of **Chinaman Well Track**, signposted "**Chinamans Well** 15.5 kilometres", to reach **No 1 Bore** 1 kilometre later. An old windmill and tank together with rusting disc plough and other implements mark the site of early pastoral activity.

Follow the low growing scrub over minor dunes to **No 2 Bore** some 4.7 bouncing kilometres later. Again windmill components and an old water tank litter the ground next to a shallow soak. A sequence of boggy patches and roller coaster undulations continue past the boundary of **Wyperfeld NP** to a flat at **Lost Swamp**, 5.2 kilometres beyond **No 2 Bore**.

Weave around the bog holes here and keep left to reach **Chinaman Well** 6.1 kilometres later – a deep timber shored shaft that is now disused and capped with some galvanized mesh. Bush camping is possible here (no facilities), and an overgrown track heads slightly west of the well to follow an open weave wire fence on the west boundary of **Chinamans Flat.**

So keep right at the well turn off to stay on the main track, and reach the **Pella Track** junction about 2 kilometres further on. Turn right here to follow the boundary of national park for 9.5 kilometres, before turning left just prior to a gate. Follow the netting fence past broad acres of crops on the right to reach **Milmed Rock Track** 8 kilometres later. Turn left and begin a north west run for 3.2 kilometres, to reach the turn off to signposted "**Hermie Strauss's Garden**".

We will continue straight, but it is worth turning left here to visit this former desert oasis on a 4.8 kilometre return detour. The garden was once irrigated by a natural

Grain silos near Yanac.

Camped at The Wattles.

spring, but that has dried to become just moist soak between a pound-like dune system. Patersons Curse lives on here with ground covers and some native pines. An old water tank and rusting iron relics are also found on the site, while energetic visitors can climb the nearby dune for a further outlook.

Back on the main track you will follow a netting fence past the property of **Booligal** (Hermann Strauss's original pastoral run) and some impressive dunes on the left. Signposted "**Lookout Dune**" is reached 9.4 kilometres from **Hermies** turn off, where a steep 500 metre walk will reward you with commanding views over the **South Wyperfeld Wilderness Area**.

Continue to **Round Swamp** about 5 kilometres later via a potentially boggy and clay topped path. A large camping area offers shade, fireplaces, tables and toilet. The centrepiece swamp is coloured with succulent plants, and is indeed quite circular in shape. A deep timber shored well is also nearby, with a mesh capping for safety.

You will negotiate a couple of smaller dunes with some lurching corrugations on the steeper western side. Nine kilometres beyond **Round Swamp** you will arrive at **Arnold Springs** to find minor local tracks and a small clump of reeds on the left, textured with scratchings, where various animals have dug for the precious water.

As the track heads more westerly, the dunes become bigger, with one especially demanding crest found 2.2 kilometres from **Arnold Springs**. A bypass track skirts this lofty peak, so don't feel compelled to charge up the more difficult path. In fact it would pay to reassess tyre pressures or fine tune your general sand driving technique rather than just give the vehicle more throttle and risk breaking something (or worse).

You will reach **Milmed Swamp** 11.5 kilometres from **Arnold Springs** to find a lovely grassed area surrounded by red gums. **Milmed Rock** is reached 1.7 kilometres later, where a small outcrop of rock marks an otherwise unblemished sea of sandy scrub.

More dunes (some with bypasses) will continue to test the driver, while offering any passengers excellent elevated views of the **Big Desert**. Some 19 kilometres later you will arrive at **Pigeon Springs** (treed area and soak), then the main **Murrayville Road** 11 kilometres later.

Turn left here and reinflate your tyres to their usual gravel road touring pressures at some point prior to undertaking higher speeds. **The Springs Camping Area** is just 5.5 kilometres down the track and is one possibility if you want to boil the billy at the same time. (**The Springs** was used by stockmen in the 1860s to water cattle on the lengthy drove from **Kow Plains** to **Nhill Station**).

Some 10 kilometres later you will reach **Moonlight Tank** – another camp utilising old stock route water points. Indeed the **Murrayville Road** owes its very existence to pioneering graziers who drove stock along this path in the mid 1800s. A number of bores were sunk along the route in an effort to maintain its viability, although these days it is only bee keepers who use the road commercially. Road conditions are usually good even for a carefully driven 2WD, but any rain quickly affects the clay road base, putting an end to any vehicle travel – sometimes for days at a time.

Travel another 6 kilometres to **Chinaman Well Track** on the left (the other end of this 33 kilometre cross country dune drive back to **Chinaman Flat**) and further on, a lookout walk on the right. **No 2 Bore** is reached 9.4 kilometres later (another abandoned water point) and **Red Bluff Track** is found 3.2 kilometres beyond that on the right, with a lookout track to the left.

Continue south past an old galvanized tank at **Wagon Flat** to reach sealed road 1 kilometre prior to **Broken Bucket Camp**. A large dam, tank and windmill mark this popular camp where basic facilities are provided. The bitumen continues past **Netting Fence Track** and broad acre cropping to **Yanac**, some 24 kilometres later. No services are available here, so continue the sealed run into **Nhill**, 35 kilometres away.

Rural mail boxes near Yanac.

TRACK 27 LITTLE DESERT

WESTERN VICTORIA

Many tracks follow a straight path through the sand ridges.

With your UHF set on scan, you will find the ***Little Desert*** *buzzing with chatter. 4WDers plying the numerous sandy tracks that criss cross this mallee scrubland may initially be puzzled with its apparent popularity, until they realise that most of the traffic is simply passing by via the nearby* ***Western Highway;*** *one of Victoria's busiest arterials. There is a strange irony in battling soft sand in low range, while listening to passing truckies warn of any "flash for cash" speed cameras.*

Fortunately the 4WD track network across the ***Little Desert*** *encourages a slower outlook, and with your radio switched off (or perhaps set to a convoy channel), it is possible to find solitude amongst this superb scrub country. Fringed by farmland, the national park is split into three sections by two bitumen roads.*

A desert in name only, the ***Little Desert*** *averages about 400 mm of rain annually, making it feel relatively lush compared to the more arid Central Australian regions. Its* ***Eastern Block*** *typifies this sense of fertility with stately River Red Gums lining the* ***Wimmera River*** *– although recent droughts have certainly tested their stamina. The* ***Central Block*** *features swamps and a couple of lookouts, while the lesser visited* ***Western Block*** *backs up to the South Australian border.*

We begin the trek in **Dimboola**; a typical western district town with a wide main street, and facades that date from perhaps more prosperous days. Head west from the town centre passing under the iconic **Little Desert** gateway arch to cross the **Wimmera River** at a new bridge. Turn left at the tee intersection and follow the main road past several side tracks and an olive grove onto gravel road.

You will reach **Horseshoe Bend** about 7 kilometres from the bridge, and **Ackle Bend** about 1 kilometre later. These camping areas are popular during holiday periods, but offer peaceful river outlooks at other times of the year. **Horseshoe** and **Ackle Bends** are accessible to conventional vehicles, but also mark the beginning of the 4WD only track system.

The **Little Desert**'s other campground option is found near an old eucalyptus distillery site, south of **Kiata** on the **Western Highway**. Again 2WD vehicles can reach the camp, but unsurfaced sand trails head from there into the **Eastern Block**. All of the park's defined camps are provided with fireplaces, tables and toilets and are big enough to accommodate larger groups. A fee is payable by overnight campers at these sites, but self contained bush camping is permitted in the **Central** and **Western Blocks** at no cost.

Follow the **Wimmera River** south along **River Track** through a potentially closed gate and via a stretch of braided tracks. These various routes have evolved because of regular river flooding and recreational use of the river, but they all merge at **One Tree Hill Track**, some 2 kilometres from **Ackle Bend**.

Turn right at this junction, but prior to the turn find somewhere to pull over and drop your tyre pressures to somewhere around 20psi (138 kPa). Lower tyre pressures together with selection of 4WD is essential to deal with the numerous patches of soft sand that will come.

Driving the sand tracks is fun, though

BASIC CHECK LIST . . .

- ☑ Soft Roaders
- ☑ Trailers with Care
- ☑ Good Clearance Needed
- ☑ Road Tyres
- ☑ Avoid Wet Weather

TRACK SNAPSHOT

TOUR ROUTE
Dimboola to Kaniva via the Little Desert NP.

DURATION AND DISTANCE
This 170 kilometre tour can be done in one day, but better spread over two or more.

TRACK DETAILS
Sandy tracks throughout most of the park, with some clay pans and minor dunes. OK for most soft roaders and trailers not a problem.

WHEN TO GO
Spring is peak season with wildflowers aplenty, but the other months are suitable providing it is not too hot or too wet – the clay pans and other bogholes are nasty when weather affected, and gates close off sections of McDonalds Highway.

CAMPING
Excellent camping at Horseshoe and Ackle Bends (fees apply) with bush camps at Stans Camp, Redgum Swamp, and Broughtons Waterhole. Caravan park at Dimboola and Kaniva.

FUEL AND SUPPLIES
Dimboola and Kaniva have most services that you need.

MAPS
Meridian Productions: Victoria's Deserts.

OTHER INFORMATION
There are plenty of other tracks within the national park, and those with time to spare can check out the other attractions. The Little Desert Lodge near the north west corner of the eastern block is a malleefowl sanctuary and worth visiting if you have time.

The mallee fowl is only rarely seen in the wild here now

Broughtons Waterhole is a nice place to stop

fairly routine and with no dunes to speak of. Soft roaders are quite suitable for these conditions and grabbing low range will probably only come in useful if you stop on one of the powdery corners. Further into the park, you may come across some sections where old car tyres have been embedded into the sand as a traction aid.

Signage is also surprisingly comprehensive right across the desert, with only short cut tracks and the border tracks missing out. In the latter case it is obvious where you are, as cleared farmland backs right onto a netting fence defining the national park boundary.

Pass **Stringybark Track** on the right to reach the next tee intersection on **Eagle Swamp Track**, 4.1 kilometres from **River Track**. Turn left at the junction with **One Tree Hill** directly ahead, and follow the sandy furrows to a minor dune 2 kilometres later. The track splits for this dune (as it will for other dunes across the **Little Desert**) so keep left to reach a clay pan on the right, 1.6 kilometres from the dune.

Mostly open country here helps **Mount Arapiles** to dominate the skyline as you reach a clump of trees fringing **Eagle Swamp** 2.2 kilometres from the clay pan. A parking area allows walkers to take a closer look at the swamp, but don't be tempted to drive onto the lake as a bogging is all but inevitable and the scars can last for years.

McCabes Hut Track is reached at a tee 200 metres later, where you turn right (left option heads to the **Wimmera River** and **Ellis Crossing**). Proceed past elevated views of **Eagle Swamp** and pass **Dry Well Track** on the right (MVO). Begin a more north westerly route through scrub, with lurching and corrugated sections especially savage near tree roots.

You will reach **Mallee Dam** about 9 kilometres from **Eagle Swamp** where you turn left onto **Mallee Track**. The vegetation thickens up now as if on cue, as you pass taller trees and potentially boggy sections of clay. An impressive stand of grass trees flags the approaching tee intersection of **Dahlenburgs Mill Track**.

Turn left here onto **Dahlenburgs Mill**

Fire is a natural occurrence in the Little Desert.

LITTLE DESERT

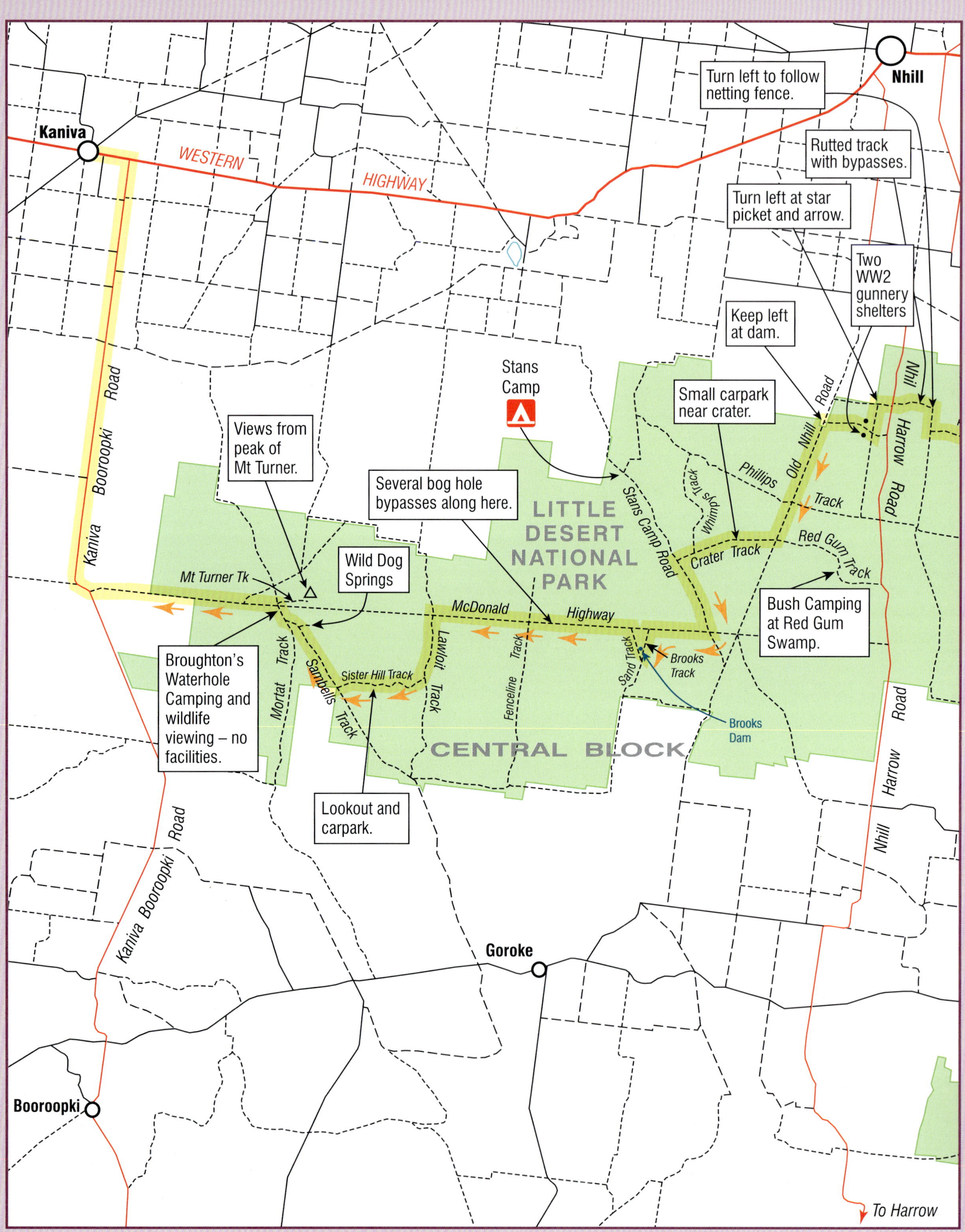

WESTERN HIGHWAY
Kiata Campsite
Wimmera River
Dimboola
WESTERN HIGHWAY
Track
Two Dams
Mathews Track
EASTERN BLOCK
Horse Shoe Bend Campsite
Mallee Dam
Dry Well Track
Track
Track
One Tree Hill
Swamp
Stringybark
River Track
Wail
Ackle Bend Campsite
Dahlenburgs Mill Track
Link Track
Salt Lake
Mallee Track
McCabes Hut Track
Eagle
One Tree Hill Track
Several parallel paths along river.
Windmill Site – car park.
Dahlenburgs
LITTLE DESERT NATIONAL PARK
Mill Track
Small dunes along here.
HIGHWAY
LITTLE DESERT NATIONAL PARK
Salt Lake Track
Eagle Swamp
Ellis Crossing
Lower tyre pressure before turning onto One Tree Hill Track.
Lears Well
Southern Break Track
West Wail Flora & Fauna Reserve
River
Good views of Mt Arapiles from here.
Olivers Lake
Wimmera
Veer right away from netting fence here.
Lake Wyn Wyn
Nurcoung Flora Reserve
Lake Natimuk
Mitre Dam
Natimuk
Mt Arapiles
Lake Tooan
Mt Arapiles Tooan State Park
WIMMERA HIGHWAY
Mt Arapiles Tooan State Park
N
NW
NE
W
E
SW
SE
S
0
2.5
5
Kilometres

Little Desert fenceline track.

Track to follow an old fence line past a MVO track (route of the lengthy **Desert Discovery Walk**) to a prominent dune 4.1 kilometres later. Excellent views take in the farmland of **Natimuk** and the increasing bulk of **Mount Arapiles**.

You will reach a triangulated intersection on the boundary of national park 7.2 kilometres from the **Mallee Track** turn off. Turn right here and follow **Southern Break** along a netting fence on your left, with sheep grazing and some cropping making use of the relatively light and infertile soils. Veer right 3.4 kilometres later (don't follow the boundary fenceline south) along a track surfaced with buckshot.

Wildlife is routinely seen in the open areas; kangaroos and emus are numerous, while eagles and some smaller birds are also common. Unfortunately the malleefowl is rarely spotted in the wild, even though it was the reason for this park's establishment back in 1955. Habitat shrinkage and years of predation by foxes and feral cats, have decimated the attractive mound building bird, to the point where a fenced off sanctuary has been built nearby.

You will reach another triangulated tee intersection 3.6 kilometres from the last, where you turn right onto **Salt Lake Track**. Head north passing **Lears Well** on the left and a clay pan on the right 600 metres later. Sections of track follow parallel paths to the **Little Desert**'s largest salt lake, 10.8 kilometres from the last turn.

A carpark on the right allows walkers to access the lake edge. This shallow pan is a great place to see animal tracks embossed into the muddy surface, as emus and kangaroos move about the park. The lake's surface is usually dry and coloured with leeching mineral, but at the time of our most recent visit some local showers had partially filled the basin with water, creating an enormous mirror to reflect the cloud formations. Recent bushfires had also caused an ash residue to collect on the lake, giving it a greyer than usual appearance.

Turn left 300 metres beyond **Salt Lake** onto **Dahlenburgs Mill Track**, veering left away from **Mathews Track** 4 kilometres later. You will reach the windmill site 1.3 kilometres further on, where a small parking area allows you to stop and contemplate the area's grazing history. Much of the **Little Desert** was earmarked for agriculture in the 1950s, and the vestiges of those pioneering developments are still found across the **Eastern** and **Central Blocks** in particular.

Several windmills were assembled to supplement the meagre surface water run off, with the now bladeless **Dahlenburgs Mill**

The Wimmera River is fringed with lovely red gum forest

Salt Lake is covered with animal tracks.

standing testament to those early works. While the metal tank has succumbed to the ravages of time, **Dahlenburgs** still features some original troughing, and makes an interesting stop over within the **Eastern Block**.

Beyond the windmill site you will pass **Link Track** (MVO) and negotiate some rough trail past **Two Dams Track** to a tee intersection at private property. Turn right and follow the netting fence for 1.1 kilometres, then turn left to continue following the fence into some rutted terrain. Pick your way past wet and boggy patches linked with bypasses to the sealed **Nhill – Harrow Road** 2 kilometres later.

Turn right for 20 metres, then swing left again to follow fenceline on the boundary of national park. Turn left 800 metres later at an unsignposted track marked with a star picket and timber arrow pointing the way. Follow the cleared land for 1.5 kilometres, turning right onto better road.

You will reach an old concrete bunker on the right 400 metres later, with another bunker a little further away on the left. These structures were used as gunnery shelters during WW2, but have now deteriorated with flaking render and some graffiti.

Beyond the bunkers you will reach a dam, where you keep left at a triangulated intersection, to reach the **Old Nhill Road**. Head south through a sea of khaki scrub to cross **Phillips Track** and reach **Crater Track** on the right. We will turn right here with **Red Gum Track** branching to the left (access to bush camping on **Red Gum Swamp**).

Follow **Crater Track** to a small carpark 1.1 kilometres later adjacent to a crater mound. It is difficult to make out the crater rim from the track, but an indistinct path brings you to a viewpoint overlooking the now vegetated formation which has a diameter of about 800 metres.

A winding section of track slows progress past **Whimpys Track** on the right and **Stans Camp Road**, 1.4 kilometres beyond that. We will turn left here, but interested visitors could head north to check out the pioneering outstation. (**Stan's Camp** dates back to the 1850s when sheep were first pushed into some pretty inhospitable grassland. A pile of ripple iron and some structural timbers are all that remain of the basic hut, while the original stock route was subsequently developed into a vehicular track that is still in use today).

Heading south from **Crater Track**, you will reach **McDonald Highway** and the turn right onto its straight as a die route crossing the entire **Central Block**. Don't let the highway title conjure up visions of arm chair comfort however – in true desert road building tradition (think **Gunbarrel Road Construction Party**) this highway is rough, corrugated and basically consists of two wheel furrows in the sand.

Turn left at **Brooks Track** 3 kilometres later to reach **Brooks Dam**. Permanent water and few visitors have encouraged a variety of birds to this lovely treed area. Over 220 species have been sighted in this national park, with the **Little Desert** being the northernmost refuge for some species, and the southernmost limit for others.

Beyond the dam, turn hard right onto **Sand Road** and make your return to **McDonald Highway**. Turn left again onto some rutted sections of track. Bog hole bypasses (some permanent) require you to actually turn the steering wheel occasionally, instead of merely using it as toe compensation, as lateral lurching bounces the vehicle from furrow to furrow.

Pass **Fenceline Track** (MVO) and turn left onto **Lawloit Track** 5 kilometres later. Turn right onto **Sister Hills Track** 3 kilometres further on, to reach a small carpark on the right, some 2.2 kilometres later. A short but steep walk crests the dune for extensive views.

Continue beyond grass tree stands to a tee intersection on **Sambells Track**, where you turn right. Drive past the turn off to **Wild Dog Springs** (often dry), to reach an intersection on **Mortat Track**. Veer right here to reach **Broughton's Waterhole** 500 metres later.

It was **Richard Broughton** who first ran sheep in this region in the mid 1800s, with waterholes such as this being a vital resource. Camping is superb near the redgum fringed waterhole, and fireplaces together with tables and chairs allow quiet visitors to perhaps catch a glimpse of wildlife coming in for a drink.

Mount Turner Track originates just a stone's throw from **Broughton's**, with the dead end trail finishing at a small carpark several kilometres in. Walkers can then follow an informal 100 metre path to a gnarly sandstone outcrop. While the peak offers only modest elevation, it is still possible to take in the southern country and look back over **Wild Dog Springs** and **Sister Hills**.

Continue west from **Broughton's Waterhole** to pass two sets of potentially closed gates, before reaching the sealed **Kaniva – Booroopki Road**. Find a place to reinflate your tyres, and follow the bitumen for 21 kilometres into **Kaniva**.

TRACK 28

GRAMPIANS/GARIWERD

WESTERN VICTORIA

This range country is impressive from the many lookouts

BASIC CHECK LIST . . .

- ☑ Soft Roaders
- ☑ Trailers with Care
- ☑ Road Tyres
- ☑ Avoid Wet Weather

TRACK SNAPSHOT

TOUR ROUTE
Halls Gap and return via tracks within Grampians / Gariwerd NP.

DURATION AND DISTANCE
You will need at least a couple of days to follow the 250 kilometre trek if you wish to undertake some of the walks.

TRACK DETAILS
Routine unsealed roads in the main, with some rough patches and sandy sections. Suitable for all 4WDs and trailers OK.

WHEN TO GO
Autumn and Spring are peak seasons in the Grampians, although seasonal track closures limit access along this trek to between November and the beginning of June. Summer is OK for touring as long as it is not a day of extreme fire danger.

CAMPING
Numerous bush camps with basic facilities are found across the national park (fees apply and prebooking required at peak times). Some restrictions for generators.

FUEL AND SUPPLIES
Halls Gap

MAPS
Spatial Vision: Grampians.

OTHER INFORMATION
The Grampians is a busy destination over the warmer months. If you are looking for a quieter camp, try some of the bush offerings at Rocklands Reservoir, just west of the national park.

*If the **Great Dividing Range** begins in Queensland and finishes in **Victoria**, then it reaches the end with a shout. The **Grampians/ Gariwerd** mark the final eruption of geology literally stamping a dot under Australia's north–south orientated exclamation mark, with sandstone walls bursting more than a kilometre skyward. Its form is a complex mix of ranges, waterways and fascinating rock formations.*

Not to be forgotten, its flora and fauna are found in abundance; these treasures enrich the landscape, and are sometimes the sole reason people give for visiting this western district national park. Ancient Aboriginal artwork and other links to Country are an integral feature too, while walking tracks criss cross the entire area.

This tour follows good roads and tracks in the main on a meandering route into valleys and over the ranges. Camping enthusiasts are well catered for, while bushwalkers and photographers will not be disappointed, and even fishers could leave here with a smile on their face.

We begin in **Halls Gap**, heading west on **Mount Victory Road** to climb 2.5 kilometres to the **Wonderland Range** turn off (carpark and trail head for several bushwalks). Keep right at the junction to pass **Silverband Road** on the left 2.7 kilometres later (access to waterfall and other **Wonderland Range** walks).

Continue west past the **Glenelg River Road** 3.2 kilometres further on, and reach the **Mount Difficult Road** 1.3 kilometres after that. Turn right here to pass **Old Mill Road** and reach **Boroka Lookout** at a carpark. A 50 metre stroll from here offers expansive views over **Mounts William** and **Rosea**, with the dissected valley framing **Lake Bellfield** through native pine and grass trees.

Return to the main road and turn right at **Mount Victory Gap** to pass the prominent peak and reach a turn off to **Reids Lookout** on the left, 1.9 kilometres later. Turn left here for a short distance to reach a carpark and lookout taking in **Lake Wartook** to the north and the imposing **Serra** and **Victoria Ranges** to the south. A walking track to **The Balconies** begins here as well.

Return to the **Mount Victory Road** and swing left to wind your way down the range, passing **Taylors Track**, to reach **Rose Creek Road** 4 kilometres from the lookout. (We will turn left here, but those who continue

Many birds inhabit the Grampians / Gariwerd including this rainbow lorikeet

for a further 2 kilometres will reach the **Lake Wartook** turn off and **MacKenzie Falls** access road 1 kilometre beyond that. Visitors can then follow a short but steep walking track that descends to the mist blown base of the falls where mosses and delicate ferns thrive).

Return to **Rose Creek Road** and turn west onto gravel to pass **Taylors Track** and **Zumsteins Track** in quick succession. **Wallaby** Rocks Track is reached 4.9 kilometres from the turn off, where you turn right onto the rougher road. A corridor of bracken and grass trees funnel you to an informal lookout on the right 3.2 kilometres later (a small carpark is found 100 metres off the track). Some burnt bushland and uneven sections slow progress as you meander past waterways to a helipad 2.5 kilometres beyond the lookout. **Wallaby Rocks** leap out from the landscape here, with excellent views to the west.

Follow a gully delineating **Sheet of Water Creek** to descend past a minor turn off on the right (informal lookout). Erosion control mounds and rough patches continue past **Lauders Track** on the left as you appreciate the dominant bluffs and rock formations. Slow down for some rocky sections and the lush headwaters of **Sheet of Water Creek** to reach a tee intersection on **Asses Ears Road**. Keep left here to cross open grassland, keeping straight past **Schmidts Road** on the right.

Trace the boundary of national park past an 1878 shepherds grave with rural views to the west, to reach **Geranium Springs Road** and its prominent rocky knoll 2.2 kilometres from the **Schmidts Road** turn off. Some 400 metres later you will arrive at **Brim Springs** – a picnic area with fireplace and table. With permanent water, the site is significant to the local Aboriginal groups, but it also became home to European settlers. A log cabin was built here in the 1840s using local timbers and surrounded by ornamental garden. Although the dwelling no longer stands, seeds from the original scented geraniums have naturalised here, with a small plot still growing within a fenced enclosure.

Continue south on **Asses Ears Road** for 2.5 kilometres, keeping left at **Glen Isla Crossing Road**. Drive parallel to the **Glenelg River** with great views through fire damaged trees to the tilted slab like structure of the **Victoria Range** with its veins of red sandstone. You will reach **Lodge Hill Road** at a tee intersection 3.5 kilometres later at **Victoria Gap.**

Turn right here (signposted **Red Rock Road**) to cross the **Glenelg River Bridge** and keep left at the **Glen Isla Crossing Road** junction 800 metres later. Follow **Red Rock Road** for just a few hundred metres to the signposted turn off "**Red Rock Picnic Ground**" on your right. We will keep left at this junction to continue the trek, but for now turn right to reach the picnic ground 1.1 kilometres later.

A defined carpark with fireplace and table are the only facilities, but this is a great spot for bird and wildlife viewing. The picturesque swamp nearby is fringed with red gum and marshy reeds, under a backgound of orange sandstone slabs. You can stroll around the wetland, but it is rather soft under foot in places.

Return to **Red Rock Road** and turn south through some potentially boggy country to pass **Mathews Track** on the left, with native pines framing the prominent formation of Red Rock. You will cross **Muline Creek** 4.5 kilometres beyond **Mathews Track** (parking area at crossing) to reach **Red Rock Creek** 2.2 kilometres after that.

Cross the bridge and drive for 2 kilometres before turning left onto **Billywing Road**, to follow a corrugated path to **Harrops Track** 700 metres later. Follow **Harrop Track** over a single lane bridge to arrive at the **Goat Track** turn off 400 metres further on. We will continue directly ahead here, but **Buandik Camp** is found 800 metres along **Goat Track** and is a worthwhile diversion. The large camp on **Cultivation Creek** has basic facilities, but bollards restrict the camping to walk in arrangements. Several walks originate here,

Most tracks are easily driven on this trek

GRAMPIANS/GARIWERD

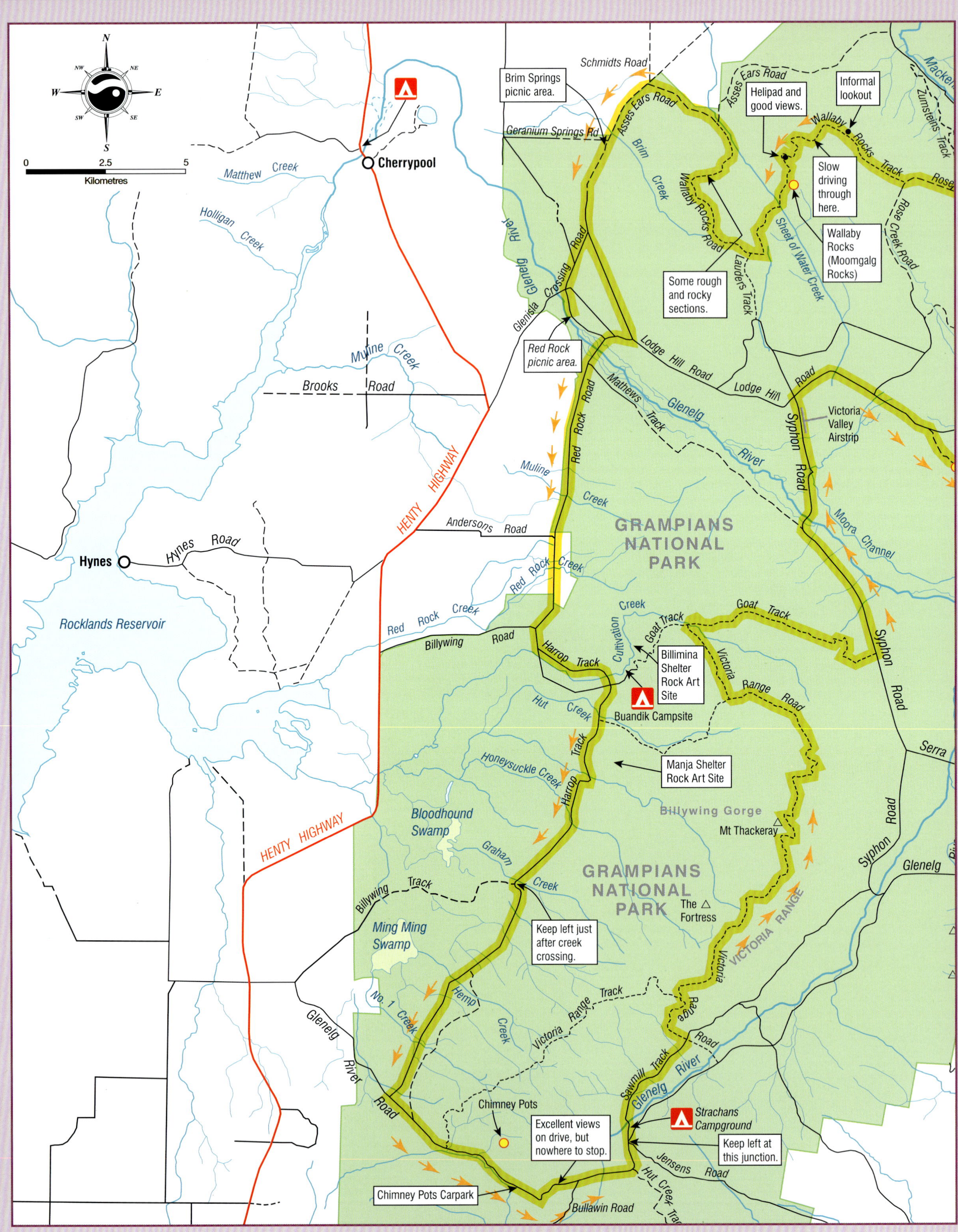

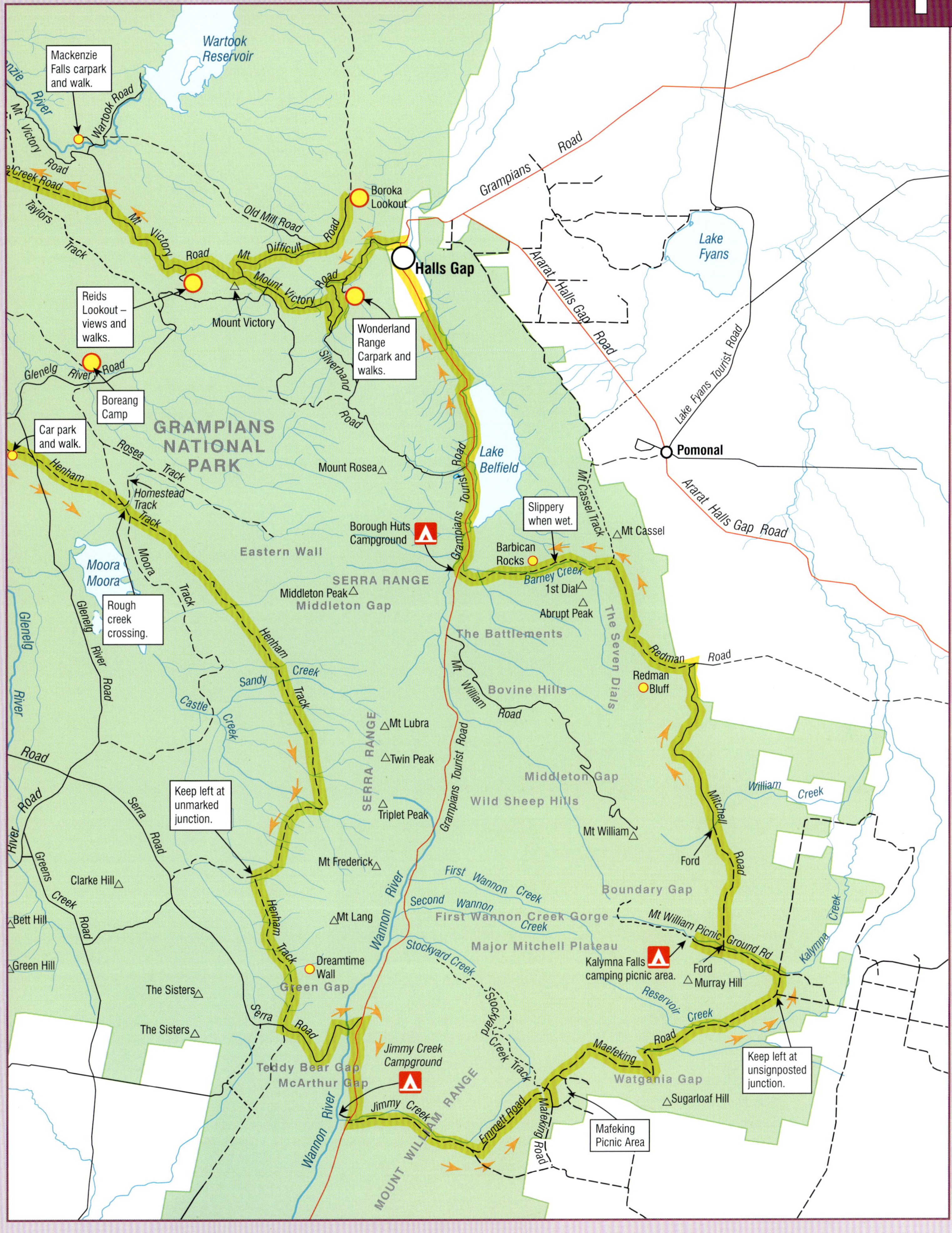
Wartook Reservoir
Mackenzie Falls carpark and walk.
Wartook Road
Mt Victory Road
Boroka Lookout
Old Mill Road
Mt Difficult Road
Halls Gap
Grampians Road
Lake Fyans
Ararat Halls Gap Road
Lake Fyans Tourist Road
Pomonal
Taylors Track
Reids Lookout – views and walks.
Mount Victory
Mount Victory Road
Wonderland Range Carpark and walks.
Silverband Road
Glenelg River Road
Boreang Camp
GRAMPIANS NATIONAL PARK
Car park and walk.
Rosea Track
Mount Rosea
Lake Belfield
Grampians Tourist Road
Mt Cassel Track
Henham Track
Homestead Track
Borough Huts Campground
Slippery when wet.
Mt Cassel
Barbican Rocks
Eastern Wall
Moora Moora
Moora Track
SERRA RANGE
Barney Creek
Middleton Peak
Middleton Gap
1st Dial
Abrupt Peak
Rough creek crossing.
The Seven Dials
The Battlements
Redman Road
Redman Bluff
Glenelg River
Sandy Creek
Castle Creek
Mt William Road
Bovine Hills
Mt Lubra
Twin Peak
Middleton Gap
Wild Sheep Hills
William Creek
Keep left at unmarked junction.
Serra Road
Triplet Peak
Mitchell Road
Mt William
Ford
Mt Frederick
Clarke Hill
Greens Creek Road
First Wannon Creek
Second Wannon Creek
Boundary Gap
Bett Hill
Mt Lang
First Wannon Creek Gorge
Mt William Picnic Ground Rd
Major Mitchell Plateau
Kalymna Falls camping picnic area.
Kalymna Creek
Stockyard Creek
Dreamtime Wall
Green Gap
Green Hill
Murray Hill
The Sisters
Reservoir Creek
Serra Road
Wannon River
Stockyard Creek Track
Jimmy Creek Campground
Maefeking Road
Watgania Gap
Sugarloaf Hill
Keep left at unsignposted junction.
Teddy Bear Gap
McArthur Gap
Jimmy Creek
MOUNT WILLIAM RANGE
Emmett Road
Mafeking Road
Mafeking Picnic Area

with the **Billimina Shelter Rock Art Site** being a popular destination.

Continue south on **Harrop Track** to cross **Hut Creek** and reach the **Manja Shelter Rock Art Site** carpark 500 metres later (walk to Aboriginal art site). Cross the sandy banks of **Honeysuckle Creek** to reach **Graham Creek**, keeping left at the **Billywing Track** junction, just past the ford. You pass other waterways draining into **Ming Ming Swamp**, with **Hemp Creek** and **No 1 Creek** requiring a slow approach. You will reach a tee intersection on the **Glenelg River Road** where you turn left onto better road.

Drive under the shadow of a sheer rock face on the left to pass **Chimney Gap** and reach a carpark at the **Chimney Pots** 4.9 kilometres from **Harrop Track** (a steep and exposed walking track that loops around this prominent feature in the Victoria Range). One kilometre beyond the carpark you will be greeted by sweeping views of the entire valley, however there is nowhere to park, so just enjoy the outlook as you head east. Pass **Bullawin Road** on the right, then **Hut Creek Track** a couple of kilometres later, to arrive at **Jensons Road** 800 metres beyond that.

Turn left at this junction to follow **Sawmill Track** to **Strachans Campground** 400 metres later. Basic facilities surround an old chimney here, with camping opportunities beyond the bollards. Wood splitters worked in the **Victoria Valley** near here from the 1870s. Redgum was harvested and cut in the sawmills throughout the ranges. Felled trees would be dragged by horse or bullock team to the mill site. Other timber varieties were milled and used for house building or goldfield tunnel props.

Head past the camp and turn left through a SCG onto **Victoria Range Road** 3.4 kilometres later.

Erosion control mounds punctuate the climb past dense tree fern and sheets of stacked rock. Broken views of **The Fortress** mark the abrupt scramble to **Mount Thackeray** (no roadside view, but parking area and demanding walk) about 9 kilometres into **Victoria Range Road**.

MacKenzie Falls are well worth the walk

Aboriginal artwork is seen at several sites across the Grampians / Gariwerd

You begin a descent at a clearing 1.4 kilometres later, to ramp down around tight bends and past house sized blocks of rock. Broken views continue to a tee intersection on **Goat Track** 10 kilometres later.

Turn right here to maintain the descent into the **Glenelg Valley** with monolithic rocks glistening in the distance. You will reach a tee intersection on **Syphon Road** and turn left onto better road, crossing the **Glenelg River** 5 kilometres later.

Remain on **Syphon Road** to cross the **Moora Channel** and pass an airstrip on the right. You reach **Lodge Road** and turn right, to pass **Rose Creek Road** on the left 2.9 kilometres later. Keep straight over a causeway to reach **Henhams Track** 2.2 kilometres later, where you will turn right (Those who keep straight for 4 kilometres will reach **Boreang Camp** to find basic facilities and walks).

Follow **Henham Track** past a walk trail head to cross the **Glenelg River Road** 2 kilometres later. Remain on **Henham Track** to drive through a SCG and past several intersecting tracks. Some sandy sections may require a tyre pressure reduction if it is warm and the sand becomes powdery, especially around the rough creek crossing near **Homestead Track**.

You will pass **Moora Track** on the right to deal with a few more slow creek crossings, where water shed from the **Serra Range** flows into **Cattle Creek**. You will reach an unsignposted corner some 14.8 kilometres from the **Moora Track** junction, where you keep left. Follow **Henham Track** past the **Dreamtime Wall** (rock climbing enthusiasts only) to **Green Gap** and the main **Serra Road**. Turn left here to climb over **Teddy Bear Gap** and drop down past a fireline track to the sealed **Grampians Tourist Road**.

Turn hard right at this junction and drive south to the **Jimmy Creek Campground**, for walks and basic facilities in a pleasant setting on the **Wannan River**. Continue south from the camp to cross **Jimmy Creek** and follow the waterway east on a gravel climb into the **Mount William Range**, to reach **Emmett Road** on the left.

Turn left here to reach an intersection on **Mafeking Road** where it intersects with **Stockyard Track**. We will keep straight here, but for now turn right onto **Mafeking Road** to reach the signposted "**Mafeking Picnic Area**" turn off on your left. A 700 metre detour reaches a carpark and information board detailing the history of **Mafeking** as **Victoria**'s last gold rush. The mining activity around 1900 saw alluvial and reef workings with a town that bustled for 20 years before being reduced to ash following a 1960 bushfire. A stone cairn and obelisk mark the site, with toilet, table and 2 kilometres of walking trail.

Return to **Emmett Road** and turn right to continue north east along **Mafeking Road**. Make a descent past the views of **Watgania Gap** to **Murray Hill** on the left, with a concrete bridge spanning the rocks of **Reservoir Creek**. Keep left to follow the fenceline 10 kilometres beyond **Mafeking** at an unsignposted junction, before turning left onto **Mount William Picnic Ground Road**. Follow this road for 2.4 kilometres to the **Mitchell Road** junction and turn right here. (**Picnic Ground Road** continues west for 1.1 kilometres to a picnic and camping area near the delightful **Kalymna Falls** and is well worth the detour).

Follow **Mitchell Road** over **Kalymna Creek** and another causeway over **William Creek** 4 kilometres later. Good views of **Redman Bluff** rise from the **Mount William Range** now as you reach **Redman Road** 10 kilometres beyond **Mitchell Road**.

Turn left to follow a gash in the landscape with fern gullies and mature trees marking the winding climb. You will reach **Mount Cassel Track** on the right (rugged link track to **Pomonal**), 5 kilometres beyond **Mitchell Road**, where you swing west over a floodway, and beneath the sandstone spires defining **Mount Cassel**. The track surface here would be slippery if wet, as you follow **Barney Creek** past **Barbican Rocks**.

Several causeways punctuate the slow descent before you reach the sealed **Grampians Tourist Road** at **Borough Huts Campground** (large camping area with basic facilities and walk in camping). Turn right to pass **Lake Bellfield** with its picnic area and toilets, reaching **Halls Gap** 8 kilometres later.

A chimney is all that remains of a timber cutters camp at Strachans Campground

Chapter 4
EAST GIPPSLAND

◀ *Jungle at Errinundra Saddle.*

TRACK 29 CROAJINGOLONG

EAST GIPPSLAND

Fallen trees are one hazard on the minor tracks

*The **Cann, Thurra, Mueller** and **Wingan Rivers** disect **Croajingolong NP** on their sometimes boisterous journey into **Bass Strait**. Their riverine forests are a highway of jungle and wildlife, while their inlets and wild coastline are popular with boaters and fishers.*

*This tour follows a lovely coastal run from the **Cann River** township to **Genoa**, taking in all four waterways on a relatively easy amble near the eastern tip of **Victoria**. Camping is popular at the designated national park sites, but there are quieter options within the state forest. Fishing and bush camping opportunities are numerous, while bush lovers will find plenty of remote coastline.*

The journey begins by heading south from **Cann River**, following the **Tamboon Road** through residential area toward the coast. An old meathouse marks the town limits, with an early saw mill and relics laying witness to this town's heritage. Native forest harvested in 2012 is slowly returning, as you pass **Gauge Track** and **Cemetery Track**.

Bass Track is reached 5.5 kilometres from **Cann River** with a parking area located at this junction. Turn right onto wide gravel here, to reach a quarry 900 metres later. Keep left at the quarry site onto a much narrower track delineated with paper daisies. Veer right one kilometre later at an old track on the left (there is a painted indicator in a prominent tree).

A rough descent with scoured ruts and uneven sections is coloured with native flag iris and Australian bluebells. The track finishes at a dead end, some 4.7 kilometres from the **Tamboon Road**, where a small group could set up a basic bush camp. A short but steep walk leads to the **Cann River** from here, with lovely sandy waterholes and a scenic creek confluence defining the waterway. It is possible to follow the river at low water levels both downsteam and upstream – with the latter option reaching a rocky choke and a series of falls.

Inky waters on the Thurra River.

BASIC CHECK LIST . . .

- ☑ Trailers with Care
- ☑ Water Crossings
- ☑ Good Clearance Needed
- ☑ Road Tyres
- ☑ Avoid Wet Weather

TRACK SNAPSHOT

TOUR ROUTE

Cann River to Genoa via Croajingolong NP.

DURATION AND DISTANCE

Allow two or three days for the 180 kilometre journey to allow sufficient time to look around.

TRACK DETAILS

Routine forestry tracks and roads with some rough sections. Low range and reasonable clearances needed for the Mueller River fording.

WHEN TO GO

Seasonal road closures limit travel to the warmer period between November and June. Holiday times are quite busy on the coast. Avoid the trek in very wet weather, when the Mueller River can rise to an unfordable level.

CAMPING

Lovely camping at designated sites on the Thurra and Mueller Inlets. Privately managed bookings at Point Hicks Lighthouse ph 03 5158 4268 or www.pointhicks.com.au Other national park camping at Wingan Inlet and Peachtree Creek ph Parks Victoria 13 1963. A ballot may be necessary for the above camps over the peak summer and Easter holidays. Other options at Choof Choof, and bush camping on the Cann River at Bass Track and the Wingan River on Link Road.

FUEL AND SUPPLIES

Cann River will cater for most needs, with Mallacoota being the next major town. Genoa has only a hotel – no other services.

MAPS

Rooftops: Cape Conran – Wingan Inlet

OTHER INFORMATION

Carry plenty of drinking water through Croajingolong as the rivers can be brackish for some distance away from the ocean, and stock graze upstream. Treat all river water before drinking.

Return to the **Tamboon Road** and turn right to reach the boundary of **Lower Cann River Conservation Reserve** and a single lane bridge over **Reedy Creek**. This wetland is a lush introduction to **East Gippsland**, with a small parking area found on the right, just over the bridge.

Continue south beyond **Bedford Track** to another bridge and wetland at **Granite Creek** to reach **Thurra Road** on the left. Keep straight past a lovely clump of grasstrees to **Broome Track** on the right. Thick coastal vegetation here includes banksia, bracken and various eucalypts.

Tamboon Road deteriorates to gravel at the **Point Hicks Road** junction 800 metres later, where you keep right toward signposted **Furnell Landing**. Follow a corrugated descent past a timber harvesting area with great views to coastal range country.

You will reach **Choof Choof Track** on the right 5.1 kilometres from the last junction. Turn right here for a rough and narrow track leading to a backwater on the **Cann River**. There is superb camping here in **Tamboon State Forest** with an elevated clearing and basic facilities, together with easy water access and landing for small boats.

Visitors can walk from here to the more popular area at **Furnell** via the river bank, or throw a line in locally. Commercial fishing ceased at **Tamboon Inlet** in 2001, but for almost 100 years prior it was a bustling landing – indeed the name **Choof Choof** arose from the exhaust sound of many fishing

The Dunes at Thurra River.

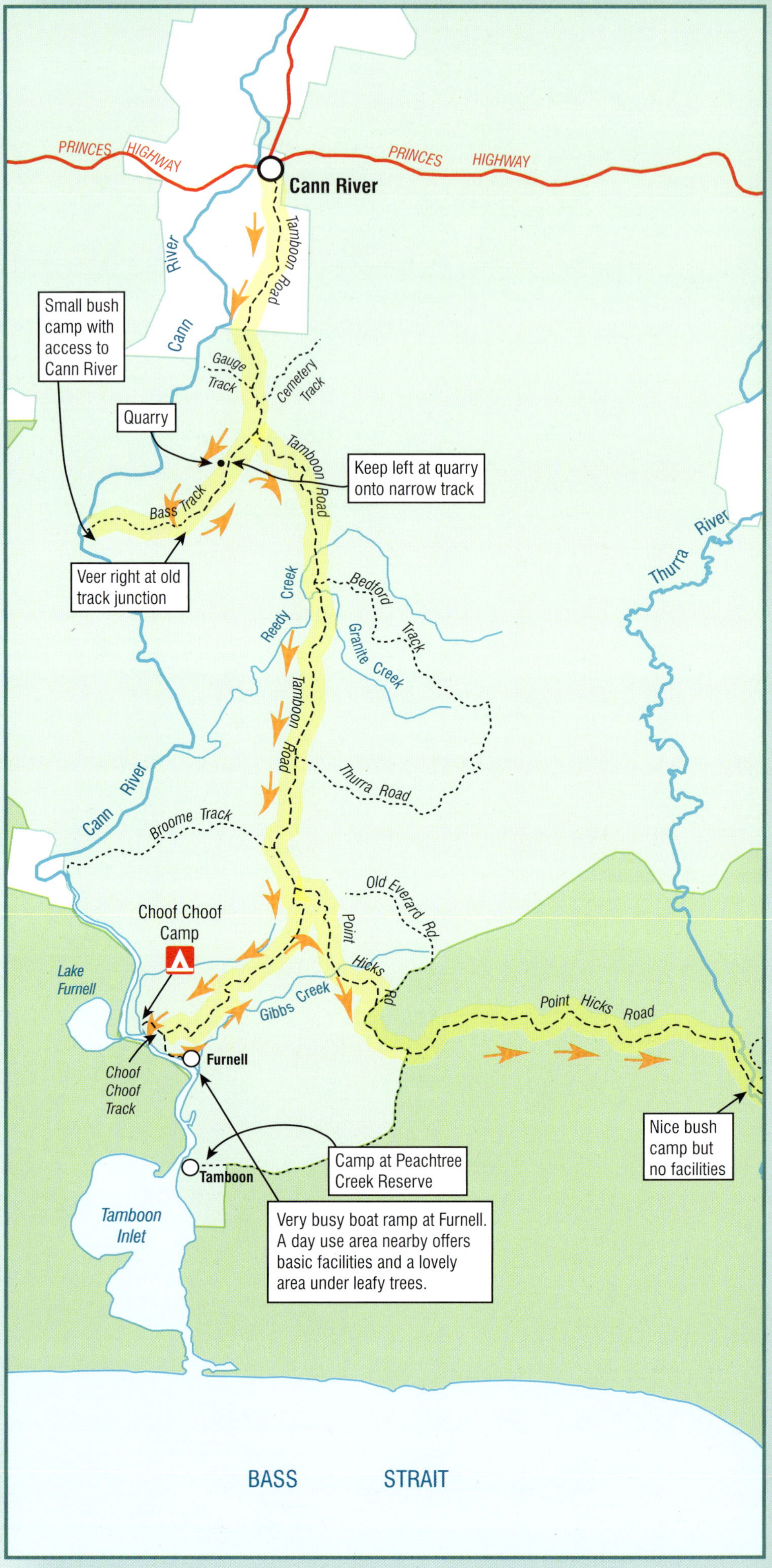

PRINCES HIGHWAY
Cann River
Tamboon Road
Small bush camp with access to Cann River
Gauge Track
Cemetery Track
Quarry
Keep left at quarry onto narrow track
Bass Track
Veer right at old track junction
Reedy Creek
Bedford Track
Granite Creek
Thurra Road
Thurra River
Cann River
Broome Track
Old Everard Rd
Choof Choof Camp
Lake Furnell
Point Hicks Rd
Gibbs Creek
Point Hicks Road
Furnell
Choof Choof Track
Nice bush camp but no facilities
Camp at Peachtree Creek Reserve
Tamboon
Tamboon Inlet
Very busy boat ramp at Furnell. A day use area nearby offers basic facilities and a lovely area under leafy trees.
BASS STRAIT

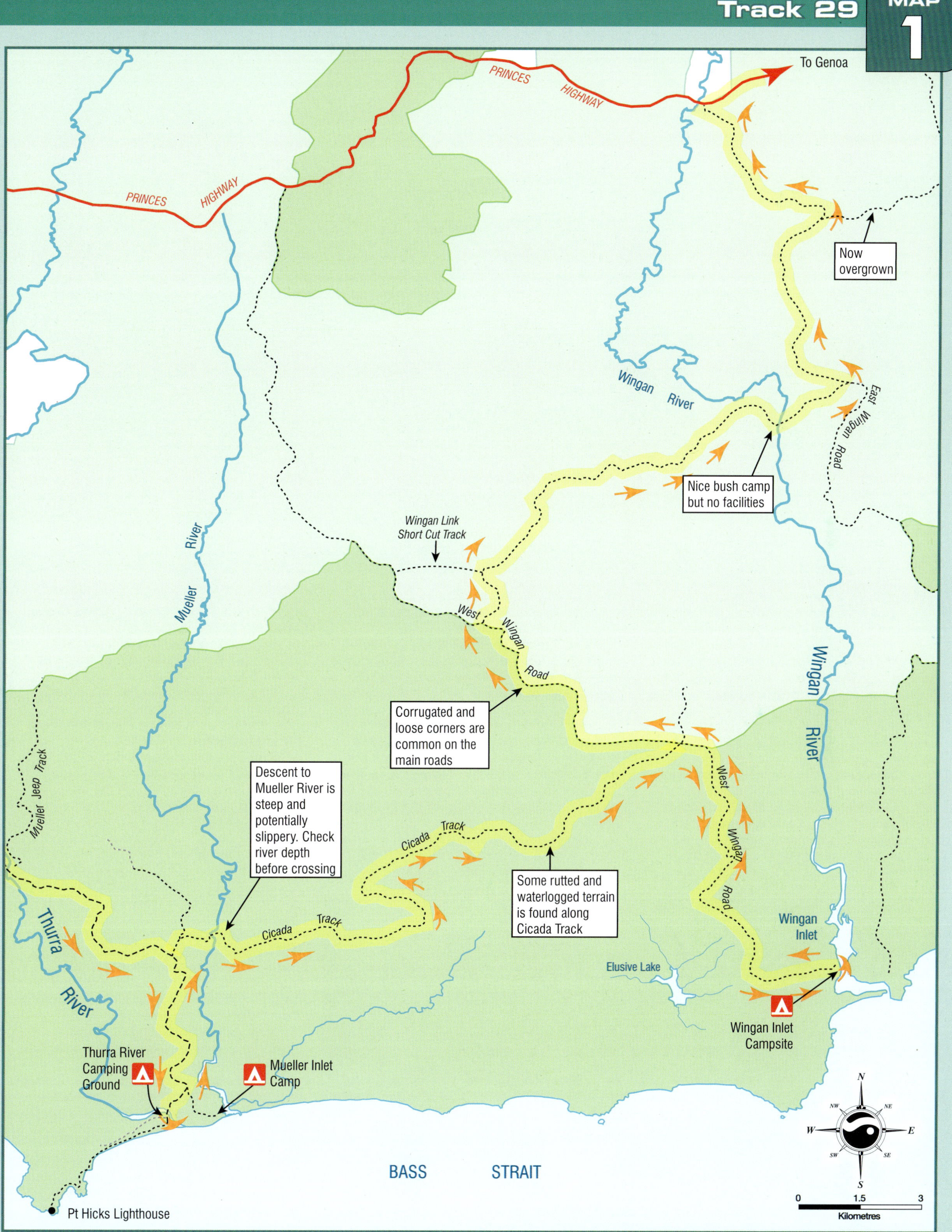

To Genoa
PRINCES HIGHWAY
PRINCES HIGHWAY
Now overgrown
Wingan River
East Wingan Road
Nice bush camp but no facilities
Wingan Link Short Cut Track
West Wingan Road
Mueller River
Corrugated and loose corners are common on the main roads
Wingan River
Mueller Jeep Track
Descent to Mueller River is steep and potentially slippery. Check river depth before crossing
Cicada Track
Cicada Track
Some rutted and waterlogged terrain is found along Cicada Track
West Wingan Road
Thurra River
Wingan Inlet
Elusive Lake
Wingan Inlet Campsite
Thurra River Camping Ground
Mueller Inlet Camp
BASS STRAIT
Pt Hicks Lighthouse
N
NW
NE
W
E
SW
SE
S
0
1.5
3
Kilometres

Treeferns crowd out some of the tracks.

boats plying the sheltered waters.

Return from **Choof Choof** to the **Tamboon Road** and turn south to **Furnell Landing**. It is only 700 metres to the small community of several houses, where boat launching is the primary activity. The boat ramp is busy, but the day use area nearby offers basic facilities and a lovely area under leafy trees.

Retrace your steps to the **Point Hicks Road** turn off and swing right for a winding downhill run over corrugated corners. You cross **Gibbs Creek** 2.2 kilometres later, with the **Old Everard Road** fanning off to the left 1.4 kilometres beyond that. Cross into **Croajingolong NP** to find **Fisherman Track** on the right 1.5 kilometres later (a right turn here leads to the small community of **Tamboon** and **Peachtree Creek Reserve** – a campground on **Tamboon Inlet** which has probably been used for millenia by local Aboriginal groups).

Keep left at **Fisherman Track** to follow **Point Hicks Road** through a seasonally closed gate with excellent views directly ahead toward **Mount Everard**. The undulating drive passes forests of juvenile grasstrees, before you reach the **Thurra River** at a one lane bridge. There is a small parking area near the bridge allowing travellers to check out this local patch of jungle. **Mueller Jeep Track** finishes on the northern side of the river near here, but it does not link with the **Point Hicks Road**.

Continue to follow the **Point Hicks Road** for 6.1 kilometres to arrive at the **Cicada Track** junction. We will turn left here to continue the tour, but for now keep straight to reach the **Thurra River Camping Ground**. The campgound is sheltered under a canopy of mahogany gum and is very popular, especially over the summer holiday period, when fishers look to wet a line.

Floods have uprooted trees along the Cann River

Nearby **Mueller Inlet Camp** is equally popular and privately managed bookings are essential for both camps. Phone the **Point Hicks Lighthouse** on 03 5158 4268 for current information, including the possibility of a ballot application. However day visitors can enjoy several walks through the area.

The surf beach walk with its wild, windswept vegetation is worthwhile, as are nature walks in the adjoining bushland. Banksia, teatree and marram grass are the habitat of some of **Croajingolong's** 265 bird species. However the vast expanse of barren dunes on **The Dunes** walk is particularly impressive. A marked walking trail guides visitors into a desert like landscape, where 150 metre high sand hills dominate the outlook. From the highest point the surrounding bushland can be seen cradling this unique valley of sand all of the way to **Point Hicks** and the open sea.

Day visitors can also visit the historic lighthouse at nearby **Point Hicks**; a rocky promontory where Cook first sighted the Australian mainland in 1770. The lighthouse was built from locally cut rock in 1888, and still warns mariners up to 50 kilometres from shore.

Retrace your steps to **Cicada Trail** and head north east along two furrows in the sand to a potentially closed gate 500 metres later. If open, begin a descent following a jungle gully on the right to a tree fern archway flagging a fording of the **Mueller**

Wingan Inlet sunrise

The beaches are usually deserted at Croajingolong

River. Stop prior to the crossing to determine its depth and flow rate, and don't continue if it looks dangerous. (My rule of thumb with a snorkel equipped full size 4WD is don't drive what cannot be comfortably walked.)

If trafficable, a loose, steep and potentially muddy descent funnels you into a beautiful waterway where inky waters reflect a fern lined gully. The steep climb out will warrant low range to deal with some rough terrain and erosion control mounds. Parking is very limited at the crossing, with just a single carpark on the eastern side and nothing close by on the west.

The rest of **Cicada Track** traverses relatively flat country, rutted in low lying places, but with a sandy base and some graveled areas where water logging is a problem. It is still a nice bush drive however, with lovely coastal forest and the occasional termite mound. Goannas are regularly spotted, with wallabies and birdlife also abundant.

You will reach a seasonally closed gate and tee intersection on **West Wingan Road** 19.8 kilometres from the **Thurra** crossing. We will turn left here to continue, but for now swing right to follow winding gravel south past **Boundary Track** then **Gale Hill Track**. You will pass **Elusive Lake Track** some 1.2 kilometres later (nice walk through banksia and stringybark to the deep fresh waters of **Elusive Lake**), before reaching a boat ramp and campground at **Wingan Inlet** (bookings essential over the peak periods; phone Parks Victoria for details 13 1963).

This shallow inlet is the starting point for several signposted coastal walks. A boardwalk over tidal flats allows you to follow the **Wingan** estuary to the ocean. Birdlife is commonly seen darting through the bloodwoods and paperbark, or wading across the flats. From the ocean beach a pink granite outcrop known as **The Skerries** is visible to the naked eye. A colony of up to 400 fur seals romp around the protected rocks. Keen eyed visitors may also spot whales or dolphin groups cruising the offshore waters.

Retrace your steps to the **Cicada Track** junction and follow the main road climb around loose bends to **Wingan Link Road**, some 7.7 kilometres later. Turn right here to leave national park and follow good track to **Wingan Link Shortcut Track** 1.8 kilometres into the journey. Keep right at this junction to continue through bushland now shrugging off previous fire damage. Broken views over the **Sand Patch Wilderness Area** mark the track's close proximity to the **Wingan River** (300 metres away, but no view through thick forest).

You will reach an open area of heathland and wind down to the **Wingan River** at a bridge, 10 kilometres from the **Short Cut Track**. There is nice camping (no facilities) just over the bridge under the canopy of some lovely mature eucalypts with banksia, trigger plants and delicate ferns irrigated by the trickling waters.

You will reach a tee intersection on **East Wingan Road** 2.2 kilometres later where you turn left to pass **McMillan Track** (now overgrown with fallen trees). Five kilometres later a forest of bottlebrush flags the **Princes Highway** and sealed road. Turn right to **Genoa** for free camping at the old bridge, and walking access to the pub, but no other services.

Mueller River crossing on Cicada Track

TRACK 30 ERRINUNDRA

EAST GIPPSLAND

Tree ferns overhang some tracks.

*The rainforests of **Errinundra** rise over 1000 metres into the moist clouds of **East Gippsland**, where consistent rain drenches the landscape. National park now protects parts of this natural jungle, and is the highlight of this tour.*

*Visitors will drive from **Club Terrace** near the **Princes Highway** to **Bendoc** in the state's north, on a rambling climb onto the **Errinundra Plateau**. A couple of inviting riverside bush camps can extend your stay here, while history buffs will get a glimpse into the early settler life and a short lived local gold mining rush.*

Begin this tour in **Club Terrace,** a one time gold mining town that has transitioned into a timber town, located just off the **Princes Highway**, 21 kilometres west of **Cann River**. A clutch of traditional forestry worker cottages form the nucleus of town, with the old fuel station and its rusty bowser no longer part of the package. Only the iconic 'Shell' sign and a lovely jacarandah remain to mark its passing.

Head north through town to pass the **Euchre Valley Drive** on your right (no longer trafficable with bridges out and overgrown).

Goonmirk Rocks.

BASIC CHECK LIST . . .

- ☑ **Soft Roaders**
- ☑ **Trailers with Care**
- ☑ **Road Tyres**
- ☑ **Avoid Wet Weather**

TRACK SNAPSHOT

TOUR ROUTE
Club Terrace to Bendoc via Errinundra NP.

DURATION AND DISTANCE
This 100 kilometre tour could be done in a day, but will take longer if you wish to do some of the walks.

TRACK DETAILS
Routine driving for all vehicles and drivers in the dry along forestry tracks and gravel roads. Very slippery in the wet on some sections.

WHEN TO GO
Potentially all year round with the exception of a seasonal closure on the detour to Goonmirk Rocks. However do not venture into Errinundra if wet weather is forecast; some roads are clay topped and become impassable when rain affected.

CAMPING
Superb camping on the Ada River and at the Delegate River near Bendoc.

FUEL AND SUPPLIES
No supplies on this trek. Stock up in Cann River or Orbost and replenish at Delegate (limited weekend hours) or Bombala in NSW.

MAPS
Rooftops: Cann River – Orbost – Delegate

OTHER INFORMATION
The Errinundra Plateau is well worth exploring further if you have the time. There are a number of opportunities for bushwalking or checking out some of the abandoned mining relics from the district's time as a small gold producer.

Continue past the timber milling plant and numerous vacant building blocks prior to the bridge over **Rocky Creek**. You will climb past the **Old Combienbar Road** on the right to reach cleared land and cattle grazing. Stock ramps, haysheds and other farming infrastructure dot the landscape as you travel beyond the elevated **Bemm River** bridge, 3 kilometres out of town.

Trace the jungle environment on your right and cross **Possum Creek** to be rewarded with scenic glimpses of the waterway at some of the road bends. Turn left onto gravel 11.4 kilometres from **Club Terrace** onto **Errinundra Road**, just prior to the **Errinundra** bridge.

Follow a corridor of yellow flower in early summer, with deep cuttings and a steady grade that is usually a feature of major logging roads (log trucks still use this route, so drive with care, and keep your headlights on). You will reach **Boulder Flat** about 18 kilometres from **Club Terrace,** where rampant blackberry is now choking the cleared land.

A brick chimney and old homestead on the left precede a cottage on the northern end of the flat, where an old shed marks **Burtons Track** on the left. Tree ferns dominate the valley here as you pass **Bolla Creek Track** and **Barrs Road**, both on the left. Cross a bridge over **Shady Creek** into **Lower Errinundra Nature Conservation Reserve**, where verdant plant growth defines the **Combienbar State Forest**.

You will reach the **Ada River** confluence at a bridge 12.1 kilometres along the **Errinundra Road**.

Excellent camping under mature eucalypts and easy swimming hole access at the river make this a popular stop. Basic facilities are provided.

Continue north past **Helmers Track** (access to private land holding at **Errinundra**) to find a deterioration in the road surface. Rough sections with poorer drainage make for a slower drive, and the largely unsurfaced track would be slippery when wet.

Pass Gays Road (now closed) to gain some elevation and excellent views over the local ranges. The birdlife is active, with rosella pairs commonly sighted darting between some massive trees. Roadside cuttings drip with walls of fishbone fern, creating a natural vertical garden around some bends.

Tall trees are common on the plateau.

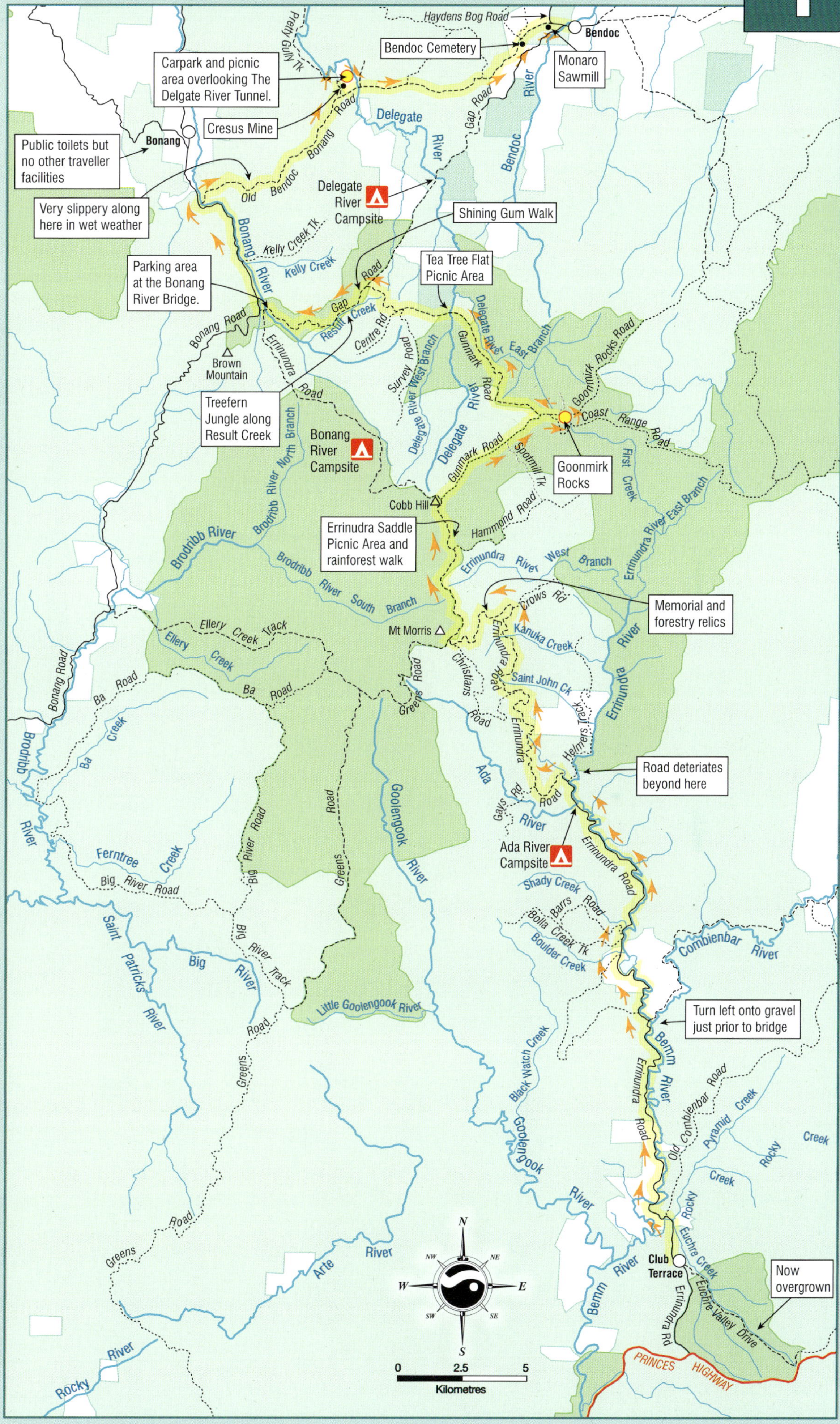

ERRINUNDRA

Christians Road marks the head of **St Johns Creek** as you climb to about 1000 metres now, reaching the **Kanuka Creek Scenic Reserve** 3 kilometres later. You will pass **Crows Road** on the right to round a spur and head in a south westerly direction on a gradual descent through lovely wattle forest. One kilometre later you will find a memorial to Frank Morris (a forestry pioneer who managed use of the timber resource on the **Errinundra Plateau**), together with some hut remains, a loading ramp, and other rusting relics.

Continue past **Christians Road** to reach a tee intersection on **Mount Morris**, with **Greens Road** branching to the left. Turn right at this junction to follow the boundary of **Errinundra NP** past a gravel pit and through harvested forest, now more than 40 years old and mature in appearance, although regrowth of a uniform size does have some ecological drawbacks.

Hammond Road flags the turn off to the **Errinundra Saddle Rainforest Walk** 300 metres later, where a tunnel of trees crowd out the sky at a small parking area. Basic facilities are provided at this rest stop, and following the 800 metre boardwalk into verdant jungle is well worthwhile.

Return to the main road and turn north through national park toward **Cobb Hill** 2 kilometres later, where you turn right onto **Gunmark Road**. Climb through black wattle and the occasional shining gum to the peak of the **Gunmark Range** at about 1150 metres to pass **Spotmill Track** (walkers only) on the right.

You will reach **Goonmirk Rocks Road** 1.7 kilometres beyond **Spotmill Track** where we will keep left to continue this tour.

Many cascades tumble through Errinundra NP

The Delegate River tunnel is impressive.

However those interested in seeing some of **Errinundra**'s ancient mountain plum pines can turn right here at the triangulated intersection. Pass through a seasonally closed gate and veer left away from **Coast Range Road** 300 metres later. Follow the track through yellow paper daisies for 1 kilometre to the easily missed **Goonmirk Rocks Walking** track on the left.

Parking is limited and the walking track largely overgrown, but those who follow the 100 metre foot trail through balckberry and stinging nettle will see some examples of this small wet forest conifer growing up to 2 metres in height near the rock outcrop. Other taller examples of the tree can be seen further along **Goonmirk Rocks Road**.

Return to **Gunmark Road** and turn right to pass a gravel pit and numerous tree stumps with plank notches cut from the early forestry days. In summer, flowering pink foxgloves on the trackside flag a private residence on the right, before **Tea Tree Flat** is reached 1 kilometre later.

This is a lovely area to stop for a break, with basic facilities and the infant **Delegate River** gurgling under foot. The road culvert itself looks to have been an old mining relic – a heavy gauge hot riveted iron tube – while the tea tree wetland is an interesting change in the landscape. A walking track heads south from the parking area to a clump of large trees 15 minutes away.

You will exit national park west of **Tea Tree Flat** to pass hardwood plantation on an elevated divide separating the **Delegate** and

Minor tracks are often slippery.

Bonang Rivers. Continue past **Survey Road** (currently closed) and **Centre Road** to reach a tee intersection on **Gap Road**, 4.2 kilometres beyond the flat.

Turn left here onto solid and well drained gravel road to follow **The Gap Scenic Reserve** westward to a carpark 900 metres later. A demanding walking track originates here taking hikers on a three hour ramble through old growth forest to two enormous shining gum trees thought to be over 600 years old.

Continue west past a wall of tree fern at **Result Creek**, where a parking area is found 1.1 kilometres beyond the old growth walk. Another parking area is reached 3.3 kilometres later at the **Bonang River Bridge**, although no official walking tracks are found at either site.

Cross the bridge and keep straight away from **Errinundra Road** on the left, to reach a tee intersection on the **Bonang Road** 200 metres later. Swing right onto wide bluemetal to follow the **Bonang River** through beautiful mature forest.

Pass **Kelly Creek Track** (closed) and fern glades to emerge at the **Old Bonang Bendoc Road,** 5 kilometres beyond **Errinundra Road**. The community of **Bonang** lies just a few kilometres directly ahead, but no services are currently available (other than public toilets), so turn right onto the **Old Bendoc Road** to cross the **Bonang River** at an aging timber bridge.

Winding road climbs into **Bendoc State Forest** now, following an earthen road covered in leaf litter, which would be slippery in wet weather. You will pass various side tracks before reaching **Pretty Gully Track** on the left, some 8 kilometres beyond the bridge.

Turn left here to pass the old workings of the **Cresus Mine**, keeping right at a junction 900 metres later for a descent to a carpark at a picnic area and fireplace overlooking the **Delegate River Tunnel**. This structure was cut in the gold mining days to redirect the **Delegate**'s flow, and expose gold bearing alluvial ore. Visitors can follow a short walk to both sides of the tunnel, but supervise children near the upstream entrance, where water gushes through with some force.

Return to the **Old Bonang Bendoc Road** and turn left past private farms to a scenic crossing of the **Delegate River** at a single lane timber bridge. Proceed past several side tracks and the **Bendoc Cemetery** to reach the **Monaro Sawmill** on your right. Sealed road paves the way now to a tee, where you keep right away from **Haydens Bog Road**.

Cross the **Bendoc River** and reach the landmark pub in the middle of town. While **Bendoc** remains a strategic centre for Victorian public services (police, DELWP), there are no other services in town and travellers need to cross the border into **Delegate** for supplies, 17 kilometres to the north.

Accommodation and camping are found here too, but camping on the **Delegate River** just out of **Bendoc** is another option. Follow **Gap Road** south from Bendoc along a sealed road for 7 kilometres and gravel for a further 1.5 kilometres. Basic facilities are found on a nice stretch of river here, popular with fly fishers.

TRACK
31 YALMY RIVER
EAST GIPPSLAND

Giant tree ferns in Snowy River NP.

*The eastern **Snowy River** region marks the transition into far **East Gippsland**, where dense forest is the norm, and only limited clearing and development marks the major river flats. Timber harvesting has been (and remains) a major industry in this sector, with state forest logging coupes and long term forest regrowth occurring on a significant scale.*

*This tour follows the **Bonang**, **Yalmy** and **Orbost State Forests** along a serpentine route flanking the **Yalmy River.** Although this river is only crossed once and largely exists out of sight in the mountain watershed country, it is a significant contributor to the jungle in the south of the **Snowy River NP**. The drive from **Bonang** to **Orbost** takes in some of this magnificent country, together with an optional (and relatively easy) low range detour if you feel so inclined.*

Monkey Top Track has some boggy sections.

Leave **Bonang** heading south on the blacktop to pass the old BP filling station (now closed) and some big pines, with **McKillops Bridge Road** on the right. You pass **Maling Road** 1.4 kilometres later and turn right onto **Rising Sun Road** 300 metres beyond that, signposted '**Yalmy Road**'. The main track veers left 100 metres later, but you need to keep right following the powerlines on a narrow track coloured with foxgloves in summer. Some tall timber and tree fern flags **Yalmy Road**, 1.6 kilometres beyond the bitumen, where you veer left.

Proceed south along a potential log truck route past **Sun Track** and the old **Rising Sun Mine**. **Snowy River NP** flanks you on the west, and **Bonang SF** to the east, with **Yalmy Road** following the boundary of these zones, almost all of the way to the **Yalmy River** crossing.

Tall wattles and yellow paper daisies usher a journey past the abandoned **Good Hope Mine** on the right, and the headwaters of the **Deddick River.** Rosellas flash through some areas of big trees, where tree stumps stand witness to earlier logging activity. Wallabies are also common through here, so take particular care near dawn and dusk, and keep your headlights on even during the day along this narrow and winding road.

Yalmy Road has a reasonable surface for the most part, although potholes and corrugated corners can catch out the driver from time to time. A patch of burnt forest with tree ferns rising from the ashes, precedes a gravel pit and **Minchin Track** on the right.

Keep straight for a further 700 metres then turn right onto **Monkey Top Track**, signposted '**Big Tree**'. The track crowds in overhead now as you reach a small carpark 1.6 kilometres later, dominated by a massive shining gum some 80 metres tall.

This location marks the end of travel for AWDs and the start of an optional detour for full size 4WDs. Smaller vehicles will probably find the back way into **Waratah Flat** just a little too rough, and low range is a welcome capability when dealing with some of the descents. So retrace your steps to **Yalmy Road** and turn south to follow the **Rodger – Yalmy Divide** to **Waratah Flat Road**, where you turn right to reach the camping area, 3 kilometres later. You will then pick up the notes for

BASIC CHECK LIST . . .

- ☑ Soft Roaders
- ☑ Trailers with Care
- ☑ Road Tyres
- ☑ Avoid Wet Weather

TRACK SNAPSHOT

TOUR ROUTE
Bonang to Orbost via Yalmy State Forest and Snowy River NP.

DURATION AND DISTANCE
This 130 kilometre journey can be comfortably done in one day, but an overnight stop at Waratah Flat or the Yalmy River crossing is worth considering.

TRACK DETAILS
Well surfaced forestry roads in the main, with some narrower tracks near Youngs Creek. The optional detour into Snowy River NP is just a little too demanding for AWDs, but no problem for bigger 4WDs with low range in the dry.

WHEN TO GO
The arterial route is open all year round, with the optional detour closed from June until November. Avoid wet weather regardless as many tracks will become slippery and impassable.

CAMPING
The designated camping at Waratah Flat has basic facilities, but bush camping on the Yalmy River crossing is very pleasant. Commercial caravan park at Orbost.

FUEL AND SUPPLIES
No fuel or supplies at Bonang or Bendoc. Travellers will need to top up at Delegate (limited weekend hours) or Bombala in NSW. Orbost has a full range of services.

MAPS
Rooftops: Cann River – Orbost – Delegate

OTHER INFORMATION
This tour is a logical extension from our Errinundra trek, but those who undertake it as a stand alone option, can reach Bonang via the main Orbost – Bonang Road. This gravel arterial winds its way through nice bush to the locality of Goongerah (camping available), before following the Bonang River into the hamlet of Bonang.

travel from beyond there.

However full size 4WDs can continue past a seasonally closed gate at **Big Tree** to squeeze through even narrower track along a very impressive and beautiful tree fern avenue. Large leafed mint bush litters the track with white flowers in the warmer months, while prunella ground covers splash purple blotches into the forest.

A few bogholes punctuate parts of the climb where water collects, before beginning its tumultuous race down the **Rodger River.** Keep left at **Bowen Link Track** some 2.6 kilometres from **Big Tree** to find native veronicas flourishing in the light now revealed by a patch of burnt forest.

You will climb to about 1200 metres before making a descent with broken views toward **Mount Bowen**. Masses of paper daisies and the contrasting trunks of burnt trees grow along the now undulating drive, featuring some climbs and descents that may have you reaching for low range.

You will reach a tee intersection on **Waratah Flat Track** 1.9 kilometres beyond **Bowen Link Track** where recent track realignments have pushed **Monkey Top Track** further west than some maps show. Turn left here to follow good track over some moist sections, and past cuttings dripping with walls of fern. You pass under the 1199 peak of **Monkey Top**, although it is obscured with thick forest, to follow an old logging road on a continuous descent.

Drive past **Rich Knob Track** on the right, 8.1 kilometres beyond the last tee, for a wider earthen road descent that would be slippery if wet. Proceed through a seasonally closed gate 5.6 kilometres later to cross the **Rodger River** at a bridge, with just a small parking area found prior.

A massive shining gum at The Big Tree.

Waratah Flat Campground is reached 300 metres later with basic facilities, including new fireplaces. A recent bushfire has robbed this camp of its previous charm, but in time the bush will rejuvenate, bringing an impressive late spring display of the Gippsland waratah.

Continue south returning to **Yalmy Road** and turn right through further fire damaged bush with broken views to the left over the **Yalmy Valley**. The road winds for 8.2 kilometres beyond **Waratah Flat Road**, to the **Deddick Trail** turn off on your right. (The **Deddick Trail** is a rewarding 4WD journey into **Snowy River NP** following steep mountain country to **McKillops Bridge** in the north. River crossings and plenty of low range work limit the 50 kilometre trek to full size vehicles and experienced drivers.)

Continue along **Yalmy Road** to pass **Rodger River Track** (MVO) 5 kilometres later, before breaking away from the **Snowy River NP** at **Lightning Track**. Keep left here for a descent into **Yalmy SF,** with excellent views to the east as you ramp down to finally reach the **Yalmy River.** Look out for fallen rock on some cuttings to find a low level bridge over the **Yalmy** with camping at clearings on both sides of the major waterway. There are no facilities, but splashing around in the **Yalmy** on a hot day is reward enough.

Follow the road south to pass **Serpentine Track** and the lovely inky waters of **Serpentine Creek** at a single lane bridge. You will reach **Pinnak Road** at a triangulated intersection (right turn on **Yalmy Road** heads uphill), where you veer left. Excellent range views open up 3 kilometres later, before you pass **Paradise Ridge Road** on the left and enter **Martins Creek Nature Conservation**

Kanuka trees are found in the moist areas.

Reserve, where pockets of warm temperate rainforest can be seen. Stands of ghostly brittle gums call this reserve home, while silver leaved stringybarks droop from overhead with metallic coloured foliage.

You will pass **Mine Track** to reenter fire damaged bush, before finding views of **Mount Pinnak** on the right, and valley views on the left taking in private land on **Sardine Creek**. The sustained descent crosses verdant **Sardine Creek** at a culvert, reaching a tee intersection back on **Yalmy Road**.

Turn left at the tee to pass **Silvertop Track** and cross **Broken Leg Creek** and its ferny banks at a bridge. Keep straight at the **Mount Watt Road** junction then turn left onto **Cooney Ridge Road** 5 kilometres after that.

Follow the forestry road past several side tracks (including **11 Bob Track** which leads to **Mount Buck** – there is a trig point and galvanised steel tower here, but no views). You will reach the **Orbost – Bonang Road** at a tee intersection, and turn right (it is a tricky intersection and difficult to see oncoming traffic, especially from the left).

Follow the blacktop for 3.8 kilometres then turn left onto **Coulsons Road** for a pleasant bush drive past some cypress pines. Keep right at **Lightwood Track** 2 kilometres later, to pass a forest studded with creamy trunked grey gums and fibrous stringybarks. You will reach **Iron Chimney Track** 2.6 kilometres beyond **Lightwood Track**, and turn right to follow a banksia lined gully on the right. **Chimney Track** finishes at a tee intersection on **Storer Track** 2.2 kilometres later, where a carpark marks a local walking trail head at **Youngs Creek Picnic Area**.

Once the site of an old sawmill dating

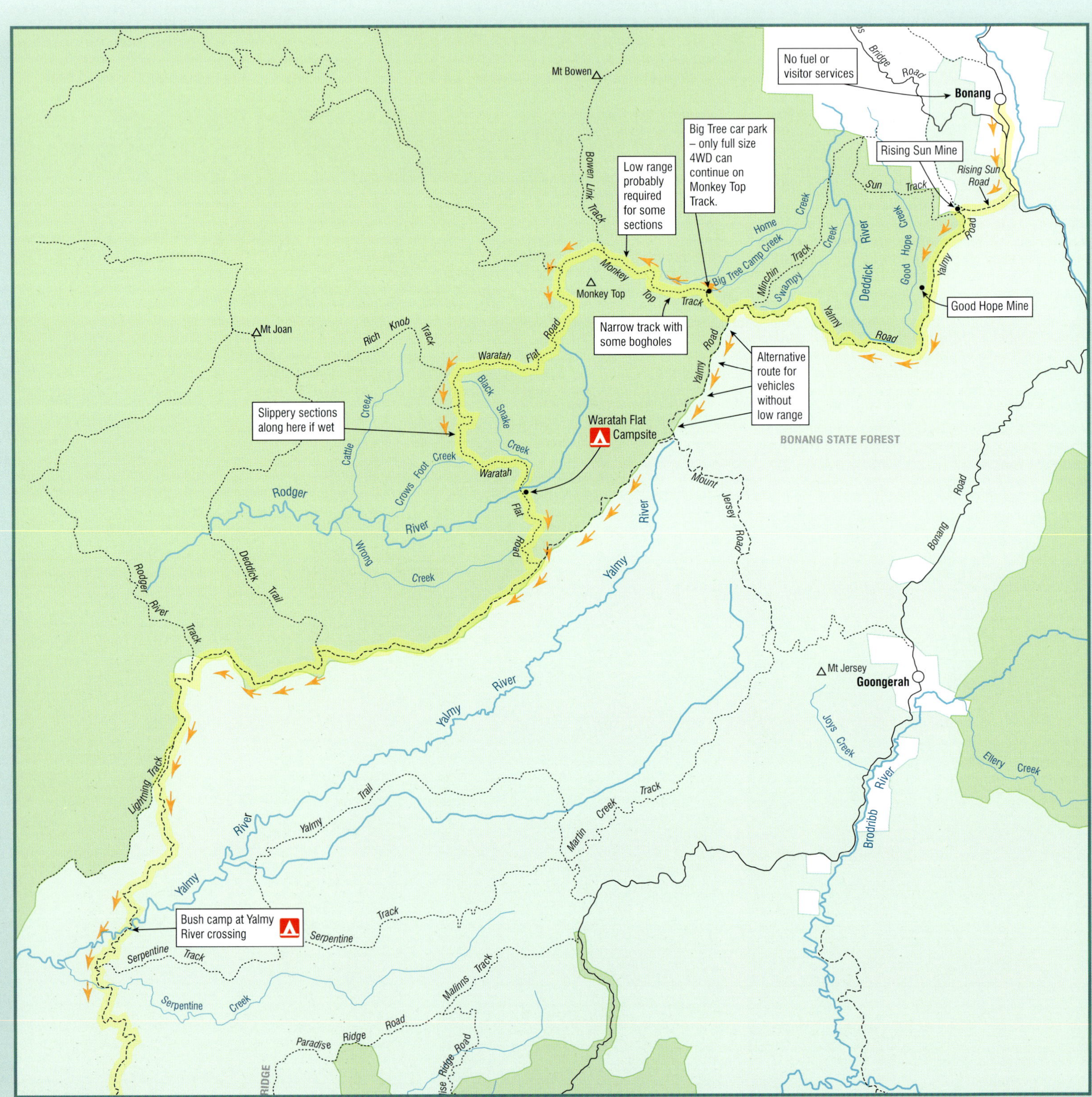

JOINS TOP OF MAP TO RIGHT

back to the 1920s, the picnic site features an old steam engine, which once powered the mill. These days basic facilities are provided here, and a popular walk to a waterfall on **Youngs Creek** invades kanuka and tea tree jungle on a fairly easy 400 metre amble.

Wallabies, kangaroos and lyre birds are frequently spotted around this area. Other walks take in the local forest, together with a more lengthy option to the old reservoir wall, once supplying **Orbost** with drinking water. (The reservoir is situated 4 kilometres upstream, where a curved dam wall was constructed in 1918. Unfortunately algal growth affected the water quality and it could not be controlled, so the site was decommisioned.)

Cross the bridge over **Youngs Creek** heading west past **Break Neck Track** on the left. Turn left onto **4 ½ Mile Track** 600 metres later, keeping staight at **Stock Track** 300 metres beyond that. You will cross a lovely waterway (nowhere to camp) then reach the **Orbost – Bonang Road** again. Turn left here to pass by open valley and farming activity, for the final few kilometres into **Orbost**.

Youngs Creek Falls are a short walk from the carpark.

JOINS BOTTOM OF MAP TO LEFT

Track 31

MAP 1

Excellent views along here

Mt Buck (No views)

Youngs Creek Picnic Area, waterfall and creeks

MARTINS CREEK NATURE C.R.

ORBOST STATE FOREST

ELLERY STATE FOREST

BRODRIBB FLORA RESERVE

MURRUN GOWER STATE FOREST

Orbost

0 2 4 Kilometres

TRACK 32 ORBOST TO BUCHAN

EAST GIPPSLAND

Ford at Bete Bolong Creek.

BASIC CHECK LIST . . .

- ☑ Soft Roaders
- ☑ Trailers with Care
- ☑ Road Tyres
- ☑ Avoid Wet Weather

*This short trek links **Orbost** with **Buchan** via a scenic route taking in parts of the lower **Snowy River**, and points of interest in the adjacent state forest. There is excellent camping at the **Buchan Caves Reserve**, and a quiet bush camp on the **Snowy River** at **Long Point**; accessed via an optional low range 4WD track. Visitors will enjoy superb scenery, visit an historic fire spotter's tower, and see a stand of naturally occuring spotted gums.*

Start this tour by heading west from **Orbost**, crossing the **Snowy River** on its concrete bridge, then turning left 500 metres beyond the river onto signposted **'Lochend Road'**. Follow this road back under the bridge for views of the old rail trestle bridge (the longest in Victoria, and used for 70 years from its constuction in 1916). You will cross the rail where trestles have collapsed on either side (now the route of the 96 kilometre East Gippsland Rail Trail from Bairnsdale to Orbost).

You will reach a tee intersection 800 metres beyond the rail where you turn right (left turn follows **Burns Road** to a lookout taking in **Orbost** and the **Snowy** flood plain). Continue east, then turn left onto **Watt Road** at another tee intersection 1.1 kilometres later (right turn to river). Trace the sealed road westward past corn fields and other vegetable crops relying on irrigation from the **Snowy River** waters. Several tracks fan off the **Orbost – Buchan Road** to access the wide river and its sandy banks.

Timber slab hut at Orbost.

TRACK SNAPSHOT

TOUR ROUTE
Orbost to Buchan via the Snowy River.

DURATION AND DISTANCE
This 70 kilometre journey is a nice day trip, but can be extended with a stay at Long Point.

TRACK DETAILS
Routine driving along the arterial route and suitable for most drivers and vehicles. The optional detour to Long Point is steep and possibly slippery; it requires low range and reasonable clearance.

WHEN TO GO
All year round, although rain will quickly affect those unsealed roads without stone topping.

CAMPING
Formal camping at both Orbost and Buchan, with an alternative bush site on the Snowy at Long Point.

FUEL AND SUPPLIES
Orbost and Buchan can provide for most needs.

MAPS
Rooftops: Snowy River – McKillops Bridge – Lakes Entrance

OTHER INFORMATION
Make time to visit the fascinating limestone caves at Buchan. Both Regal and Fairy Caves are open for guided tours all year round, or you can explore other cave systems in the company of one of the local guides.

You will reach the community of **Bete Bolong** and an avenue of exotic trees including pittosporums and mature oaks. Turn right on the **Buchan Road** 4.3 kilometres beyond **Watt Road**, to find some lovely old rural architecture with settler farm houses and a purpose built slatted shed. Poplars define the route out of **Bete Bolong** as you swing more westerly away from the **Snowy** and begin the climb.

Broad acres of cropping backs onto **Waygara SF** and a narrowing of the bitumen beyond here. Several forestry roads fan off on either side, before you reach **Long Point Track** about 10 kilometres from the start of the climb.

Full size 4WDs equipped with low range can turn right here for an optional detour to **Sandy Point**. The turn is a little difficult with limited vision, but keep left 200 metres later away from **Back Break Track**, to follow a good surface of gravel topping.

You will wind your way through bushland, passing a minor spur track to the left, before selecting low range about 4 kilometres into the drive. A sudden descent into a gully is followed with a climb back up to ironbarks and the **Wood Point Flora Reserve**. Then a sustained final drop off over erosion control mounds invades some jungle, before reaching a camping area at **Long Point**.

Informal terraced sites and small clearings on a river bend provide a nice outlook, although the only facilities provided are table and seats. Sandy river access and shallow margins make this a nice spot to splash around in the warmer weather, but the water smoothed rocks and sheer slope of the vegetated east bank are a visual attraction in their own right.

Return to the **Orbost – Buchan Road** and turn right to head north along some winding road where a bridge spans **Wall Creek** and its gully of ferns. You will reach **Monument Track** 4.6 kilometres beyond the bridge, where you turn left on the apex of a corner, to be confronted with a rather steep track beginning. The rough and rocky introduction improves to a routine but potentially slippery route over leaf litter and a gradual descent.

Cross **Jack Creek** on an old timber bridge, where massed tree ferns have taken hold. The climb out over erosion control mounds continues to a junction 2.5 kilometres beyond the blacktop. We will keep left here to continue the tour, but for now swing right to the old **Stringer Knob Fire Tower** and its amazing structure built from two massive trees spliced together and tied back with steel guy ropes. The 28 metre tall pole and fire spotter's cabin was built in 1941 in response to the disastrous 1939 bushfires. There is no access to the tower (nor any views in the area) but the site is well worth seeing and the explanatory signs quite interesting.

Continue west on **Monument Track** for a descent to a tee intersection, where you keep right away from **Tuckerbox Track**. Continue past some broken views to reach the **Mottle Range Flora Reserve** 5.5 kilometres beyond the tower. Some specimens of naturally occurring spotted gum (the only such stand known in Victoria) are found over the next 700 metres, before reaching a tee intersection on **Mottle Range Road.** (These blotchy yellow and grey trees are most impressive over summer when their trunks shed their old bark to reveal an attractive new skin).

Turn right here to pass **Tara Range Link Road** 3 kilometres later, and descend to **Bete Bolong Creek** 800 metres beyond that. The rocky ford flags a sustained climb past mossy rocks and **Seven Mile Road** on the left. One kilometre later you will keep left on **Mottle Range Road** at the **Tara Road** junction to follow **Torr Creek** and its jumble of vegetation.

The ferny views frame some nice forest with banks of bracken reaching to the water in the complex mountain gully folds. You cross **Torr Creek**, reaching a tee intersection on **Gilberts Road** 600 metres later. Turn left to pass **Kings Road** here, and arrive at **North Boundary Road** 500 metres after that. Keep straight on **Mackiesons Road** to find some cleared land and range views. Follow a corridor of mature trees with farmhouses and pastoral infrastructure punctuating the drive.

You will reach the **Buchan Road** at the locality of **Buchan South**, where you turn right onto sealed road. Cross **Tea Tree Creek**, keeping straight at the B**uchan South Road** 700 metres later. Pass the **Timbarra Road** and **Buchan Cemetery** to be greeted with broad views over the rounded hills of the **Buchan Valley**. Keep right at the **Old Buchan Road** for further views and a panoramic vantage point over the township. Arrive in **Buchan** to find the rebuilt pub and cafes, together with great camping and other activities in the **Buchan Caves Reserve**.

The track to Long Point requires low range.

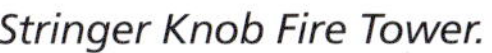
Stringer Knob Fire Tower.

ORBOST TO BUCHAN

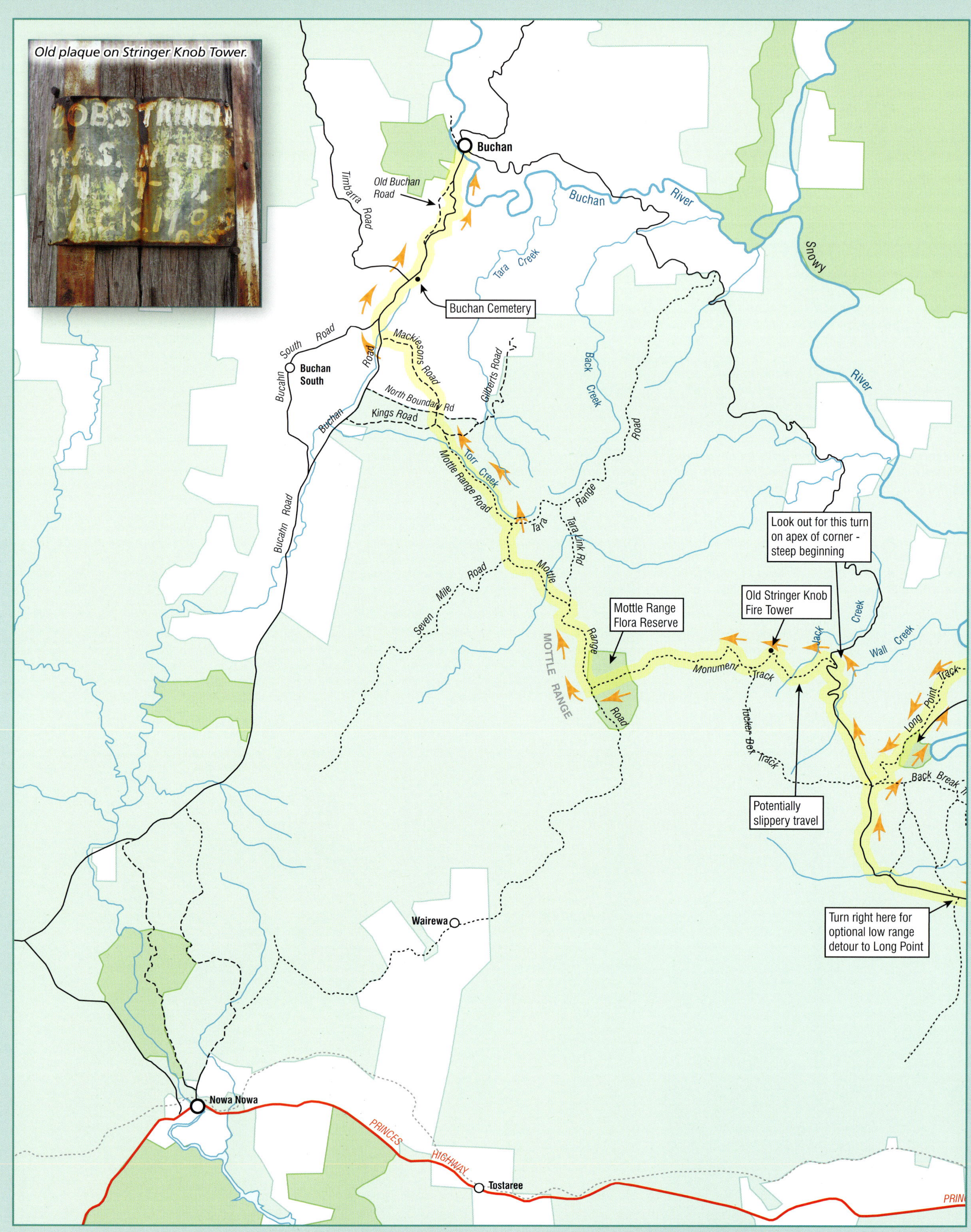

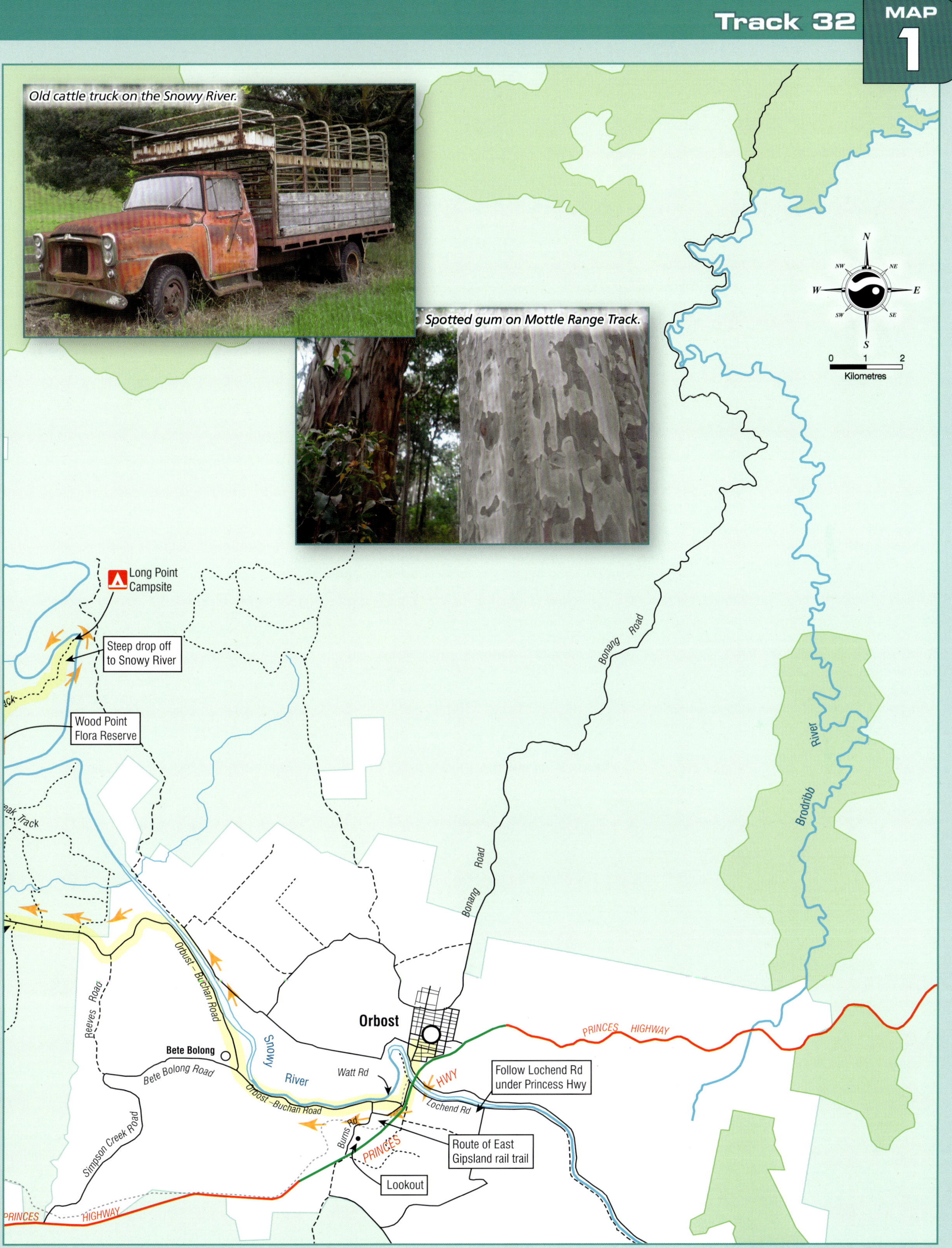
Old cattle truck on the Snowy River.
Spotted gum on Mottle Range Track.
N
NE
E
SE
S
SW
W
NW
0
1
2
Kilometres
Long Point Campsite
Steep drop off to Snowy River
Wood Point Flora Reserve
Track
Bonang Road
Bonang Road
River
Brodribb
Orbost–Buchan Road
Beeves Road
Orbost
Bete Bolong
Bete Bolong Road
Snowy
River
Watt Rd
HWY
Follow Lochend Rd under Princess Hwy
Lochend Rd
Orbost–Buchan Road
Burns Rd
PRINCES
Route of East Gipsland rail trail
Lookout
Simpson Creek Road
PRINCES HIGHWAY
PRINCES HIGHWAY

TRACK 33 TIMBARRA RIVER

EAST GIPPSLAND

Pasture and deciduous trees define the Tambo Valley.

BASIC CHECK LIST . . .

- ☑ Soft Roaders
- ☑ Trailers with Care
- ☑ Road Tyres
- ☑ Avoid Wet Weather

*The **Timbarra River** gathers on the high plains of north east Victoria, before drifting south to merge with the **Tambo** near **Mount Elizabeth**. Its contorted passage splits the **Nunniong** and **Nunnett Plains** in the north, and widens through the semi cleared land of **Timbarra Settlement.***

*This tour follows an easy passage from **Buchan** into the **Timbarra Settlement** before climbing over a series of high plains. This alpine environment is captivating country, and well worth soaking up, before you descend to the **Tambo River** at **Swifts Creek.** There are camping opportunities aplenty en route, together with one of the best kept bush huts in this state.*

Leave **Buchan** heading south on the **Bruthen Road**, turning right onto the **Timbarra Road** 4 kilometres further on. Follow this good sealed road past grazing sheep and old stockyards to a four way intersection two kilometres later. Keep right here (left turn to **Stonehenge Caravan Park**) to be greeted with awesome views over the **Buchan Valley**.

Bushland transitions from cleared pasture as the road begins to wind a little more and you reach **Windarra Road** on the left. You will pass **Mainline Track** for a slow climb along **Spring Creek** where tree ferns shelter in the state forest.

Cross **Spring Creek** at a culvert to pass **Little Bull Flat** and **Sunny Point Track** on the right. A clearing at **Bull Flat** marks **Bull Flat Track** turn off and a cluster of cypress pine before you pass **Switchback Track** on the right. You will reach the crest of **Dividing Range** at **Dinner Hill Gap**, with **Mount Victoria Road** breaking away to the left.

The Washington Winch is well preserved.

TRACK SNAPSHOT

TOUR ROUTE

Buchan to Swifts Creek via the Timbarra River and Bentley Plains.

DURATION AND DISTANCE

Allow two or three days for the 140 kilometre journey if you wish to soak up the High Plains atmosphere.

TRACK DETAILS

Well surfaced forestry roads in the main, with ruts and gutters in places, but suitable for a well driven AWD. The optional detour is a little rougher, probably requiring low range and reasonable clearance for comfortable travel.

WHEN TO GO

Seasonal road closures apply on some sections of this trek between June and November, so plan your trip here in the warmer months.

CAMPING

Lovely camping at Bentley Plains and on the Timbarra River with basic facilities. Other bush camps possible as shown on map, with commercial camping options at Buchan, Stonehenge and Swifts Creek.

FUEL AND SUPPLIES

Buchan and Swifts Creek have most services.

MAPS

Rooftops: Snowy River – McKillops Bridge – Lakes Entrance

OTHER INFORMATION

Swifts Creek is a small and welcoming town that has milled timber commercially since the late 1940s, and still relies on this important industry. A prominent pub and wood fired bakery seem to keep most travellers happy, with camping and other accommodation options available on the peaceful Tambo River.

Enjoy the last few kilometres of sealed road on a descent past **Holy Hell Track** for views over the **Timbarra Valley** at **Pretty Boy Saddle**. Swing left onto gravel at the fork, away from **Nunnett Road** for a descent to the **Timbarra River South Nature Coservation Reserve**. Deep cuttings and rocky embankments precede river views and a camp with basic facilities on the **Timbarra River**.

Cross the bridge and follow good gravel past **Scorpion Creek Track** to the **Timbarra Central Camp**, 1.4 kilometres beyond the bridge. There are some lovely river camps along this stretch of river at **Gordons Gully**, some with rapids and natural spa baths and others close to the basic facilities. It is a popular location during holiday periods in the warmer months, and the recent addition of site numbers may mean that a booking system is under consideration.

Follow the **Timbarra Road** further north past a series of other access turn offs as you pass elevated river views and some unfortunate patches of blackberry. The camping area at **Timbarra North** is reached 3 kilometres beyond the **Central Camp**, marking more basic facilities and the end of bush camping for a while.

Open grazing country and private land defines the **Timbarra Settlement** with cottages and orchard trees clustered along the poplar lined river. Cascades rushing through rocky chokes can be seen from some places (no access) and there is a lovely cottage at a creek crossing where blue flowering chickory has naturalised.

Cross the **Timbarra** at a timber bridge to find excellent views of the river with stockyard and ramps preceding a series of gates (leave as found) and grids. More huts and weekenders mark the drive eastward as you leave the river and climb into thicker bushland.

Pass **Running Creek Track** on the left and **Big Hill** on the right to be greeted with broken views from the rocky outcrop. You will arrive at a tee intersection at a location known as **The Volcano**, some 7.5 kilometres beyond the last bridge.

Turn left here (right track to potential bush camp at **The Volcano**), to reach another tee intersection 300 metres later on **Nunnett Road**. Turn left onto this wider logging road to pass **Jungle Creek Track** and **Running Creek Link Track** through lovely forest.

Six kilometres later you will reach the **Glenmore Logging Camp** – a group of four disused forestry workers huts at a potential camp with basic facilities. These weatherboard huts are in poor condition, but recent renovations may continue and bring them into better shape.

Keep left on **Nunnett Road** 100 metres beyond the huts to pass a logging coupe and seasonally closed gate. Continue past **Running Creek Track** on the left and **Rainbow Track** on the right as you climb to about 1000 metres of altitude. Keep left at the **Mellick Munjie** junction, some 8.7 kilometres beyond the huts taking the high road past **Ah Chow Road**. Continue over **Wombat Flat** to the **Nunnett Plains Scenic Reserve** with **Gronows Track** on the left where seasonal wildflowers colour the plain.

Graceful snow gums are home to rosellas and flame robins, as you reach the plains proper where several tracks fan off. Cattle still graze parts of these high plains, and brumbies are occasionally sighted. These wild horses are the descendants of horses first set loose in the late 1890s by miners and graziers. The animals multiplied in the wild and were rounded up for military purposes during WW1. Since then, numbers have again increased to what some would say are worrying levels.

Cross **Bluewater Creek** at a culvert, to head north past **Pig Plain Track**, which marks the northern boundary of the **Scenic Reserve**. Large moss covered boulders flag **Nunniong Plains Track** on the left, 4.7 kilometres beyond **Bluewater Creek**.

Reasonably capable 4WD vehicles can turn left here for a very scenic link to the **Nunniong Plains** further north. Even vehicles not equipped with low range can make their way down to the river here, and make a judgment on whether they are capable of the rutted exit. AWDs and those less confident can remain on **Nunnett Road** to pass some nice camping possibilities (no facilities) on the **Timbarra River**, to arrive at the plains later via a slightly longer route.

Those turning left will descend to a bridge spanning the **Timbarra** where reeds sway in the clear water flow. There is excellent camping here with shade and ready river access, although no facilities. A rutted climb breaks away from the river and is quite trafficable if dry, taking travellers over a rocky knoll to another camping area two kilometres later.

You will reach a tee intersection on the **Nunniong Road** 500 metres beyond that, where you turn right, and in 300 metres arrive at a large open plain. A number of tracks weave through the **Nunniong Plains**, with a hut and camping area found 2 kilometres to the west.

Head back south from **Nunniong Plains** on the main road, passing several smaller plains and plenty of slender snowgums. With an altitude of about 1200 metres, there is regular snowfall and abundant rain to irrigate a range of subalpine vegetation on the plains. Fortunately much of the southern part of the **Scenic Reserve** has escaped the ravages of a bushfire that struck other parts of the area in 2003.

Nunniong Road winds past a number of side tracks, with both alpine ash stands and logged areas marking the descent. You will pass the substantial logging tracks of **Flinns** and **Sawpit Roads**, before reaching a seasonally closed gate and tee intersection, with **Bentley Plains Road** branching to the

Swifts Creek and its community is worth a stop

Glenmore Logging Camp

Moscow Villa is well maintained.

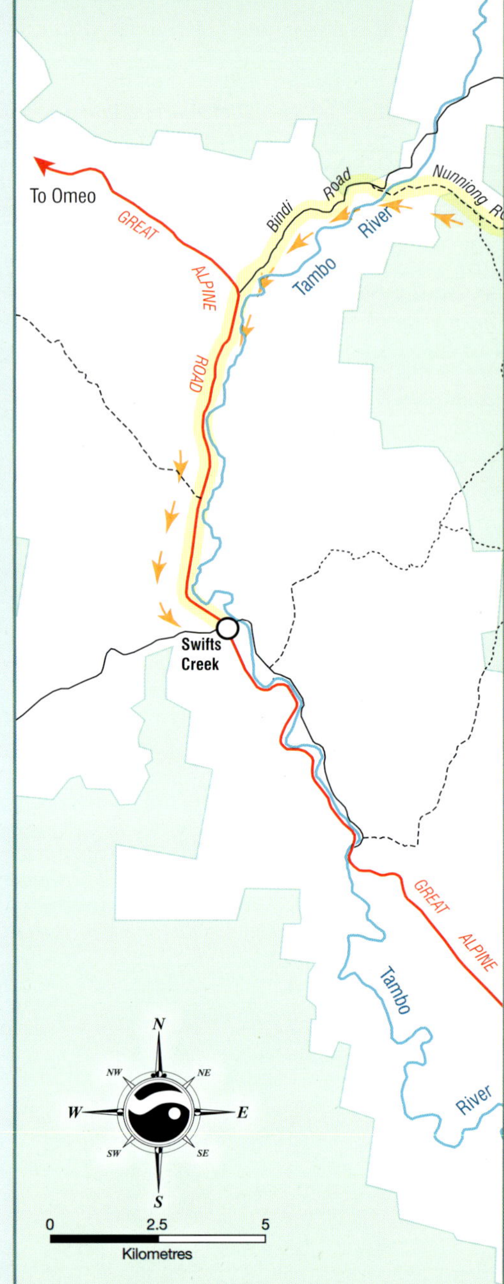

left.

Turn left here to trace the descent past a gravel pit and a verdant fern gully all of the way to the **Bentley Plain Reserve**. **Moscow Villa** is the centrepiece feature on arrival, with a large well maintained log wall hut dating from the early timber cutting days welcoming visitors to the plain. Another smaller and less impressive hut is found 200 metres away at the campground.

Basic facilities are provided at this scenic location, and a network of walking tracks criss cross the **Bentley Creek** wetland. Bottlebrush and snow heath colour the alpine meadow, while sphagnum and other mosses grow in the moister pockets. An isolated stand of old pine trees marks one corner of the plains, where visitors may find some shelter. The **Douglas Reserve Walking Track** is especially appealing with substantial galvinised boardwalks penetrating the jungle at the back of **Moscow Villa**. Longer walks to **Bentley Creek** check out parts of the reserve's eastern corner; just be aware that hot summer days and the smaller wetland wildlife can attract the resident snake population.

Retrace your steps from here to the last tee intersection, and keep heading west for 500 metres to **Escarpment Track**. (You can turn left here, to find the **Mount Nugong Fire Trail** 2 kilometres later. A steepish access track leads to a large tower, and although there is no access to the structure, some broken views can be made from nearby rocky outcrops.)

Nunniong Road drops away from **Escarpment Track** offering some views as you reach **Flukes Corner** and the **Washington Winch** site 200 metres later. This elaborate set up of winch cables, suspended pulleys and lofty supporting timber pylons illustrates the methods used to extract felled trees from the steep forest slopes. An abandoned steam engine (built in the USA and the only one of its type in Australia) together with explanatory notes give visitors an insight into the amazing techniques of the early timber harvesters.

Gravel paves the way past mossy boulders and messmate forest, although parts of the roadside verge have fallen away, so bunting and star pickets define some sections of the fragile road edge. Pass several side tracks on the serpentine descent with great views to be had from a hairpin bend, 8 kilometres from the **Washington Winch**.

Corrugated corners continue to the **Tambo Valley Golf Club** where the blacktop returns. The valley drive passes the **Old Bindi Road** before crossing the **Tambo River** and meeting the **Bindi Road** shortly after. Turn left here to pass some nice old farming properties with olive groves and poplars lining the **Tambo**. You will reach the **Great Alpine Road** 4.6 kilometres later, where you turn left to arrive at **Swifts Creek** some 8 kilometres after that.

Bentley Creek flows through some impressive forest.

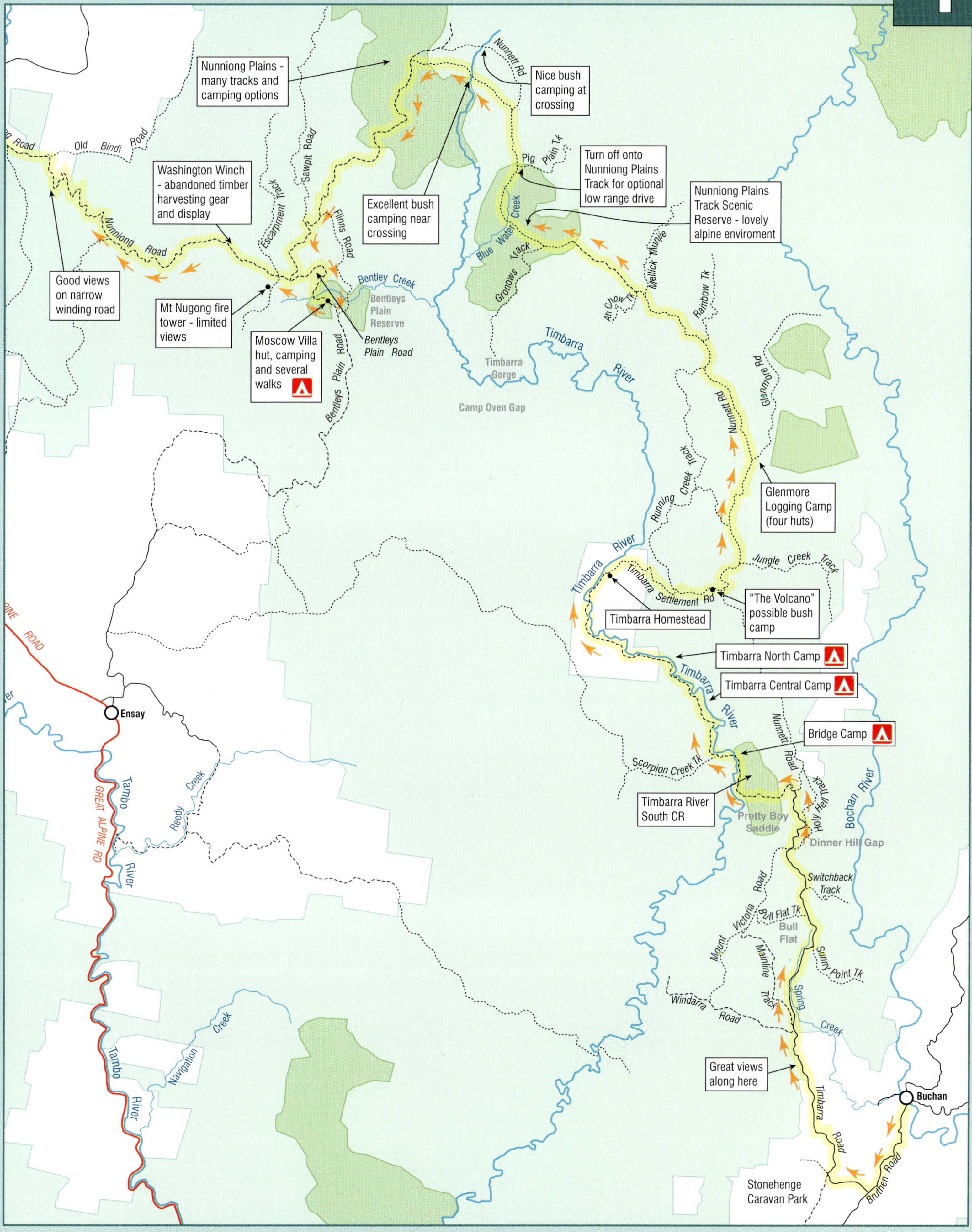

Nunniong Plains - many tracks and camping options

Nice bush camping at crossing

Washington Winch - abandoned timber harvesting gear and display

Excellent bush camping near crossing

Turn off onto Nunniong Plains Track for optional low range drive

Nunniong Plains Track Scenic Reserve - lovely alpine enviroment

Good views on narrow winding road

Mt Nugong fire tower - limited views

Moscow Villa hut, camping and several walks

Glenmore Logging Camp (four huts)

"The Volcano" possible bush camp

Timbarra Homestead

Timbarra North Camp

Timbarra Central Camp

Bridge Camp

Timbarra River South CR

Great views along here

Old Bindi Road
Nunniong Road
Escarpment Track
Sawpit Road
Flinns Road
Nunnett Rd
Pig Plain Tk
Blue Water Creek
Gronows Track
Bentley Creek
Bentleys Plain Reserve
Bentleys Plain Road
Timbarra Gorge
Camp Oven Gap
Timbarra River
Ah Chow Tk
Mellick Munjie
Rainbow Tk
Glenmore Rd
Running Creek Track
Jungle Creek Track
Timbarra Settlement Rd
Scorpion Creek Tk
Nunnett Road
Holy Hell Track
Bochan River
Pretty Boy Saddle
Dinner Hill Gap
Switchback Track
Mount Victoria Road
Bull Flat Tk
Bull Flat
Sunny Point Tk
Mainline Track
Windara Road
Spring Creek
Timbarra Road
Buchan
Bruthen Road
Stonehenge Caravan Park
Ensay
Great Alpine Rd
Alpine Road
Tambo River
Reedy Creek
Navigation Creek